WHERE ARE YOU?

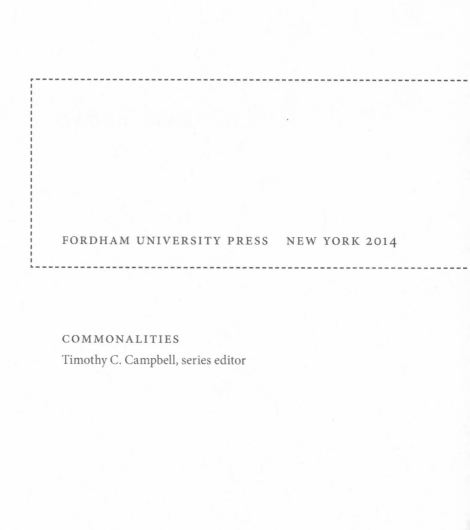

FORDHAM UNIVERSITY PRESS   NEW YORK 2014

COMMONALITIES

Timothy C. Campbell, series editor

WHERE ARE YOU?

An Ontology of the Cell Phone

MAURIZIO FERRARIS

Translated by Sarah De Sanctis

Fordham University Press has no responsibility for the persistence or accuracy of URLs for external or third-party Internet websites referred to in this publication and does not guarantee that any content on such websites is, or will remain, accurate or appropriate.

Fordham University Press also publishes its books in a variety of electronic formats. Some content that appears in print may not be available in electronic books.

Library of Congress Control Number: 2014939960

Printed in the United States of America

16 15 14   5 4 3 2 1

First edition

CONTENTS

FOREWORD: TRUTH AND THE MOBILE PHONE

Umberto Eco

In this book, Maurizio Ferraris shows how mobile phones are radically changing our way of life and have therefore become a "philosophically interesting" object. Now that they have also assumed the functions of a palm-sized agenda and pocket computer with an Internet connection, mobile phones are less and less a tool for oral speech and more and more a tool for writing and reading. As such, they have become an omnicomprehensive tool for recording—and we shall see to what extent words like writing, recording and "inscription" prick up a Derridian's ears.

The first hundred pages of this "anthropology" of the mobile phone are also fascinating for the general reader. There is a substantial difference between talking on the home phone and talking on the mobile phone. On the home phone, one could ask whether someone was home, whereas on the mobile phone (except for theft cases) one always knows who is answering, and whether they are there (which changes our situation of "privacy"). On the other hand, home phones allowed one to know where the caller was, while now there is the problem of where she might be (besides, if she answers "I'm behind your back" while calling through a foreign mobile company, her reply is traveling half the world). Nevertheless, I do not know where the person who answers me is, but the phone company knows where we both are—so our ability of escaping the control of single individuals is counterbalanced by a total transparency of our movements with respect to Big Brother (Orwell's, not the TV one).

One can therefore make some pessimistic (paradoxical and hence reliable) reflections on the new "homo cellularis." For instance, the very dynamics of the face-to-face interaction between Tom and Dick changes, being no longer a relation between two people: the conversation can be interrupted by the cellular insertion of Harry, so the interaction between Tom and Dick proceeds only by fits and starts, or stops altogether. Thus the main instrument of connection (my being constantly present to others and the others to me) becomes, at the same time, the instrument of disconnection (Tom is connected to everyone apart from Harry). Among the optimistic reflections, I like the reference to the tragedy of Zhivago, who after years sees Lara from the tram (remember the final scene of the film?), doesn't manage to get off in time, and dies. Had they both had a mobile phone, would we have had a happy ending? Ferraris's analysis oscillates between the possibilities that the mobile phone opens up and the castrations it forces upon us: first of all the loss of solitude and of the silent reflection upon ourselves, as well as our being condemned to the constant presence of the present. Transformation does not always coincide with emancipation.

A third of the way through the book, though, Ferraris moves from the mobile phone to a discussion on themes that have become increasingly interesting to him in the past few years, such as the polemic against his original masters, from Heidegger to Gadamer to Vattimo; against philosophical postmodernism; against the idea that there are no facts, only interpretations; up to a now complete defense of consciousness as (poor Rorty) the Mirror of Nature. Of course, with a lot of common sense—and it is a shame not to be able to follow step by step the foundation of the sort of realism that Ferraris calls "weak textualism."

How do we get from mobile phones to the problem of Truth? By way of a distinction between physical objects (like a chair or Mount Blanc), ideal objects (like Pythagoras's theorem) and social objects (like the Italian Constitution or the obligation of paying for drinks in the pub). The first two kinds of objects exist also outside of our decisions, whereas the third kind becomes, so to speak, operative only after a recording or an inscription. Given that Ferraris also attempts a somehow "natural" foundation of these social recordings, then the mobile phone presents itself as the absolute device for any kind of recording.

It would be interesting to discuss many of the points made in the book. For example, the pages dedicated to the difference between recording (like a bank statement, a law, or any collection of personal data) and communication. Ferraris's ideas on recording are extremely interesting, while his ideas on communication have always been a little generic (they seem like they have been bought in Ikea, to use the metaphor of a previous pamphlet of his against him). But in the space of a Bustina[1] one does not go into deep philosophical discussions.

Some readers might wonder whether a reflection on the mobile phone was really needed to reach conclusions that could have been drawn from the concepts of writing and "signature." Of course, a philosopher can be prompted even by the reflection on a worm to build an entire metaphysics, but perhaps the most interesting aspect of the book is not that mobile phones allowed Ferraris to develop an ontology, but rather that his ontology allowed him to understand, and make us understand, mobile phones.

ACKNOWLEDGMENTS

The idea of a collective intelligence—the dream that, by connecting to a network, people could create some super-intelligent totem—seems bizarre to me. But without friends, students, colleagues, even relatives and obviously without masters (one of whom unfortunately died a few years ago), this book would not have been written. Which perhaps would have been better, but still, the book is there, and acknowledgements are needed—and, as is appropriate, have to be written down.

I thank everyone, and full heartedly, but first of all my friends from the LabOnt (laboratory for ontology) at the University of Turin, who have been a source of ideas, elaborations, and reasonings that otherwise would have never crossed my mind: Tiziana Andina, Carola Barbero, Cristina Becchio, Cesare Bertone, Stefano Caputo, Alessandro Gatti, Alessandra Jacomuzzi, Pietro Kobau, Alessandro Lancieri, Luca Morena, Alessandra Saccon, Alessandro Salice, Daniela Tagliafico.

For the same reason I am indebted to the 2004–5 graduate students in philosophy at the University of Turin, with whom I tested this book and from whose reactions and relations I received suggestions of various kinds: Giulia Alberti, Elisabetta Audisio, Alessandra Berlese, Marco Bertello, Davide Biasoni, Laura Borlengo, Maria Teresa Busca, Fabrizio Calzavarini, Raffaella Cavalletto, Davide Coero Borga, Maurizio Dale, Barbara D'Alessandro, Laura Teresa Di Summa, Davide Passio, Sara Gennaro, Davide Grasso, Alessandro Lomartire, Gemma Lupi, Carola Marucci, Giuliana Racca, Erika Sampò, Davide Saraniti, Alessandra Scotti, Fabio Scuderi, Fabio Straforini, Maria Grazia Turri, Nicolò Valenzano, Simona Verlengia, Antonella Vitielli.

My friends Barry Smith and Leo Zalbert, from the IFOMIS in Leipzig and Saarbrücken, saw this work as it was taking shape (initially in a very short observation to Smith about his objection to Searle, then in its definitive form in Saarbrücken, in January 2004). Kristòf Nyìri of the Hungarian Science Academy saw its conclusion and pushed me to hurry up with it.

I thought that maybe the way to an ontology of the mobile phone could be possible thanks to my friend Armando Massarenti and my brother Gabriele Ferraris, who welcomed its first, fragmentary, sketches in the Sunday issue of "Il Sole 24 Ore" and in "Torinosette." I also owe a lot to other friends: Gian Maria Ajani, Andrea Bottani, Mauro Bussani, Rosa Maria Calcaterra, Richard Davies, Michele Graziadei who offered me comments and suggestions on previous versions. I owe the first impulse of writing on social objects (and a number of other teachings) to Roberto Casati. I perfected the idea thanks to Achille Varzi's objections during the first Italian conference on analytic ontology in Padua (July 2003), as well as in many informal conversations.

Anna Donise could only read the book *in extremis* this time as she was writing one herself. But she heard a lot about it from me, to the point that, I am afraid, she was not surprised—she found in it many of the things she said to me.

TRANSLATOR'S NOTE

The book you are about to read was written in 2005: It was the dawn of smartphones (at least outside Japan), and tablets—invented only three years before—were far from common. The iPad wasn't released until 2010.

Now, in 2014, forty-one years after the first call was made with a cell phone, Maurizio Ferraris's work acquires an almost "prophetic" valence: As you will see, the following pages insist on the cell phone not so much as a tool for speaking but rather as a tool for writing, and—as such—cell phones are seen as handy but capacious personal archives (think of all the e-mails, music tracks, videos, notes, etc. that are treasured in our phones). The natural and successful marriage of cell phone and computer, now fully realized in tablets, is often hinted at and, in a way, predicted.

If I say this, it is not to praise Maurizio Ferraris as some kind of psychic visionary but to underline that his theory of documentality (the first traces of which can be found in the present book) actually did touch on something real that was going on back in 2005 and is happening all the more today.

The book is therefore still incredibly relevant, and interesting also for a nonspecialized audience, as it unravels the philosophical core of what has become perhaps the most important of our everyday objects. The first part is focused on the analysis of the cell phone, while the second sketches a philosophical theory (later developed in *Documentality* and in the *Manifesto of New Realism*, one of the most-debated books in contemporary continental philosophy) that accounts not only for the cell phone but also for a number of objects whose ontological status we rarely reflect upon, such as promises, professorships, and theatrical plays.

A note on the translation: Although the book is subtitled "An Ontology of the Cell Phone," I use the British phrase "mobile phone," as it allows me to keep a number of puns (and, more important, theoretical arguments) based on the fact that the cell phone is, indeed, *mobile*, its mobility being the very condition for its constant and ubiquitous presence with us— which, as we will see, has tremendous consequences.

WHERE ARE YOU?

INTRODUCTION: WHERE ARE YOU?

The number you have called is currently unavailable.

—VODAFONE AUTOMATED REPLY

Where has he gone? Where is he now?

—TOLSTOY, *WAR AND PEACE*

"*Phile Mauritie, ton beltinon kai ton timiotaton he historia tes emailes he kat'akribeian* . . . Hmmm, how does this manuscript go on?" This is how, in September 1997, my friend Alfredo Ferrarin replied to my suggestion that "per e-mail" (Italian for "via e-mail")—one of the most recurrent terms for a decade now ("I'll send it to you via e-mail")—could be read as the title of an Aristotelian treatise: *Perì Mail*, or "About Mail," "On Mail," "Mail," just as there are the *Perì Hermeneias* and the *Peri Psyches*. But, indeed, how does this pseudo-treatise go on? In 1999 I started to give a continuation to the manuscript in a short article on e-mails, writing on paper and the internal writing through which our mind, ever since Plato, has been represented. Now, years later, I might have managed to complete it, getting to the conclusion that, despite the appearances, *the mobile phone is a writing machine*. How is this possible?

In January 2001, in Syracuse, I was walking with Jacques Derrida and we were talking about mobile phones. The topic was philosophical and not technical. I claimed—with a dogmatic attitude—that mobile phones are stupid machines while computers are intelligent, maybe because I thought that on a computer one can write intelligent essays whereas, on the phone, one could produce only stupid texts. I was obviously wrong, and not only because on the computer one can very well write monumentally idiotic essays, but mostly because—as Derrida pointed out—in time, mobile phones were going to centralize all the functions of a computer with the addition of the one feature that computers were lacking: being with us at all times. We started reasoning about this and projected on the spot a dialogue over mobile phones. Then, for three years, nothing came of it, as often happens when one thinks (and it is the most mistaken of thoughts) one has time. In the meantime, I kept following my own trail for the *Perì mail*.[1]

In August 2004 the Hungarian philosopher Kristóf Nyìri, during the yearly Wittgenstein congress in Kirchberg, proposed a duo with Derrida on the topic, at the conference "Seeing, Understanding, Learning in the Mobile Age," held in Budapest from April 28–30, 2005. The basic idea was that the *mobile phone* was leading to some uncalculated transformations, precisely with regard to seeing, understanding, and learning. Since the fundamental question that one asks when speaking on the mobile phone is, "Where are you?"—an absurd and unthinkable question in the age of home phones—I suggested to Kristóf that "Where are you?" also constitutes a philosophical *Grundfrage* or, in simple terms, an interesting issue: the *mobile* prospects a *mobile ontology*, and not only a mobile party—as, with a vague Hemingwayan reminiscence, commercials seem to claim ("it's all around you"). I said I was going to talk it over with Derrida, and I did: it was the content of one of our last phone calls. I called him again at the start of October, but he did not answer; I tried again on the mobile phone but I got the answering machine. On the morning of October 9, a friend called me on the mobile phone: Jacques was dead. All that is left of him are writings and recordings, and above all a reflection on writing that, as time goes by, seems to increasingly grasp the essence of a present that is very relevant to us. But in what way?

The question "Where are you?" grasps the essence of the transformation induced by this tool, which is not simply a wireless home phone. In fact, it suffices to reflect a little to find out that mobile phones are much more for writing than for talking (think of the boom in text messaging). They became a kind of computer (the two devices are in fact already united: you write with your phone and call with your computer); they even turn into a sort of credit card for paying the bill at the supermarket or donating to the victims of a tsunami. At this point, asking what a mobile phone is, what kind of object it is (which is the meaning of the term *ontology*), becomes philosophically interesting. This is so mostly for a reason that I will extensively argue for in Part I: with mobile phones we do not witness a triumph of oral speech, but of writing and even ideograms, that is, the writing that does not copy speech, but draws things and thoughts. The problem of *inscription*, as well as its role in the construction of social reality, comes to the fore, rather paradoxically, precisely through a tele*phone*—a machine for speaking at a distance that nonetheless, as a *mobile* phone, seems to become something completely different.

Thus far, all is clear—you might say—even too much so: technology holds some unexpected surprises. But what is this story about social reality? What does it have to do with mobile phones? I hope the reader does not think that the construction of social reality I am talking about is something like having a chat, arranging a meeting, or maybe lazily commenting on the events of the past day—as it happens in the long phone call making up the novella by Alberto Abrasino, *La controra*. Believe me, it is nothing like this. Also—and it is not hard to understand this—as much as we can lengthen texts, as much as the SMS (*short* message service) can become an LMS (*long* message service), it is just unlikely that sooner or later we will receive the entire *Recherche* by Proust on a mobile phone: it is simply handier to read it at home.[2]

No, social reality is not this, yet it has to do with writing. Search your pockets, open your wallet: you will find bus or train tickets, bar or supermarket receipts, and other receipts as well from your credit or debit card transactions. Then, once back home, look into your drawers, ransack your many "papers" (which we call that way without thinking, and yet with such preciseness): you will find other inscriptions and records, bills, receipts, sale records, cards and letters. If we kept them all, we would have the most perfect reconstruction of our social life, our public life (bills) and our private life (letters). If we consider that there are entire buildings (post offices, ministries, banks, libraries) whose *raison d'être* is to keep these inscriptions, then the role of writing in the construction of social reality will seem quite obvious.

Now, also note this: for the past twenty years, an increasing percentage of these inscriptions have been stored in computers (think of the inconceivable e-mail archives we all have, discovering in dismay that we wrote more in five years than Leibniz did in his whole life) or in cards with a memory such as, for instance, New York underground tickets, which work like a modest credit card. Well, it would not be difficult to prophesize that, sooner than we can imagine, these inscriptions will all end up in our mobile phones, which will be turned into wallets, IDs, train tickets: the mobile phone will swallow them all.

Am I exaggerating? Playing the Jules Verne of the mobile phone? Showing off because I once went to New York on a trip? Absolutely not. It is already so with regard to the payment of Italian train tickets: you get the reservation on your mobile phone and the ticket inspector knows not only where you are (seat 55) but also what your name is. Therefore, thanks to the possibility of storing inscriptions, the mobile phone becomes a great constructor of social reality; this is the theoretical point I wish to call your attention to.

Let us step back, for a moment, and look at the story behind writing this book or, if you prefer, to the novel about this essay. In Kirchberg I saw, for the first time, the American philosopher John Searle. While listening to his conference, I recalled that thirty years before he had had a ferocious dispute with Derrida, contesting his basic thesis: the decisive role of writing in the construction of social reality. And, still listening, I remembered that ten years before Searle had written a book on social reality in which he tried to grasp what he defined as "an immense invisible ontology": the tissue of norms, rules, institutions that, according to Searle, rises above physical reality. We cannot touch it, but it is very important for us.

This theory presents many qualities, but is afflicted by a fundamental flaw: the belief that the essence of social reality depends decisively on the many molecules of a piece of paper that can turn into a banknote and not on the few molecules, for example, of the governor's signature that makes it valid. Searle's idea is, in short, that a man can be a prime minister, a professor, or a husband; a piece of paper can be a banknote or a restaurant bill, and that social reality is built upon physical reality. Fair enough: it is so, in a way. But what is it that turns a human body or a piece of paper into something else, allowing for such a metamorphosis? The many molecules of the physical object or the few molecules of the ink for the writing? For all I have been saying, it is the latter: namely the limited molecules of writing, on an ID or a letter of appointment; very rarely on the skin—and when it happens, such as in Auschwitz or in Kafka's *Penal Colony*, it does not augur well. That is, precisely what Derrida claimed and Searle firmly refused to take into consideration. Besides, had Moses descended Mount Zion with some unwritten stones, the physical object would have hardly turned into the social object "ten commandments."

In conclusion, it is in Kirchberg that I had the—however weak— illumination: without thematizing inscriptions, it is impossible to solve the enigma of social ontology,[3] that is, to answer the question "what is there between the earth of physical objects and the sky of ideal objects? What is there between chairs and theorems?" It is not an easy question, because we know from Hamlet that, in between, there are more things than our philosophies can dream of:[4] obligations, promises, bets, christenings and funerals, weddings and divorces, Nobel prizes and jail convictions . . . more or less, all the happiness and unhappiness of our lives.

This is it, I do not want to beat around the bush with this tale of missed opportunities, writings, readings, meetings and phone calls ended with a phone ringing in vain. It does not matter much to the reader to know what I had in mind when I thought of a pseudo-Aristotelian treatise or while I was in Syracuse or Kirchberg. What matters is that the core of the problem lies precisely in the mobile phone (which, in the years between Ferrarin's e-mail and Searle's conference, had become a formidable writing device).

In Part I, I propose a *theory of writing*. Mobile phones are everywhere, tying us together with an invisible wire—while being wireless—and at the same time, unlike home phones, dislocating presence. But most of all, mobile phones have letters and not only numbers on their buttons; this is not only due to a mnemotechnical function (as in some old rotary phones) but rather to the fact that they are really writing machines. Is this the acme of modernity? In a way, yes, but only to a certain extent. If, for example, science fiction has not insisted much on this possibility of transformation of presence, it is because it was already there, from cave paintings to station newsagents. And, from the very start, it had a very specific function: not only to communicate but, first of all, to build an immense invisible ontology, that is, the network of inscriptions, communications, and registrations that defines social reality. First moral of the story (I will try and draw a few out of this book): who said that treatises, after all, are nothing but papers was not wrong, but only if he admitted that papers are not only those (who knows for how long) cluttering our desks, pockets, folders, and wallets, but also computer *blips*, sim cards and neurons in people's heads.

Second moral, then: treatises are only papers solely for paper people. In real life, someone who fails to keep a promise remembers very well that she is in the wrong, otherwise remorse would be inexplicable.

This is, therefore, my fundamental thesis. Social objects, as I shall extensively argue, consist of *inscriptions*: on paper, magnetic memories, and people's minds; and, from this perspective, the allegiance between phone and computer guaranteed by the mobile phone represents a formidable tool for constructing social reality. To demonstrate this thesis, I illustrate the most evident transformations of presence induced by mobile phones in chapter 1. In chapter 2, I argue that these metamorphoses depend on the fact that mobile phones are writing machines. In chapter 3, I claim that writing has to do more with recording than communication: Derrida wrote this in 1967, namely in an age when there were neither computers nor mobile phones, and they were not even dreamt about (suffice it to think that in *2001: A Space Odyssey*, released in 1968, normal typewriters are used and Hal is only for thinking). Finally, in chapter 4, I illustrate and argue for the role of recording in the construction of social reality.

This reality will be thematized in Part II, centered on social objects. Reviewing the (rather few) available theories, I try to answer the question: what is constructed through recording? It is a delicate matter, on which it is easy to be mistaken. Some say that through recording you construct nothing at all, because no one would be willing to obey, say, a law whose consistence was more or less that of a postcard where, instead of receiving "love and kisses from Prague," we got the Emperor's Message with norms and impositions on tax, waste disposal, and the protection of public green spaces. Some, exaggerating in the opposite direction, claim that you construct everything, absolutely everything—not only social objects but also theorems and numbers (that is, ideal objects) and even physical ones. The underlying idea is that the reality of the external world is investigated by science, which proceeds by way of theoretical constructs, so that (thus the reasoning goes) tables and chairs, mountains and rivers, in the end, are the outcome of social constructs or even of alembics and almanacs in people's minds, be they crazy scientists *à la* Strangelove or solipsistic philosophers like Fichte.

Obviously, it is not so: in their absolute form neither anticonstructivism nor constructivism are acceptable, being false and nonsensical. Even with the most powerful mobile phones, computers or virtual reality devices—or with the magic power with which a Golem is made—it is impossible to build physical objects like tables (they are fabricated by carpenters according to a preexisting theory and not on the basis of Ikea catalogs as absolute constructivists think) or mountains, or ideal objects like number 5 or Pythagoras's theorem. These things can be recorded or calculated, photographed or archived through a writing system deposited, for example, (*increasingly*) on the mobile phone.

Nonetheless, things are different in the case of social acts, such as promises, treatises, contracts, and social objects deriving from them, be they capitals or trade unions, banknotes, or medieval knights, birthday parties or graduation ceremonies. Here recording is not an accessory—although important—element (Mount Blanc and Pythagoras's theorem exist independently from their recordings, but it is certainly good to know they are there, and this is exactly what records make possible). Vice versa, in relation to social objects, recording is a constituting factor. This is no laughing matter: the late Mattia Pascal (consider him as a real person) is there, speaking, and yet *socially* he is no more, by virtue of the death certificate. Absolute constructivists—that is, as we shall see, postmodern philosophers—would draw the conclusion that maybe he was really dead, thereby making a banal categorical mistake: in fact, that man undoubtedly exists, as a physical object, as a biological organism and also as a person endowed with consciousness, memories, intentions. Instead, he does not exist as a social object: his is what is very exactly defined a "civil death." The opposite therefore holds true: civil life, as well as the paper-related existence of all social objects, *constitutively* depends on records, that is, on what I will call, more technically, *inscriptions* (that is, on modern and ancient mobile phones). And this, I claim, is the right interpretation of an often misunderstood Derridean expression: "there is nothing outside the text." Outside the text there is an entire world, but without inscriptions there is no social world.

Here is, therefore, my fundamental thesis: social ontology lies on a writing system, which can very well do without mobile phones (it already existed in the age of Sumerians and Pharaohs), but which mobile phones perfectly embody, allowing or promising the connection to all the systems for oral or written communication; the access to all record circuits (writings, images, music); the possibility to check one's bank account, to pay for bus or opera tickets and, if one wishes to, to download this book so as to read it on the train. All of this while, perhaps, a text informs one of the prime minister's resignation, the change in the interest rate, Juventus (Italy's most storied soccer club) winning the championship, the fact that one has left the country and now the roaming services will be dealt with by another company, or even (hopefully not, but these things happen) that "it is over between us."[5]

Part I

PERÌ MAIL: THE PHARAOH'S MOBILE PHONE

On November 6, 1824, from Egypt, Champollion wrote to his brother: "I passed my hands over the names of years which History has completely lost record of, the names of Gods who have had no altar raised to them for fifteen centuries, and, hardly breathing for fear of reducing it to dust, I collected a certain tiny piece of papyrus, the last and only resting place of the memory of a King who, when alive, may have found the immense Palace of Karnak too confining for him!" Ah, if only the pharaoh had had a mobile phone! Yes, had he owned one, and had the reception been good in the pyramid, what would he have done with it? He would have *spoken*, of course, but mostly he would have *written, recorded, constructed*. To verify this claim, I will develop the following topics in Part I:

1. *Speaking*. "Is that you, my love?" "No, I'm her husband." Here is the point. There is a big difference between being on the phone and being on a mobile phone. In Heideggerian terms, it would be a "being-on-the-phone" versus a very different "being-on-the-mobile-phone." With the mobile phone, a sentence like "Hello, is this the Heideggers? Can I speak with Martin?" ceased to exist. No, the message—apart from unpleasant accidents—reaches *him* and not someone in his family; yet, on the other hand, he could be anywhere. Used as we are to finding someone, when we do not manage to do so it makes us feel rather anxious. The most menacing of all messages is, "The number you have called is currently unavailable." Vice versa, a real ontological isolation takes place when we find out that there is no reception and we start looking for it, frantically. We feel lonely, yet until fairly recently

that was always the case, because we were always without reception, and it is not only a matter of speaking.

2. *Writing*. In fact, mobile phones are not only machines for speaking, they are also writing machines. E-mails and mobile phones today are virtually identical, and they do not only convey phonetic writing but also ideograms—:) :-) :-(;-)—that is, the kind of writing furthest from speech that you can think of.

3. *Recording*. Why do we write? To communicate? It is not so obvious. Given that mobile phones today become Gameboy and PlayStation equivalents, agendas and address books, watches and alarm clocks, cameras and recorders, the prevailing element is that of recording, if not even capitalization—so much so that the functions of mobile phones and credit cards tend to overlap.

4. *Constructing*. Recording does not only build capital; in general, all social objects that once rested on a desk, as I mentioned in the introduction, will move to the mobile phone. For the moment, we can only check the transactions in our bank accounts but, sooner or later, I bet our national insurance numbers, our driving licenses, IDs, and passports—which today are all paper or plastic documents—will be incorporated into the mobile phone. We will be able to say, "this is my *corpus*" (my address book, my identity, my money, my archive).

The moral of the story is easy to find. Wearing ourselves out analyzing the culture of television and images, we failed to see the boom in writing over the past thirty years that has culminated in the mobile phone. Maybe we were blind to it because it was too obvious—to the Pharaoh, to Champollion, to Kafka (if you want to find out how it ends, skip to the epilogue of this book)—and too ancient. What is at stake here is more than just a technological evolution; it concerns our way of being in the world—both physically and philosophically—because here we are no longer dealing with just a "mass communication system" but a "mass recording system." The sooner we realize this the better.

1

SPEAKING

The Italian word for mobile phone is *telefonino*, literally "little phone": a strange diminutive for such a powerful device. What is it about a mobile phone? Does it simply increase our ability to speak, to carry sounds to a distance, that is, literally, to phone? It seems that way, at least if we look at its name, designing its function in a univocal way—and not the inventor's name, unlike the case of the guillotine (what did Victor Hugo say? "Christopher Columbus couldn't get his name attached to his discovery. Guillotin couldn't detach his from his invention.") Yet, things are not so simple.

I am on a train. The person I call answers. He says "hi" without asking "Hello, who is this?" He doesn't have to, because my name, which is stored in his address book, appears on his mobile phone. Also, most of the time I dial the right number, since it is listed in my address book: what used to be the phone equivalent to print errors vanishes, and yet they were so common with the old rotary phones, and only a little less so with the later keyboard phones. We no longer dial the wrong number; the worst that can happen is to be told that the number dialed "is not in service," but that is another story.

These are some effects of writing that inaugurate our *peri mail*: the mobile phone is also an address book, an alarm clock, a stopwatch, a notebook, a camera, a recorder. For the patient ones, it also encompasses an agenda, as well as images, videos, films, music, a lot of stuff—and in a fairly small space. It is a complete transformation, which I will elaborate on later—not to the point of boredom, I hope. Yet the most "abyssal" or "inaugurational" transformation—as someone fond of big words would put it—is this: As soon as the other party answers, one feels compelled to ask, "Where are you?" Here is the starting point from which I will begin to disentangle an immense invisible ontology.

Mothers and children. Until a few years ago the question would have seemed absurd, almost idiotic: Where do you expect me to be? I am here, I mean there, where you are calling me. The home phone even allowed for topographic verifications: during the Battle of Berlin in April 1945, you could easily find out how far the Soviets had advanced; all you had to do was call a phone number in the suburbs and if someone answered in Russian, then the Soviets were already there. With the mobile phone it is completely different. The message can reach us anywhere, and, in turn, we could be anywhere ourselves. This is why what was superfluous with the home phone becomes essential with the mobile phone, and I am far from exaggerating given that, with the spread of mobile phones and texting, even the "where-are-you?-mails"[1] were born: messages, mostly sent from mothers to their children, whose *only* content is, indeed, the question, "Where are you?"

The mother (an unstoppable social figure, unlike partners or bosses) has absolutely nothing to say to her child; in a way there is nothing that matters to her apart from knowing where the child is. The child, though, always has a response—namely to answer, "I'm at Gino's," and then hang up, leaving her mom with an unanswered follow-up question: "And where is Gino?" The mother might as well get a satellite navigation system, like those installed in taxis or used by the electronic sensors in intelligent missiles.[2]

"I'm right behind you!" Yet, beyond maternal worries—proving how mobile phones create not only independence but also new forms of dependence, on both sides—this "where are you" issue lies at the basis of infinite requests, precisely because, given the difficulty of locating the interlocutor, finding out where he is becomes an informational good of primary importance: "Where are you?" "On the train, I'm arriving." "Where are you?" "Platform 4." "Where are you?" "At a meeting, I'll call you later." Note that meeting points in airports and train stations are disappearing: In the age of location-based mobile phones they are no longer needed.

In Japan, a country that is particularly sensitive to mobile phones, the question "where are you?" turned into a game. There is a small community whose members, throughout the day, update one another on where they are. A contented mind is a perpetual feast, but the game, even outside Japan, still holds some surprises. In fact, a variation of the *Grundfrage*, the fundamental question—"why something instead of nothing?"—for instance, is offered by the much more crucial one expressed in conversations like, "Where are you?" "I'm right behind you." In this situation we thought we were communicating at a distance, but we were in fact like the children of the past, talking (or rather trying, in vain, to talk) through empty cans tied by a thread. In fact, at times, the voice comes from two sources: the mobile phone and the space behind us, where our interlocutor is.

Or take the following hyperbolic case: If two people have signed up with two telecommunications companies from different countries, the answer, "I'm right behind you," has to travel half the world to reach the interlocutor's ear.[3] A French advertisement, a few years ago, redacted the full list of these weird situations, including the embarrassing one I mentioned above: "Is that you my love?" "No, it's her husband." "La donna è mobile" is a possible situation, in theory, thanks to a strictly private device like the mobile phone—unlike the semi-public home phone.

How do I look? There is also the variant of videophones. In a commercial that was popular some time ago, a girl sent her picture and asked, "How do I look?" [In Italian, literally, "How am I?"—Trans.] In fact, here we also have the overturning of normal conversational rules (we usually ask, "How are you?," although often we do not really care much). Between the two situations, though, the first is the really decisive one: "Where are you?" The second, as funny as it may be, is based on a pun. The girl asks, "How am I?"; but she is not alluding to her mood—which is instead what we talk about when, in phone conversations or in public, we ask someone, "How are you?" She asks, "How am I?"—meaning, "How do I look?"—in the same way in which, in a typical matrimonial scene, one asks one's partner before going out if he or she is well dressed and looking decent.[4] In the case of "Where are you?," on the contrary, the question is unequivocal. We want to know precisely where our interlocutor is. In a way, we generalize the call-in television quiz question, "Where are you calling from?," with the *crucial* exception that here we ask not the caller, but the person we are calling.

Transformations of presence. If we compare the question "where are you?" with the situation of two speakers being face-to-face and physically in the same place, it is hard not to notice how many things change. Obviously, ever since it became possible to send letters—or better yet, letters addressed to a general delivery—this presence has started to vacillate, but some things stayed the same. Also it is quite unlikely that the two would ask each other, from one general delivery to the other more than once a day, "Where are you?"—"On the stairs." . . . "At the supermarket." . . . "At the post office picking up your damn letter." . . . "Look, I don't mean to criticize, but with this 'where are you' thing we'll end up doing nothing all day." And so on.

It is well-known that our modern and postmodern times have brought about a proliferation of "non-places" (Augé 1992): shopping centers, freeways, waiting areas in airports; places that are all the same in terms of how they look and what they have to offer and yet are dislocated all over the world. Well, one has to admit that the objective non-place, the utopian place (literally, *utopia* means "in no place") of the postmodern age pales in comparison to the subjective non-place: namely the difficulty in locating our interlocutor and the apprehension deriving from it. It is almost a universalized version of the angst described by Proust: a phone call in the middle of the night from Albertine, and the Narrator does not have a clue of where she might be—at the theater? With her aunt? With another man? Albertine is a liar, and the Narrator has no way to check.

At least as a start, these transformations should be taken seriously, in this *mobile ontology*—in its two meanings of "mobile ontology" and "ontology of the mobile phone." I will try to expose them briefly before drawing some philosophical conclusions, going through four major points summed up in four words: objects, subjects, knowledge, and possibilities.

MOBILE ONTOLOGY

Objects. The transformation from the home phone to the mobile phone might simply look like a matter of shrinking and losing wires. It is not so simple, though: cutting loose from an immobile support and becoming smaller while, at the same time, getting more powerful, the mobile phone emancipates itself: it loses its proverbial shackles—just like books that are no longer tied to monastic libraries—becomes pocket-size, and travels around the world. It makes things possible that were never seen or done before and that, with the old home phone, were not even imaginable.

First, a little history, reminiscent of Nietzsche who, in *Twilight of the Idols,* narrates how and why the real world ended up becoming a fairy tale.

Here we could tell how the home phone ended up becoming the most mobile device in the world. The story of this mobilization is interesting in itself, because in theory phones should allow communication *without* moving, whereas airplanes, for instance, allow communication (provided that it is only about communication) *by* moving. This principle was proved wrong by the famous dialectic for which, when the phone was invented, it was believed that people would have no longer traveled, while the almost contemporary invention of the airplane led people to travel even more. And now we travel round and round, taking our phones with us, switching them off only during takeoffs and landings (if we are on a plane, that is; it does not happen if we are in a car, train, or ship). Story time:

1. It begins with a home phone—fixed, black, nailed to the wall (you talk into it while standing next to it; keep your calls short, please). The connections between parties are established by hard-working and stressed-out women operators who work the telephone switchboards of large telecommunication companies. We remember them from classic Hollywood movies.

2. Then the phone adapts some nomad-like qualities. It now can be found on tables and desks, and it even can be moved a little bit, locally; if you want, you can use an extension cable to place it elsewhere, and its color (usually light gray, at times a coquettish burgundy) also makes it a bit more pleasant to look at.

3. The phone becomes polymorphous: big, for the desk, or smaller, for the bedside table. You can finally answer incoming calls from your bed, early in the morning (a typical scene in detective stories: "Charlie, do you realize what time it is?") or late at night before falling asleep.

4. The rotary phone has company, the keyboard phone. For a long time the two models—think of them as analog versus digital, it is the age of the first digital watches after all—coexist. Then the keyboard phone takes over and the rotary phone becomes *conceptually* obsolete, since it cannot offer many of the keyboard phone's features, especially those related to writing (likewise, digital watches are slowly taking over analog ones).

5. Phones are no longer a prerogative of phone companies. You can buy them anywhere, in different shapes, made in the Far East—by the emerging economies of the "Asian Tigers." The phones are cheap and often do not work well. This happened about twenty years ago, and thinking back to those times I still feel a shiver for the sense of freedom induced by that quiet revolution.

6. Quiet but not silent. At this point every household has multiple phones. Picture this: all phones ring at the same time, everyone rushes to pick up the phone only to quickly hang up again when realizing another family member is already on the phone. In the end, everyone's conversations are cut short, or one is engaged in continuous collective conversations, in the inadvertent and domestic anticipation of phone conferences.

7. The cordless phone partially solves this problem, still a landline phone but wireless: it is the dawn of mobile phones.

8. In the meantime, doctors and professionals in other disciplines equip themselves with ingenious portable devices called *pagers* that alert them when someone is trying to get a hold of them. *Pagers* signal the dawn of the "where are you" era. Their purpose, though, is typically limited to brief informative (numeric) and not affective exchanges—any mother who would have imposed a pager on her child in all likelihood would have been likened to the Grand Inquisitor Torquemada.

9. Meanwhile, the phone has begun to travel. It appears in cars and in airplanes, terribly expensive but exciting (I am both on a plane and on the phone). We also start installing phones on trains, but too late: phone booths in train cars largely remain empty, because in the meantime the mobile phone has arrived.

10. Yes, it has arrived, and phone booths start disappearing. Phone cards, a former symbol of modernity, become the objects of modern art collections. As an exercise, those who are old enough should try and remember what it was like long ago, when to make a long-distance call from a phone booth you needed half a pound of change.

Thus, the metamorphosis begins and, dramatically (it is the story of David and Goliath, or Jacob and Esau) the home phone becomes the double of the mobile phone,[5] or more exactly it tries catching up but fails hopelessly, like a loyal but unlucky dog.[6] In turn, the mobile phone becomes analogous to the computer, which more or less will give in to the prevalence of the phone. This story, then, is not only a supplement to the *Twilight of the Idols* but also a new chapter of the *Will to Power*.

I deliberately use "will to power" because, since 2002, mobile phones have outnumbered home phones; there are now seven billion mobile phones, an impressive army: imagine them all together, like the terracotta army of the Chinese emperor; a menacing legion not only for its number, but also for its location. Now: where are the mobile phones? If one were ethnocentric, one might be tempted to say that they are all in Italy or other so-called developed countries, or rather, on the trains on which we are traveling at any given time. But it is not so: for instance, there are eight mobile phones for every hundred people in Africa, where obviously the home phone never did too well. This circumstance reduces the so-called digital divide, that is, in short, the gap between who is connected and who is not, which turns into a matter of having or not having a mobile phone. Now the *to have or not to have* issue turns out to be much more easily solved than, say, the installation of Internet points "across deserts and caravans" (as Henryk Sienkiewicz, the author of *Quo vadis?*—that is, "Where are you going?" and not "Where are you?"—would say). Mobile phones can also be found on the Ganges, and not only from the Manzanares river in Spain to the River Rhine in Germany.

As Manzoni said in his *La pentecoste*, referring to another "signal," that of the Holy Ghost: "When the people's signal / Located you on the mount / and opened in your lips / the spring of the Word / . . . Thus the Spirit's voice / multiply resounded: / The Arab, the Part, the Syrian / heard it in their sermon."[7] Yet this is not a miracle. Rather it is a paradox of the mobile phone, whose diffusion seems much different from that of other technical wonders. Without going back too much in time—such as to the gap between those who had bronze weapons and those who had iron ones and beat the hell out of the former—it is a fact that cars and airplanes in what used to be called the Third World are often quite poor quality. With the phone, given the rather low costs, things are different and there are interesting aspects related to this.

1. Traditional communities, while looking with distrust at (or even rejecting altogether) the refrigerator (like Mormons) or television (like radical Muslims), do not hesitate to get a mobile phone. Obviously, there are complicated situations (where pictures are forbidden, the mobile phone can turn out to be problematic, if it has a camera). And Quakers, who should only quake before God, are starting to experience the anxieties that can be caused by a phone ringing.

2. The poor are traditionally excluded from the access to advanced technologies. With the mobile phone, though, this is not so: there are homeless people with a mobile phone, *precisely because* one can very well have one without needing a house for it. The mobile good *par excellence* can do without immobile goods; its owner, though, not quite.

3. Children use mobile phones—and the Internet and computers in general—to access goods that have a very high value also for adults, such as printing, publishing, graphic design, building a website, and perhaps writing one another with no supervision by adults. This, at least in relation to writing, seems to have been predicted by Plato, who defined writing as a *paidia*, child's play (*Phaedrus* 277 e). Yet, if the game is of interest to adults, it is another story, also because kids are smarter and quicker. This is all very much unlike during my time as a child, when they told us that our generation will go to the moon—we did not, but in any case we were supposed to do that once we grew up, like the astronauts we saw on television.

Subjects. The object changes, and subjects seemingly change with it. As I remarked, "being-on-the-mobile-phone" appears to be very different from "being-on-the-phone": it is a wholly different form of *Dasein*.

The "being-on-the-phone" constitutes, after all, an occasional fact: not long ago one could still realize that, for some reason, one had "been on the phone" all afternoon and be afflicted by it. On the contrary, with the mobile phone we are *always* on the phone. The "being-on-the-mobile-phone," thus, multiplies the ghosts (or perhaps *specters*) we carry around—as advertising companies know very well, ensuring that, thanks to our discretely evolved mobile phone, we can carry our entire office with us at all times. In order to achieve the same situation without the mobile phone, one would have to imagine a world in which, every two or three meters, including deserts and mountains, there was a phone booth and a letter box at *our* disposal and no one else's, just like the Emperor's Message.[8]

Like death in Heidegger, the mobile phone is *only ours*: no one—in principle—can answer someone else's phone, just like no one can die in place of someone else, because the mobile phone, like death, is an individual property following us like our shadow. It is the *Jemeinigkeit*, the "always mine" character of the mobile phone, one might say without overstating the fact.[9] One could at most call Tom to speak with Dick, who is with him, if Dick's phone is switched off or has no reception. Not to mention that to use someone else's phone, even just to answer it, one needs to be in a relationship of trust, confidence, almost intimacy (it is almost like using someone else's toothbrush or, given the data contained in mobile phones, like ransacking someone else's handbag or drawer). Or, at least, a strong hierarchy or chain of command has to be in place: imagine a general ordering a soldier, "Give me your phone!"

With the "being-on-the-mobile-phone" it is therefore a matter of *ubiquity* and *individuality*: they can find you, only you (individuality) everywhere (ubiquity). And this is really a huge transformation. Before, we would leave the house and leave the phone behind. Now, it is no longer like that. Wherever we are, someone can find us and vice versa. Therefore, if someone calls us and we do not answer, or our phone is switched off, then it means something. *Ex silentio*, one can deduce a lot: "His phone was off between 10 AM and noon, he probably had class. The signal was weak between 1 and 5 PM, he was on a train; off again from 6 to 8 PM, possibly a conference. But why was his phone off at 9 PM?" The guy just must have been dead tired, but the point is that his whole world can be reconstructed through a *tabula* of absences and presences.[10]

If then we chose to turn off the phone simply to work in peace, to accomplish the intra-mundane asceticism Weber talks about (I bet Jean Buddenbrook would have turned his mobile phone off), we might even feel guilty for it; and yet it is hard indeed to get anything done with all those calls coming in. So much so that today company consultants suggest not reading e-mails and turning off the phone for at least one day a week.

Also, a missed call on the home phone might mean absolutely nothing (maybe they just dialed the wrong number), whereas with the mobile phone, because of its personal character, it is another story: a missed call is at least a notice or even—as young and maybe even not so young people know—an act transforming something that is in the person's mind ("I am thinking of you") into a social fact ("I notify you that I am thinking of you").[11] Hence an entire semantics and pragmatics of something that, otherwise, would be utterly generic and asemantic: "call me back, I am out of credit," "do not give too many missed calls at the wrong hours" and, mostly, "do not forget that a missed call means something only from someone in a relation to you, otherwise it is nothing but noise."

And, as we know well from the stories of kidnapped people, when an unexpected voice answers the phone it is rarely a good sign. Think of the tragedy that happened a few years ago: in the West Bank two Israeli soldiers are captured; the wife of one of them calls him to ask, "Where are you?," and a terrorist replies, "All is fine, we have just slit your husband's throat." The reprisal is immediate: an intelligent missile hits a Palestinian notable following his phone's signal.[12] Think also of the case of Giuliana Sgrena: a colleague phones her and hears only a scream and hurried steps in the rain; this is how the world finds out about her kidnapping. A few days later, again on Sgrena's phone, the journalist receives a call: it is Arabic music, maybe a message to decipher.

Also in ordinary life, we act accordingly. Even those who decide not to use a mobile phone, thus entering a special category, a kind of Native-American reservation, have to act accordingly. Until recently they would have represented a silent majority, now they are like the Japanese on an island, unaware that the war is over, precisely because they do not have a mobile phone. Among the others, the "normal" people, some no longer have home phones and use only their mobile phones. Some use a landline only to access the Internet, but maybe soon, with more powerful and evolved mobile phones, this will be pure archaeology. Finally, some persist in the amphibious use (who knows for how long) of both home phone and mobile phone, but we can bet that, in the end, the mobile phone will prevail. In these cases, though, particularly interesting situations emerge, which one might call—in academic jargon—a phenomenology of moral action, a psychology of communicative action, and maybe even a theory of subjectivity and inter-subjectivity; in short, big stuff. Just a few notes for now:

1. If both home phone and mobile phone ring, which one do you pick up? Some would respond: the mobile phone, which is certainly for you. Others would object: the home phone, which is more institutional, just like telegrams used to be. Thus starts a conflict between different views of the world: between existentialists fascinated by the *Jemeinigkeit* on one hand, and fanatics of the third person and the world seen from the outside on the other.

2. Home phone answering machines are obsolete. In the age of the mobile phone they make little sense: either people already reached you on your mobile phone, or they left you a voice mail, again, on your mobile phone. More importantly: You receive text notifications telling you who called and when—all of this has made answering machines obsolete as such. Not to mention the text telling you that the customer you called is now available: as I said, there is an enormous eye watching you, only, it looks like an ear.

3. "I'll pass you over." This used to be a very common sentence. The phone would ring in the house, one would pick it up but they were looking for someone else. "I'll pass you over," a shout to get the guy's attention and he came. The whole scenario has almost entirely disappeared, leaving no trace at all in the memory of the youngest. The presence, that used to be dislocated in the first case, now is total. Not so much "all around you," but rather "everyone around you," stalking you.

4. We have anticipated this: "Hello, is this the Heideggers' residence? Can I talk to Martin?" This is another sentence that is vanishing, and not only because of the increase of single people. It would be odd if someone called a mobile phone and asked such questions (odd and, frankly, a bit scary. It happened to me once: someone called me on the mobile phone and asked "Hello, is this Ferraris' residence?" I shuddered: did he think I live in a phone?). The mobile is not in a house, it is in a person's pocket: it is *precisely that person*, the phone number is the code for a first name, and it is precisely names that we are calling when we phone.[13]

5. The phone is ringing in vain: that is another experience that is becoming a thing of the past. Yet, used as we are to finding people, not managing

to find them is now particularly worrisome. The most threatening sentence, as I said, is "the number you called is currently unavailable," but replacing it with an alternative, say "the customer might be engaged in another conversation," is rather daunting as well.

6. Two people are walking down the street chatting. Suddenly a phone rings and one of them answers, starting to talk and gesture to the third absent party and not his former interlocutor. A good question would be: where, exactly, is the person who answered? This holds true also for those who seem to talk to themselves, especially when it is hard to notice the mobile phone because they have an earpiece.

7. The connection-induced isolation can also become a deliberate choice, more or less like when, to say goodbye, we say "See you." Which means: "See you later, as late as possible, and anyway, not here and not now, not in the time and place in which, in fact, we are seeing each other." Well, with a mobile phone you can do the same: someone calls you and you cut the call short. Hence the increasing human disconnection generated by phone connection, which can be summed up in three scenarios: Tom and Dick talk; Tom talks to Dick, Dick is on the phone; and Tom and Dick are both on the phone, and that's it.

Knowing. "Enigma intercepts everything, from voices to phone calls to texts to e-mails to websites: all is digitalized, uploaded onto a hard drive with a backup copy in case of manipulations, and all can be immediately handed over to policemen or magistrates in their offices, whether a few yards or hundreds of miles away: fluxes of encrypted data traveling on dedicated lines, protected by passwords on both ends. All can be searched through search engines and shared from an inquiry to another, discovering whether the phone used by a supposed Islamic terrorist turns up again in a drug inquiry by recognizing a number, a computer, a word."[14]

The very least one can say, at this point, is that the phrase "Hello, who is this?" is an anachronistic question. I have suggested before that asking "Where are you?" universalizes the call-in television quiz question—Where are you calling from?—with the crucial difference that now the question is addressed to the person called and not the caller. Upon closer analysis, however, things are more complicated than this, on many levels.

While we lost our certainty about our interlocutor's location, given that he could be anywhere (even anywhere in the world: with an advanced enough mobile phone he could be at the North Pole, as many commercials tell us), we acquired a power that was unthinkable before: when they call us we see the caller's name on the lock screen and can decide whether to answer or not, without resorting to the screening function that used to be an attribute (and a quality) of answering machines.[15]

As I have stated, there is also the promise of absolute knowledge, at least for someone—say, a Big Brother. It is true that we, as private customers, have no idea where our interlocutor is, so much so that we have to ask him. This is not so for others, though, the mobile company, for instance. They know very well were we are, even though they usually do not care one bit. If I am not mistaken, they know the approximate location within a hundred yards. This, as is known, becomes relevant when trying to track someone (remember how it used to be in classic movies, when the runaway or the kidnapper had to be kept on the phone to find out where he was? Now, we know right away.) All the traffic, including e-mails and texts, is recorded and deposited somewhere. It is said (and apparently true) that the CIA recorded the all of our conversations, chats, and correspondences (that this could be of any use, is another story). The point is that, there is no harm in having it all recorded because, as we say, "you never know": someday this immense data library could turn out to be useful.

Absolute knowledge can also manifest itself in more relative and domestic applications, such as the Austrian system HAPO—acronym for *HAndel und POlizei*, "Trade and Police" (Graf 2005, 99–100)—in which 460 police officers are connected with 300 businesses of various types (shops, banks, petrol stations). Nothing like Metternich, Silvio Pellico, and Spielberg! Here we go for the short and concrete: someone pays with a fake note at the tobacconist, the latter notifies the police who, in turn, notify all the other businesses and the guy is caught within half an hour, maybe at the petrol station, where he is trying to fill his tank paying with counterfeit money.

Closer to home we find a different, less powerful kind of knowledge manifesting itself in students with access to resources that enable them to cheat in tests and exams. They can use not only snippets of information obtained through an illicit exchange (a picture of a math test sent from one desk to another) but also the equivalent of entire textbooks courtesy of the storage capacity and applications of mobile phones. This entails unpleasant assessment-related consequences (it is hard to catch the cheaters), although apparently pedagogues and professors are mostly busy trying to prevent students from texting one another about matters that are scarcely related to the topic covered in class—and to knowledge in general. Notwithstanding this, the incurable human optimism has led to projects of employment of the mobile phone in distance-learning programs.[16]

To step even lower (or perhaps higher, one can never tell) on the ladder of knowledge: there is a cognition embodied in the mobile phone that would make anyone owning not an Enigma, but just a phone with which to call a mobile phone, think. In fact, the mobile phone is an object you *call*, that you can call to find out where it is, therefore to gain the knowledge of the object's whereabouts. Unlike all other objects, that seemingly enjoy hiding from us, the mobile phone cooperates, asks to be found: in short, it answers loud and clear (and perhaps on the notes of Bizet's *Carmen*) to the question, "Where are you?" It is indeed enough to call it (hence the frustration of not finding our car in a parking lot: if only we could call it with a phone!). At times, moreover (and films already exploited this scenario), together with the mobile phone, you also find its owner, dead, in a car's trunk. But this, luckily, is another story.

Also, it is not only about knowing where the phone (or its dead owner) is. The mobile phone, just like a GPS or a modest Japanese *mogi* in the games of localization I mentioned above (Licoppe and Inada 2005, 72–73), can tell us where in the world *we* are: it can answer Scheler's question on the position of man in the cosmos, or Jules Verne's queries, whose characters spent a lot of time trying to establish, with archaic devices, where on earth they were (think of the *Voyages extraordinaires*).

Scire Aude![17] (Dare to know!) Nonetheless, knowing who is calling you, where he is, who called you while someone else was calling you or when you did not hear the phone, how much credit you have, and so on can produce an equally important side effect: a feeling of *not knowing*, which would have been inconceivable not that long ago. As I mentioned before, in theory, the possibility of anonymous calls is gone, given that the phone's lock screen displays the name, or the number, of the caller. This is very true, but *precisely because of that* when we see "private" or "unknown" number on the screen we are overcome by anxiety. Who could that be? Now, not long ago we used to get home while the phone was giving its last rings, rarely wondering who it could have been. "They'll call again." Just like all those who called while we were outside, perhaps a legion, who left no trace on our old black device.

Possibilities. Do you remember the famous final scene of *Doctor Zhivago*? Jury Zhivago (Omar Sharif) thinks he recognizes Lara from the tram, gets off the tram, tries to reach her in vain, collapses, and dies. The scene is excerpted in Nanni Moretti's *Palombella rossa*: The protagonist interrupts a water polo match to watch, together with the spectators on the bleachers, the final scene of the film. Everyone shouts at characters: "Turn around! Turn around! Turn around! . . . Knock! Knock! . . . Let him off! Let him off! . . . Run! Run! Run! . . . Shout! Shout!!! . . . NOOOOOOOOOO!!!" Oh, if only Lara and Jury had had a mobile phone!

So, with the mobile phone, plausibility itself changes; a *nouveau roman* is created and this *seems* particularly interesting because it touches not only our real world (that is all around us and that we more or less know) but also the possible worlds, those defining logical necessity. It would not be the first time. Distance communication between spirits has been the fantasy of the eighteenth-century seer Emmanuel Swedenborg, who was severely criticized by Kant.[18] The simple telegraph had already made this fantasy a reality; then the telephone was invented and the whole thing became even more banal. Until the telephone remained a home phone, though, it did not influence much our fictional imagination. Of course, as I was saying before, Proust wrote prophetic pages on the phone, when he was looking for Albertine without finding her (had Albertine had a cell phone he would not have left her alone for a second). Yet, these were only episodes. Now everything has changed, and narrative imagination has to deal with this situation. Albertine has disappeared? Where is the problem? Call her and you will find her—unless the mean woman has turned off her phone.

On the contrary, the greater part of films (and even more television series) that have come out in the past few years find their condition of possibility, their *transcendental* (to use a big word) in the mobile phone. The plots intertwine with increasing speed, precisely because everyone knows everything within seconds. With the consequence, far from paradoxical, that the action can become the side effect of a network of phone calls, just like a set of e-mails can trigger a stock market crash.

BEING AND RECEPTION

Being-on-the-mobile-phone. At this point, one might wonder whether the rise of the mobile phone—and the existential revolution (or confusion) deriving from it—might not be an opportunity to rewrite (instead of occasionally parodying) *Being and Time*, perhaps entitling it *Being and Reception*.[19] We would thus redefine the canonical ways in which our being in the world manifests itself. In favor of this transition from time to reception is the fact that the mobile phone seems to satisfy some of the fundamental requisites of the *Dasein*, as we can easily demonstrate.

1. The first aspect regards the *Dasein*, the being in the world, that reveals itself as being connected. It is precisely in this sense that being depends on reception, because without reception there is no connection. I will come back to this shortly, but for now I suggest a thought experiment (that for me was, instead, a real experience): suppose your mobile phone falls into a drain. The world withdraws. Immediately a hierarchy is formed, at first affective and then professional, of the people to notify that you will be unavailable for a few hours, until you get a new phone.

2. Another characteristic, a fundamental but despicable one, is *inauthenticity*, namely the bad faith with which we come to say that the mobile phone, like death, concerns only others. Not us, no, *we* do not need it. This attitude has prevailed for a long time, generating various prejudices on the mobile phone, seen as an uncivil and primitive device (in Hungary it was called "Bulgarian phone"). Then, within a short time things changed and, at least in principle, a different kind of relationship was established with it, including an etiquette and a sentimental education: when to call, how to call, how to leave the table if you get a call (perhaps using the excuse that "there is no reception"). One could even imagine that, in the future, the mobile phone will be compulsory for all citizens (maybe it is already for detainees in probation). It is an Orwellian fantasy, albeit a plausible one.

3. Then there is the "forever mine" individual character of the mobile phone, its *Jemeinigkeit* I mentioned above. In fact, it is a completely different experience than the home phone—and certainly a much less tragic one than the always-mine character of death. On the contrary, where there's life, there's hope, hope to call and be called, and also a certain ease in doing it discretely (think of the complicated system of signals that Heidegger and Hannah Arendt had invented in Marburg at the time of their relationship: a mobile phone would have made things so much easier).

4. There is also the notion of *Zuhandenheit,* the being at hand, of the mobile phone, making it into the emblem of what Heidegger calls "intramundane entities," that is, in plain language, the devices populating our everyday life. I will not insist much on this point because I will tackle it extensively in

chapter 2, where I will argue that the mobile phone has all it takes to be the absolute device, the device of all devices, the most useful of them all.

5. The *Befindlichkeit*, the being situated and the emotional feeling, of the mobile phone, seems to describe precisely those "moods" (*Stimmungen*) Heidegger attributed such great importance to in *Being and Time*: namely the fact that knowledge—absolute knowledge or the very relative and transient knowledge deriving from the mobile phone that I talked about earlier—is, after all, not much, compared to the affective importance it can, or cannot have, for us. Studies agree on this point (Nyìri 2005b, 151–217): the mobile phone has an emotive character that is much more pronounced than the home phone's because, as I said, it regards only us; it is intimate, and it is used for much more private conversations than those we would be willing to have on a home phone or via e-mail.

6. We could also look at the Heidegger of *Language Speaks*: in fact, language now speaks with us, with the mobile phone—and in a rucksack now typical of city dwellers (after having been a stable of mountaineers, tourists, and hermits), who progressively equipped themselves with a computer and, indeed, a mobile phone.

I will not play the postmodernist! Yet, something does not quite fit: the mobile phone, instead of describing a new way of life, confirms and emphasizes what we have known for a while—some things never change; it is not by accident that old situations (such as those described in *Being and Time*, which was written some ninety years ago) still hold true. How is it possible? Heidegger's idea was the following: the world is at the subject's disposal, so examining the subject means knowing the being through which the access to the world is granted. But do all these transformations really require a revision of our *Dasein* and therefore, if Heidegger is right, the world and the huge number of beings that make it up? Nothing is less certain than this, and the phenomenology we have looked at so far seems to demonstrate this.

To begin with, I discussed the question "where are you?" as if it were a radical transformation of presence; but this is not necessarily so. When I ask someone, "Where are you?," I am trying to situate her in space just like when I am looking for my glasses on the desk. The real transformation would be, say, "*When are you?*"—not: "When are you going to be home?" or "When are you in the office?" but "When are you?" with no further specification, almost as if the interlocutor had turned into a purely temporal event (which, obviously, does not happen). The feeling is therefore that presence stayed the same, and only the access mode changed: our correspondent is a body occupying a physical space just like he was with the home phone, only we do not know where he is. Also, "being in a chat room," for instance, does not equal being in a virtual space: it is just like being on the phone. Claiming that human presence truly changes would be like alleging that a man on a horse is present differently from a man standing.

This suggests that—contrary to what Heidegger would posit—it is not subjects that transform objects, but rather objects that transform subjects. It is not like an aggressive man who finds a stick subsequently turns violent; once the stick is found, aggressiveness increases, and this demonstrates that the least true of all sayings is *si vis pacem para bellum*. It is not true: once you have weapons, you use them, and not for peace, but for war (so much so that *parabellum* has become the name of a kind of bullet). It is therefore a matter of clarification: *dislocated* presence (that we get from walking instead of sitting and using a mobile phone instead of a home phone) is one thing; *deferred* presence (that can be achieved with any kind of recording, like a piece of paper, a magnetic trace, a text, in which reception does not coincide with transmission) is another thing. In neither of these cases do we have a *transformed* presence, though. Simply, the availability of new information creates the possibility for previously unheard-of discourses; or, rather, it provides us with the conditions to inaugurate a new language game, with different rules. What rules?

Connections. I mentioned earlier the topic of connections, which might seem like the opposite of the solitary monologue of the soul, namely confessions, but in reality they are not. On the contrary, if Augustine or Rousseau were reborn today, in the age of the mobile phone, they might write *The Connections* instead.[20] In fact, it seems like the crucial transformation concerns our connection to the world, the negative counterpart of which is announced through the feral news that there is no reception.

When there is no reception we are isolated, exactly like in the pre–mobile phone age, only, before, we did not know; just like, before e-mail, we did not receive mail while we were traveling or on holiday and just like, in the pre–answering machine age (there was such a time, and in many respects it was a great time indeed) if someone called us and did not get a hold of us, that was it. So the taxi driver (like the antihero in Martin Scorsese's film), always in a car and therefore never on the phone, used to be the paradigm of isolation and metropolitan loneliness, the portrait of the potential solipsist, escaping his isolation through a brakeless loquacity with his clients. Today you are lucky if they respond to you at all, given how busy they are on their phones.

We bid farewell to the daydreaming of the solitary walker, whose *reveries* Rousseau tormented us with: now there has to be reception, of course. Yet, precisely because of its fulfilled promise of absolute connection, the mobile phone can at times generate the effect, previously unheard-of, of a *radical isolation*, even in completely normal situations. There is a very simple way to feel lonely, detached from everything, even in the middle of a big city: leave your mobile phone at home. At this point, the specters of our correspondents start populating our imagination and feeding our anxieties (only few have Samuel Beckett's confidence: he had a phone that could only make calls, but not receive them). If a proof was ever needed that man is a political animal, here it is. Without the mobile phone we feel naked, even more naked than if we forgot our wallet or documents, and this already seems like a good argument to suggest—as I mentioned and will extensively argue in the following chapters—that the mobile phone constitutes an eminent social object, just like credit cards and documents. Indeed, it is not only about being called but also about calling ("being-on-the-mobile-phone" is a twofold situation), and good luck in finding a public phone that is still in operation in the age of the mobile phone. If it is urgent, you can try and beg passers-by to use their mobile phones but, funny enough, all of a sudden *everyone* will say that they do not have it on them (and this is the logical consequence of the *Jemeinigkeit*).

On the other hand, even with the phone in our pockets, we always live on the brink of catastrophe. Tragedy ensues when the bars on the screen decrease and we realize, *horribile visu*, "there is no reception"; it is almost like realizing "there is no escape." The possibility of being anywhere and constantly available suddenly disappears and we regress to the age—that now seems antediluvian and yet it was only a few years ago—when a railway journey meant you were unavailable to the rest of the world, apart from your travel companions (with the undoubted advantages of being able to read, write, or daydream in peace, but this is obviously another story). So, a restaurant, a gallery, a lift can turn into a deadly trap. What did Derrida say, in times that now seem remote,[21] while re-evoking the pleasure of the first intercontinental calls at a reasonable price and with a credit card instead of a pile of change? "I hear your voice and the Atlantic recedes." Here, instead, the abyss opens up, and one starts looking for a signal like a water diviner in search for water (with one's mobile phone usually balanced in a horizontal position, because one has to be able to look at the screen). Maybe one runs into other people engaged in the same behavior. We pity and understand one another, like a bunch of Tournesols in *The Adventures of Tintin*.

Lights and shadows. After this magnification of the marvels of technology in one of its small but powerful products, I will try to outline some points. I will establish them by retracing the transformations on which I had focused my attention: objects, subjects, knowledge, and possibility.

Ontological verifications: objects. Times change, so do we, and objects certainly change as well. But I challenge anyone to demonstrate that in the postmodern world the following three principles no longer hold true for the mass of physical objects constituting the ordinary thread of our experience.[22]

The world is full of things that do not change.[23] It is almost incredible that there are so many theories in the history of science and so many new notions populating our lives; yet there are constraints that do not change, and they are largely those that have to do with our perceptive apparatuses: that is, the things that have to do with the way in which we are built. Also innovations have to accept them. For example (I shall come back to this extensively in chapter 2): pens, knives, screwdrivers are old tools, in some cases (like knives) archaic; mobile phones, the mouse, and memory sticks, by contrast, are very modern and were unheard-of only thirty years ago. What do they have in common? The fact that they are handheld and can be grabbed, providing that you want to use them (because with a microprocessor alone, you are not going to achieve much). There is nothing to do, no postmodern wand will ever alter this situation, and this is because the ecological boundaries stay unchanged, determining the objects' stability.

Hence the second principle, which builds on "handiness" and all that it entails: *the world is full of medium-sized things*, neither too small nor too big.[24] Feet, hands, arms are the traditional units of measurement and define the foundation of our relationship with the world: this must mean something. Even when we speak of the speed of light and cosmic or microscopic distances, we are still bustling about things within reach, places a few steps away from us, and so on. The mobile phone does not render us ubiquitous; it limits itself to propagating our voice and writing, just like carrier pigeons used to do—it only does it better. Vice versa, the mobile phone does not bring "all around you"; it simply (and it is already a lot) multiplies the connections with what is not directly around you: namely, to employ again the vaguely emphatic expression I used before, it multiplies ghosts. These are the greatness and misery of technology: if history, as Manzoni's anonymous wrote, can be defined as "an illustrious fight against time," technology seems to present itself as an unrelenting struggle against space, as the attempt at loosening the boundaries that keep returning, because even on a spaceship traveling at the speed of light you will still have to move to grab the razor, the laser, or the interplanetary mobile you forgot in the other cabin.

The core of the matter lies in the third principle I wish to enunciate: *the world is full of things that cannot be amended*, and this incorrigibleness or unamendability constitutes a serious topic.[25] Things, deep inside, do not change because they cannot be corrected: they are as they are and not otherwise, and there is nothing we can do about it. Things present boundaries to our actions and define the range of possibilities of what we can do. We can say that the yellow table in front of us would look green if we looked at it through blue lenses, or black if we turned the light off, but we cannot but *see* it yellow in the present condition—while we can very well stare at the fire *thinking* we are witnessing an oxidation rather than the intervention of the phlogiston.

Ontological verifications: subjects. Subjects change, too, as I was saying. But subjects are nothing but a special kind of object, an object of great interest to us, of course, but that shares with the others a huge number of physical constraints. So that—contrary to what postmodern thinkers thought— human beings cannot do what they want with themselves. And even if they could, they would not necessarily want to, because in our world it is not only a matter of knowing or not knowing but also of being beautiful and ugly, just and unjust, pleasant and unpleasant. Also, experience can teach us a lot. Long before mobile phones, as soon as computers appeared, people started writing prophetic books that in the majority of cases turned out to be mistaken. Take Jean-François Lyotard's *The Postmodern Condition* and skip the analysis of the "end of the metanarratives" of modernity and the subsequent transition to the postmodern paradise that sent so many of us into raptures for the last two decades of the past century. Get to the point: the conclusion. From the text it emerges that democracy was going to be realized through everyone's access to computer terminals, as well as the creation of a collective intelligence and so on.[26] Ignore, for a moment, the fact that in many places in the world Lyotard's predictions are far from reality and that, paradoxically, it is the mobile phone that takes the lead instead of the computer; look at the places where Lyotard's predictions, at least in part, came true. Many people in gloomy rooms or maybe laundrettes, reading and writing with a rarely happy look. How did the poem go? "Painted on these shores / is, of the human people, / the magnificent and progressive fate,"[27] And then what changed?

Along the lines exposed earlier, the most manifest point is that the physical world, with its constraints and characters, did not disappear. Between the bag of change required for a phone call and the virtuality, there is only a difference of weight, not of essence, given that in all cases we are dealing with objects. It is precisely a physical object that allows for the displacement (not the annihilation) of presence. Yet postmodern thinkers seem to confuse *light* with *nonexistent* and *nonexistent* with *variously interpretable*. They clearly never did a very simple experiment: if you unplug the computer, it turns off and the connection to the Internet is gone.

Furthermore, communication is not the only thing that matters. I will elaborate on this in chapter 2 in the section on the mobile phone, but for now I will anticipate the trick: there is not only the ability to know, but also the ability to desire and to feel pleasure or pain. All these functions are not merely theoretical because, indeed, they cannot be reduced to a simple passage of information. This is why reading Bill Gates's biography might be surprising, in the sense that he, at least, does not seem to have noticed this. On one hand, in the age of "tele-work" (that is, in the age when all data can be effortlessly transmitted) he claims to never leave his office for more than five hours, sleeping time included. On the other hand, Bill Gates tells us that for several years he maintained a long-distance relationship, a parallel life if you will, with his future wife. They lived in different cities and continuously called each other on the phone. "What do you think, enough work for today?" And they left different offices to go to different cinemas, but with the same film on (and afterward, obviously, asked each other "So what do you think?"). To be honest: this does not and cannot work, unless you are Bill Gates.

A third consideration. Inventions can change people's lives, but we must wonder *whose* life. The mobile phone is one of the few sophisticated technical devices that almost everyone can afford. Even if you are homeless, and therefore cannot have a home phone, you can get a mobile phone. (How did Rilke [1910] put it? "And one has nobody and nothing and one travels the world with a trunk and a crate of books.") It is a universally certifiable fact. In this sense, we witness a radical transformation; and yet the hypothesis that true poverty, in the age of total connection, consists in lack of information still seems deeply idealistic (not to say unrealistic). When I read statements of this kind, as much as they are supported by valid arguments, I am reminded, once again, of certain claims by Heidegger that true poverty is the poverty in the world, now manifesting itself as lack of connection. Heidegger's thesis (1929–30) is that the stone has no world, the animal is poor in world, and only man has the world: which, in a way, is true. Still, there is the question of how come, as men, we can be both "rich in world" and, at the same time, radically poor, even with a mobile phone in hand. The pensive analyses maintaining that those who lack a mobile phone generally have less work, make less profit, and are not married might depict a representative reality, perhaps, but suggest that it is one thing to be poor in world (that is, to lack a mobile phone), while to be really poor (to have no job, money, or family) is another thing—so much so that one can have no mobile phone without being really poor.

A fourth point. I repeat: Inventions can change people's lives. For the better or the worse? A line in a song by Paolo Conte goes like this: "the car: what a commodity!"[28] Let alone computers, mobile phones, the Internet. Think of how a professor's life changed. Before, if you had to leave for a few days you had to bring along the typewriter, books, and photocopies (if there were any), and if you were nowhere near a phone you practically disappeared from those who knew you. Now it is no longer so, and our lives can be organized on the basis that everywhere you go, you surely have a great part—if not all—of what you need. The *clerici vagantes* are provided with every comfort. And think of how an employee's life changed. You can work from home—and might even get bored. Many people are telecommuting today, perhaps working different hours and on different schedules due to different time zones.

Yet, once again, be careful not to play the postmodernist! That is, do not believe that this simple transformation (which is genuine and considerable) automatically translates into emancipation, or even marks a real improvement. The guy at the bar in a suit with the mobile phone and the laptop might be a professor, a business man, or an employee tired of being home. But he could also have no office, and maybe not even a home, like Julia Roberts in *Pretty Woman* "I'm home when I'm naked." As for the discovery of the work-from-home, be careful: in Naples there is a lot of underground work, a form of work-from-home, that is more intense than any form of tele-work ensured by computers and postmodern mobile phones.

One last point. Mobility sounds great, and rightly so. Yet one must realize how tiring and time-consuming it is to move around. Usually, in fact, this circumstance is seen and presented as desirable: accomplished people are always on the move. One can argue that these are blinkers created by an enormous ideological distortion (it is appropriate to say so) if we consider that, at the lowest level of desirability and social hierarchies, there are migrants.

Ontological verifications: knowledge. Knowledge changed. Yet, nowadays we are dealing with a different type of access to a knowledge that, as such, has always been essentially written. We have not entered a new world: at most, provided that we own a mobile phone and a computer, our libraries have expanded—with the obvious and inevitable redundancies that follow. The theoretical point is still this: we are not dealing, *pace* McLuhan, with a triumph of the image but rather—as I will argue in chapter 2—with a boom of writing, that is, a monotonous extension of the traditional ways of transmission of knowledge.

In short, those who believe that through e-learning one can reach a world of intellectual intuition, with access to the things in themselves as well, is only cultivating, technologically, the childish delusion that one can learn a lesson by putting the book under the pillow. I already mentioned the pedagogic hopes connected to the advent of mobile phones and e-learning in general, and we can all verify the usefulness of a Google search. But that all this has to do with knowledge in general is another story, because on Google you can easily find all the information you need to join a Satanic sect or a neo-Nazi organization, or to perform the most traditional of religious practices.

And the mobile phone is no exception. Here is, for instance, a list of services it currently offers (Katz 2005, 285): proselytism, religious services, prayers, offers for the dead, pictures of miracles, even a *Mobile Rosary*, a rosary you recite with your phone. There is nothing wrong with this, but it is quite obvious that it does not fit with the idea (coinciding with the advent of personal computers) of a community that, through informatics, was supposed to flourish in rational discourses, practicing Rousseau's principle with which Kant opens his essay on enlightening: *Réveille-toi, sors de ton enfance!*

Ontological verification: possibilities. In conclusion: possibilities change, and so does the imagination. But to what extent do they change? Remember the examples of the transformation of narrative imagination produced by the mobile phone. In fact, besides the narrator of the *Recherche* and Doctor Zhivago, Mme. Bovary and Manzoni's Nun of Monza ("The wretched woman replied") too would have benefitted, at least from the point of view of narrative, from the mobile phone. But we should not forget that the resources offered by the mobile phone, like any device, are limited. That is, the thing, for better or worse, constrains us: it can ensure *something* precisely inasmuch as it cannot ensure *anything*, because it is endowed with some physical properties and not others and, mostly, because those properties are *physical*— otherwise, it would not be a thing but a thought in someone's mind.

Here is an example that will come in useful in chapter 3, when I will discuss "truth." Indiana Jones, in *Raiders of the Lost Ark*, finds himself fighting against a brawny guy with a scimitar, and then he remembers he has a gun and the conflict is solved in a flash. The idea is simple. There is a narrative convention for which a duel must be on an equal footing; we accept it, and yet it takes nothing to change one's weapon (that is, object, with the constraints it entails) and the convention we had silently accepted and that gave meaning to the story is gone. The lack of mobile phones made situations of extreme suspense possible, because people could not be warned of some decisive fact.[29] That is where all the tension was; now it could no longer be the same.

For that matter, though, a slingshot can overthrow a giant, and this principle holds also for a number of less insidious tools. For instance, one of the most typical—and most bizarre—characteristics of Anglo-American countries is the absence of shutters in front of windows. In Alfred Hitchcock's *The Birds*, the fowls would not have been able to get into the house: it would have been enough to close the shutters and that would have been the end of the story. Shutters could have kept the aliens in M. Night Shyamalan's *Signs* from intruding into the farmhouse and the protagonists from locking themselves in the basement. And in Christopher Nolan's *Insomnia* Al Pacino could have fallen deep asleep even in the perennial daylight of the Arctic summer—all he would have had to do is pull down the shutters.

The conclusion? It's simple: *every* technical invention—from the club to the lever to the wheel, from the sail to gunpowder to sticky notes—changes people's lives. But life remains situated in a world that has its laws and enforces them, and with all the mobile phones in the world I will never be able to conceive a novel or film where colors have no spatial extension (i.e., a corresponding colored body). Already Descartes, *Matrix*'s forefather, remarked: the stuff of dreams, or the painters' fantasies, presents a constant feature.[30] They are not at the subject's disposal, and not even the powerful daemon, who persuaded us that $2+2=5$, would ever be able to change these constraints. In other words, no technology, no omnipotent daemon could ever alter propositions like:

All bodies are extended.
All bodies are colored.
There is no color without spatial extension.
There is no sound without duration.

See for yourself.

THEORY OF OBJECTS

The recipe for ontology. Time to turn off the phone and take stock of the situation. So far I have examined an object, the mobile phone, and in the remaining chapters in this Part I will unveil many of its secrets. I will reveal that it is not a speaking machine but a *writing* machine; that writing is not only useful for communication but, even more essentially, for *recording*; and, in the end, it will become clear that the act of recording is the necessary condition to *construct* the immense invisible ontology of social objects, which I will investigate in Part II. Now, starting with an object is key to my strategy.

Postmodern thinkers, rightly sensitive to world transformations produced by objects, make the mistake of resolving this universe of things into a vague world and a "spirit of the time" in which everything is confusing. They are not equipped—like a great deal of philosophers—with a good theory of objects, since they dream of a world at complete disposal of the social construction by omnipotent subjects.[31] And yet: before speaking—usually, although not always—subjects think. Yes, but what do they think about? There is no thought that is not a thought of *something*, as is well known by those who are left disappointed when they ask, "What are you thinking?" and get in response, "Nothing." No, you cannot think of nothing and even if, by hypothesis, you thought of nothingness, you would still be thinking of something.

It is therefore not surprising that ontology as the theory of objects is among the most ancient philosophical specialties (although its name only dates back to the seventeenth century):[32] things possess their own identity— an essence, what philosophers call *eidos*—and that essence is the circumstance for which a chair without a seat is not a chair, namely it is not that given kind of being. And it would be wrong to think that a physical investigation can solve everything. The operation is already problematic for natural objects: if I see a wave breaking on the shore, is it exactly the same thing as a water drop splashing on the floor? It would seem that way (it is H_2O in both cases) but, unlike the drop, the identity of the wave is not physical but morphological, given that the molecules breaking against the shore are not those of the wave we saw far away (Varzi 2001). Or take borders (Morena 2002): where does the hand begin and where does the arm end? It is hard to say—and thus very hard to accuse someone of taking the whole arm when they were offered a hand. The science of physics is even more useless to explain social objects like the Berlusconi government in 2005 or the Torino soccer team after the Superga accident. In the first case many components have changed, in the second all of them have: then what defines the identity in time of the two social groups?[33] What can be done, then? Returning to the mobile phone I will illustrate the recipe for ontology: its ingredients are making explicit, distinguishing, and reifying.

1. *Making explicit* means taking out the enormous degree of implicitness that lies in objects as well as in everyday life. As I have shown, certain objects can be very enigmatic, even more so now that, in addition to the physical space, we have a cyberspace: one in which strange entities exist— such as web pages or computer files, that are not "present" in the same way as a table or a chair, but at the same time are certainly not merely ideal constructions. What is their nature?[34] This difficulty begins already with the mobile phone, that has many more resources than a home phone, and the interesting bit is that a great part of these services[35] have emerged little by little; no one—not even phone companies—could have predicted this evolution that goes way beyond the sphere of speaking (Bert 2005). From a *technical* point of view, the mobile phone in fact permits all types of

actions, including to write, photograph, play, customize, record, or listen to music; from the space-time continuum point of view, it grants us mobility and independence from the context, which has repercussions on the *social* level. And we can notice all this only after making it explicit.

2. *Distinguishing* means recognizing the peculiarity of a given kind of object with respect to others. In regards to the technological developments, consider the case of the e-book that, a few years ago, was meant to replace paper books: unlike text messages, it turned out to be less successful than expected. Why? Precisely because of the scarce distinction of the peculiarities of the paper book, a hardly replaceable object: its essential character, in fact, lies not only in the simple transmission of ideas or words, but also in doing so through a handy support, quick to consult and annotate, easy to transport (without the problems accompanying us when we travel with a computer or tablet)[36] and furthermore apt for being lent, given as a present, or used to furbish the house.[37] And, once again, the mobile phone seems like an excellent example: if the e-book promised a lot and offered little, the mobile phone ensures much more than was expected.

3. *Reifying.* The aim of all these operations is reifying: that is, offering a concrete body to impalpable functions (think of the spending power, reified by a banknote or a credit card) and mostly transforming into an object something that *prima facie* is not. And here the advantages of the object appear in all their might: it is the case of the clock, materializing the passing of the time by imitating the sun's course; or think of the computer desktop, where complex functions are turned into icons representing a desk, a bin, a mail box, and folders. It is here that powerful objects emerge, like the mouse: shaped like a rodent, it works as a hand. For this reason, once again, I began this ontology with the mobile phone, which—as I will argue in the following chapter—works as an absolute object precisely in that it is, so to speak, a mouse that needs no computer. Through the mobile phone I am trying to reify social reality and its anthropological, sociological, historical, economical, and geographical objects (Montuschi 2003)— just like people (much more serious and laborious than me) in Switzerland and Korea reify time through clocks and watches.

Existent objects and inexistent objects. The most complete taxonomy is the one proposed by the Austrian philosopher Alexius Meinong (1904) who, for the sake of exhaustiveness, aimed at deconstructing what, for him, constituted a prejudice toward the real. In fact, Meinong proposed to classify as "objects" not only those objects that common sense naturally tends to consider as such (namely physical objects) but also those that are usually located in the subjects' heads. In this case, "object" does not only apply to, say, the desk and the computer in front of me, or the book in your hands, but also to all the different thoughts that might occur in my mind and yours, just like a physical ailment we might have in this moment or we might have had in the past, or even the relation between, say, the table and the computer (the first is *bigger* than the latter) or between you and the window (say it is *on your left*).

Meinong starts from the consideration that even when an object does not exist in time and space, as logically contradictory (for instance, a square circle) or *de facto* (a golden mountain), when we speak of that object we believe we are referring to something. In the same way, we are convinced we are referring to something when we say that Mme. Bovary was bored in her provincial city, or that she never got to know Count Mosca. Hence the need for a formal doctrine that would deal with all objects, regardless of whether they exist or not.[38] It is a Copernican revolution presenting as a prejudice something that many—the majority of people—regard as a solid truth. Yet, if objects were only material, a sentence like "Object: request of a Visa for the United States" would be unintelligible, given that the only physical thing in it are the United States (the visa does not exist yet, and the request is a social object existing in time rather than space).

A hero of reification, Meinong is also a hero in *making explicit* and *distinguishing*, as emerges from his great taxonomy (see accompanying diagram). The general sphere of objects (*Gegenstände*) includes *objects* (*Objekte*), such as tables, square circles, and chimaeras, and *objectives* (*Objektive*), namely the content of linguistic enunciations, the object we refer to when we speak of something,[39] or rather when we predicate something (for instance, when we say that a rose is red). Objects therefore can be categorized as existent, nonexistent, and subsistent.

Existent objects are situated in space and time (trees, tables, the computer screen in this very moment, the page of the book when you read it) and, with their imposing presence, determine a prejudice toward the real. Inexistent objects can be objects *de facto* (a golden mountain), *de jure* (a square circle), or formerly existent (the Roman Empire or yesterday's walk, that can also be classified under the category of inexistent objects *de facto*). Subsistent objects include numbers, geometrical properties, relations (for instance,

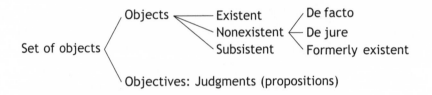

the computer is smaller than the table, a newspaper is bigger than a hand), which we never find as such but always are exemplified into something.

This universal registry, though, has its limit, denounced by Bertrand Russell (1905): *It is contradictory to speak of nonexisting objects* and wonder, for instance, if the current king of France is bold, because there have not been kings in France for a while. We should limit ourselves, if possible, to what is or can be.[40]

There is another problem with Meinong's system. Objects are proper objects, objectives are propositions regarding objects: the white snow is the object, while "the snow is white" is the objective, namely a judgment. Furthermore, Meinong is ambiguous enough on this point, because by "objective" he seems to designate both judgments and the state of things they refer to.[41] Still, for the purpose of my argument, which is more limited, we can do without them.

Finally, the third problem: The classification is not balanced, at least for the work I am proposing. Meinong's tripartition includes existent, inexistent, and subsistent objects. An existent object is, of course, a physical object. A subsistent object is a number, a relation, or a theorem. I might as well call subsistent objects *ideal* objects, in which we could easily include the objects nonexisting *de facto* and *de jure*, which are indeed kinds of ideas. I have thus reduced Meinong's three categories to two, but something has yet to be covered. On one hand, in my categorization, it is hard to claim that the Roman Empire is an ideal object like a triangle: had Romulus not founded Rome, the Empire would not have existed, unlike Pythagoras's theorem and the number 5. I therefore must find a place in which to categorize it. On the other hand, in Meinong's categorization, something like right-hand traffic is not accounted for. It does not exist like tables or chairs, nor like a number, yet it is not inexistent either. So, how to categorize it? I propose to create a new family of objects: *social objects*. In short, in revising Meinong, here is the alternative classification that I will use in the rest of the book:

Physical objects exist in time and space.

Ideal objects exist outside time and space.

Social objects require modest portions of time and space and begin in time.

First, there are *physical* objects: Mountains, chairs, tabernacles, and so on. This little is certain: these objects do not depend on subjects, given that it would be rather odd to claim that the snow on Mount Blanc depends on our will. Obviously, artifacts—and today, to an extent, organisms—can be constructed: but once they are built, they possess a life of their own with respect to the builder and everyone else. If a tabernacle was found in ten thousand years, possibly there will be no trace of the rite it was destined to, and it is plausible that no one will have thought of that object for thousands of years: yet it will still be there, with all its characteristics. Moreover, the fact that chairs are such only for humans (and maybe for cats) and tabernacles are such only for humans does not mean that their physical properties are determined by humans or cats. Postmodern thinkers try to hide this fact by claiming that physical objects are reduced to subatomic particles and are therefore the product of the scientists' theoretical constructs; yet it is certain that those very thinkers would not be happy if their doctor's diagnosis turned out to be a simple theoretical construct. There is a macroscopic level on which objects are really solid and independent and, hopefully, a diagnosis is correct.

Second, there are *ideal* objects. They are not constituted by a subject, in the sense that the properties of a triangle, of the principle of noncontradiction, or of an arithmetic operation do not depend in any way, as for their essence, on the construction of a logician or a mathematician. They are discovered and not invented, exactly like a continent. Here subjects intervene only in the phase of their socialization: I discover a theorem and publish the outcome. Obviously, one could object that axioms can be chosen and therefore outcomes can be constructed, and that my view of ideal objects is sharply Platonic. I do not deny it, but Platonism seems to satisfy deep intuitions, for instance, the fact that the discoverer of a theorem (like a historian or a geographer) is not awarded the Nobel Prize for Literature.

Finally, there are *social* objects. Unlike physical objects, they do not exist independently from someone's belief in their existence (but this does not make them arbitrary: try to leave a bar without paying and you will get the idea).[42] Unlike ideal objects, they begin in time. My promise started, say, on Friday, November 17: before that, it did not exist. This does not imply, though, that social objects depend on my will once they have been constructed as such. The promise I made on Friday, November 17, might keep haunting me even if, in the meantime, I changed my mind or forgot about it (others will remind me). Note a point that will become decisive in the rest of the book and which is the key point: social objects need a physical support that is not imposing, because it consists of an *inscription* on paper, magnetic memory,[43] or a person's mind.

In a nutshell, one might formulate the following framework:

1. In the world there are *subjects* and *objects*. Subjects refer to objects (they represent them, have them in mind, do something with them), that is, they are endowed with intentionality;[44] objects do not refer to subjects.

2. Objects are of three kinds: (a) *physical objects* (mountains, rivers, and human and animal bodies) existing in time and space independently from the subjects knowing them, even if they might have made them, like in the case of artifacts (chairs, screwdrivers); (b) *ideal objects* (numbers, theorems, relations) existing outside time and space and independently from the subjects knowing them who, nonetheless, after knowing them, can socialize them (for instance, the publication of a theorem: it will be the publication that will begin in time, not the theorem itself); (c) *social objects*, which do not exist *as such* in space but subsist as traces (inscriptions, records in people's minds) and, through these traces, acquire duration in time; they depend, for their existence, on the subjects who know or use them and who, in some cases, constituted them.

3. This last circumstance warns us that social objects, for which construction is necessary, depend on social *acts*, whose *inscription* constitutes the *object*.[45]

Note that the fact that certain objects do not need an inscription, while others require it imperatively, plays a primary role in my classification. On one hand, there are chairs and mountains existing independently from our thought of them, theorems being discovered and not invented and so on. On the other hand, there are social objects not existing without acts that constitute and inscribe them. The reason is very simple. On one side, I want to preserve the independent character of a great quantity of objects; on the other, I wish to point out that objects requiring the intervention of subjects (because there is no promise without a promisor and a promisee) are something profoundly different from a pure product of subjectivity.[46]

Still, if what interests me are social objects—and if I have just suggested that the primary ingredient, or better, the *necessary* (but not sufficient) *condition* of the construction of social reality which those objects are part of is inscription—why on earth have I decided to talk about the mobile phone? Could I not speak of, say, the typewriter? The answer is easy: The mobile phone is a *writer*, a tool for writing as well as a support *on which* to write. Time to verify this claim.

2

WRITING

An old advertisement said: "The phone: your voice." Is it still true? It does not seem like it. Already in 2005, when this book was first published, another commercial proclaimed: "When shut, it looks like a simple, very small mobile phone (4×2.4 inches), 1 inch thick, but when you open it, it reveals itself for what it is: a mobile phone that has little to envy personal computers for, with a full keyboard, a 2.75-inch screen, and Wi-Fi and Bluetooth. The expected price? Around $900."

Yes, it was expensive, just like some less ambitious mobile phones that support e-mails. Soon it became much cheaper and within a few years it became pure archaism. But there is a reason why this advertisement makes us smile, and not because of the marvels of technology, but due to a philosophical mistake regarding the mobile *eidos*. What this special phone truly is, as the advertisement puts it, is a personal computer, a machine that does many things but that, essentially, is for writing. True. Nonetheless, the point is that now—and ever since their first appearance—even the most modest mobile phones are already writing machines.

As I have already mentioned, mobile phones have letters on their buttons, and not only numbers. Letters are not present for mnemotechnic reasons—like in Maigret's old rotary phone, where "Alma 2327" stood for 2562.2327 and "Alma" indicated a real phone district in Paris whose numbers all started with the same four digits—but they are for writing text messages.

Also, numbers themselves are not only for "dialing the number" of the person we are trying to reach, but occasionally for sending a text message that, say, during an exam, would suggest to a friend that America was discovered in 1492 (here the number is a date); for setting the alarm (here the number is an hour); or for getting a result using the phone's integrated calculator (here the number is not a code, as in the case of phone numbers, pin codes, or debit cards but a real number: an ideal object).

And even if we decide to use the phone only to speak, it still will implacably write to us—at times in a perturbing and slightly annoying way[1]— telling us that the customer we called is now available, that our accounts were replenished, that we only have three euros left, that we have left Slovenia and entered Croatia, that we must go to vote, the particulars to attend a papal funeral, or (if we are Muslims in England) that the time has come to face the Mecca and pray.

Here is the system, or at least what Hegel would have called system: the allegiance, and not the opposition, between the phone and the writing machine. I will try to sketch, half in jest, a phenomenology of the mobile phone.

Thesis: The telephone. In the beginning was the word: telephone, radio, television. Not long ago, it seemed like writing was the vestige of an age that is in the process of disappearing, and that the future was going to be tied to speech and images: two functions apparently much more immediate, primary, and intuitive. Yet, the point is: the speech that circulates at a distance through the mobile phone or the radio, just like the overflowing images in cinema and television, are a prosthesis of writing and not its antithesis (they perform a distance transport, like letters). It is not by chance that the radio initially presented itself as a wireless *telegraph*. In other words, writing has always been present behind the media world and its manifestations, ready to come to the fore as always in the past, ever since the Sumerians and even before.

Antithesis: E-mail. It is not surprising that, at a certain point, there was a boom of writing: the computer, e-mail, the Web. It is an apparent opposition and a real continuity, because what the oral system guaranteed was writing itself, which has moved back to the front of the line, taking its rightful place. Do not believe those who say that we are dealing with a creolization in which writing becomes a variant of speech: it is not true and I will demonstrate it.

Synthesis: The mobile phone. Everything that can be said about e-mail, PCs, and the Web today holds also true for the mobile phone, which— uniting in the same limited physical space all the functions listed hitherto (telephone, radio, cinema, television, e-mail, web, data archive, and so on)—is a candidate for replacing the absolute tool: the tool that, for Descartes and Hegel, was the hand. Proving the fact that German is a philosophical language, in Germany mobile phones were called with a curious Anglicism: *Handy*. And here is, in our hands, at a hand's reach (*Zuhandenheit*, as Heidegger would put it),[2] the absolute tool, the machine to end all the others because it sums them all up. A handy machine, a writing machine.

Once this point is clear, I shall clarify what *writing* means. It is usually regarded as a means of communication, but it is such only accidentally. I shall get to this. For now, let us scroll together the pages of the system.

TELEPHONE

Primary and secondary orality. In the beginning was the word, then along came writing. This is what is continuously professed, and with a great deal of confidence—presupposing, moreover, that it is possible to determine at least approximately when writing began.[3] Yet, like in all great philosophies of history, in order to make figures add up, it is necessary to resort to Vichian courses and recourses: barbarity, apogee, decadence, and the return of barbarity.[4]

In this case, there would be a primary orality (that of the famous societies without writing) and a secondary orality. This second orality could be defined as returning illiteracy, but in the past century it was understood instead as the creation of a global village in which—just like in ancient villages, but at enormous distances allowed by the radio and the phone—people return to speaking, thereby abolishing the distance.

In the twentieth century, the great theoretician of primary orality was Walter J. Ong (1912–2003),[5] and his equivalent for secondary orality was Marshall McLuhan (1911–80).[6] The first described the characteristics of societies without writing, the latter suggested that through media such as the radio, the return of that original orality is realized. It is evident that all this can hold true only if we assume that between orality and writing there is an abyss, that is, to use a philosophically correct expression, a difference in essence. I will examine those differences in essence, supposing that they exist.

The enunciations that are formed in oral culture are paratactic instead of hypotactic: they possess more coordinates than subordinates. They are aggregative instead of analytical, full of formulas that cannot be disaggregated. They are therefore redundant, conservative, close to human experience, emphatic, and participative. Writing, on the contrary, seems more abstract; it permits the linearization of thought; it induces silent reading, and is a prerogative of those who are really capable of abstraction, which is strange, because Ambrogius surprised Augustine precisely for his being able to read without spelling.[7] Now, Augustine, like Plato and Aristotle before him, does not exactly seem like someone incapable of abstraction. In some cases, the idea (as old as Plato) reappears that writing is a poison for memory, which is weakened by the possibility of saving memories on paper and not in the mind. This, however, is in conflict with another idea: namely that societies without writing have no history (i.e., the codification of memory in texts and documents, and therefore the capitalization of knowledge).

To sum up, the essences at stake are as shown in the accompanying table. As a first consideration, they do not seem at all to be great contrapositions. Adorno theorized paratactic writing. Moreover, experience is full of abstractions and selections (empiricists were not fully wrong after all) and societies without writing are full of very abstract formations, that is, drawings. Finally, memory and history are not antithetic; they rather seem to be the same thing. The conclusion is that, probably, we are not dealing with differences in essence, for the reasons I have just enumerated, but mostly because *it is difficult to find a society completely without writing*. If we do not take these circumstances into consideration, we will not understand much and, in our quest for essences, we will miss the core of the matter. In fact, once we postulated these enormous distinctions, we can go wild in finding hybrid forms, insisting on the fact that writing in the age of e-mail and text messaging features traces of oral speech. Would it not be better to ask ourselves if oral speech instead reveals its belonging to writing, and if therefore the contraposition between orality and writing is not a matter of essence, thereby not constituting a real antithesis?

For example, Homer, who was illiterate, used formulas; mobile phones, when sending texts, do it as well. One could conclude that texts represent a hybrid formula between written and oral forms in which, who knows why,

Orality	Writing
Parataxis	Hypotaxis
Experience	Abstraction
Memory	History

the latter prevails. Yet one could also legitimately claim that, on the contrary, in the oral speech of the illiterate Homer there already was some writing, precisely because he used repetitive formulas, recurring to a sort of internal writing. And if this is not sufficiently recognized it is because there is a (long-lived and prejudicial) predilection for oral speech and its warmth and immediacy. In short, behind this apparently neutral analysis there is a hierarchy (speech is more important than writing) and an axiology (speech is better than writing), stemming from the idea that the voice is life and soul, while writing is death and body.[8] Yet, it is not a matter of overturning the hierarchy; it is a matter of demonstrating how fragile the distinction itself is.

Examples. Will the examples of the prevalence of orality, of the creolization or the general oralization people talk about so much (or rather write about, given that we usually find these opinions in essays and more or less scholarly documents) hold up to closer scrutiny?

I will start with the use of *formulaic expressions.* It is supposedly typical of oral speech, as we often read: in e-mails, in fact, there are formulas, clauses, and acronyms, creating a written-oral hybrid or creole (Baron 1998a; 1998b). I assume the reference is to abbreviations like ASAP ("as soon as possible") etc. The point is: I have just written *etc.*: is this an intervention of oral speech into writing? I do not think so. It is hard to pretend that there is a return of orality, unless such a return was always there from the beginning, from Roman tombstones and medieval codes, which were filled with abbreviations—among which the infamous @, standing for *apud* (at), just like i.e. stands for *id est* and & for *et.* If then I receive an invite to a party or a ceremony, written in elegant italics, I will probably find at the bottom right, in the place reserved for the signature, a formula (not different from ASAP, only less peremptory): RSVP, *répondez s'il vous plait.* And sooner or later I will find myself below a tombstone on which RIP will be written: *requiescat in pace.* An intervention of orality into writing? Creolization?

Good for those who believe it. We have to do with obvious abbreviations of alphabetic writing, both at a syntactic level (*Still waiting!* Instead of *I am still waiting for you!*) and at a grammatical level (B4B = *business for business*; CU = *see you*; U2 = *you too*; GOOD4U = *good for you*; ASL = *age, sex, location*).[9] Now, all these abbreviations existed long before e-mail, and therefore before the supposed creolization.

Next, *linearity*. If we assume that linearization (from left to right, from right to left, downward, upward, and even in boustrophedon) is the characteristic of writing, then I challenge anyone to find something more strictly and rigorously linear than an e-mail: it tries to get rid of extra lines so as to save space, but it would be inconceivable with no lines at all (unlike what can happen with a handwritten letter where one can insert a monogram or a drawing). Furthermore, the fragmentation of our correspondent's text when replying to him point by point is the most written thing there is:

> At 09:20 01/04/2005 + 0100, you wrote:
> Can I have 200 words by April 7?
> Certainly. My abstract on the web is almost 2000 characters as it is.

On to the little drawings, the *ideograms*. Texts contain them, they are called *emoticons* or *smileys*: :-) :-(:-/ ;-) (happy, sad, indifferent, cheeky, and so on). Now, I would really want to know in what way all this could constitute a symptom of the prevalence of orality. Hegel (1830, § 459), although without a mobile phone, already understood this very well. Ideograms (because this is what it is about) are the essence of writing, a writing that can *radically* do without speech, and this is why they tempted a radical intellectualist like Leibniz, who was a passionate researcher of a language for thought. Take also Frege's (1879) ideography: even here, you will find something similar to the e-mail or mobile phone ideograms. In e-mails and text messages, at most, we find a pathography rather than an ideography: the abbreviation of a feeling rather than an idea.[10] In fact, smileys are called *emoji* in Japanese and *emoticons* in English: that is, *emotion icons*; even though, in China and Japan, for these emoticons they use not only smileys but also the ideograms standing for "laughter" and "cry."

Then there is the terrible *chat*: here is an example where conversation is synchronic, like a phone call. In fact, this is an instance of intervention of oral speech in writing, with the use of interjections, little syntax, and so on. Nevertheless, using this as a decisive proof would be like claiming that *gulp* and *pant* in comics, as well as very normal signs in any text—even a very literary one—like exclamation and question marks, are the symbol of a creolization. On the other hand, it would not consider that chats, unlike phone conversations (at least in those not spied on by Enigma), are *permanent*, just like writing. And if we admit that chats constitute not only a little slower phone call, but also a permanent one (at least in principle), we would have to admit that text messages are like very fast letters, and again permanent ones (at least in principle).

Counterexamples. One last thing worth noticing is that these examples all favor orality. For this reason they systematically neglect counterexamples that come out in favor of writing.

The fax. Here is a device that was very modern twenty years ago (although it was invented in the second half of the nineteenth century) and that is now relatively obsolete, apart for an element I will mention in Part II, that is, the possibility of transferring *signatures* (and I am talking about real and substantial signatures, able to undergo aesthetic evaluation and graphologic analysis, not about the ghostly "digital signature"). Now, why is fax never mentioned? Because it is old? And then why, when it was a novelty, was it hardly ever mentioned? It was only mentioned when people tried to understand the etymology of its odd name. The fax is the example of the triumph of writing: that is, a letter, even handwritten, passing through telephone cables, traditionally destined to the transmission of orality. No one ever wrote an essay on the fact that orality has been creolized by writing. At least, no one I know of.

The answering machine. Shortly before faxes, answering machines became a stable in our homes and offices. Obviously, there were those who wrote epistolary novels, in which the correspondents are two, usually a he and a she, never reaching each other on the phone and leaving each other messages on the answering machine. The idea is rather obvious; still, it is curious that no one drew the conclusion, namely that if you can write epistolary novels with answering machines, it is because the famous answering machine, just like the fax, was a piece of writing, a mountain or perhaps a continent in the sea of orality. Precisely like writing, in fact, the answering machine is a *record*, allowing not only for the transfer of a message in space but also its deposit in time: the novel of answering machines would be nothing different from the *Liaisons Dangereuses*. We could even use our answering machines to take notes, phoning them to ourselves, just like we can save a text by e-mailing it to ourselves: that is, using a means of communication toward others as a recording tool for ourselves.

E-MAIL

Writing. Given these premises, the boom of writing we witness everyday should not come as a surprise; I do not mean only the pervasiveness of computers, e-mail, the Web, text messages, credit cards with relative signatures, debit cards with relative pin codes, and so on, but also the fact that high-tech stores are really huge depositories of writing machines. There is an apparent opposition and a real continuity here, because, indeed, what guaranteed the supposed system of orality was writing, which now comes to the fore. If this is the problem, it can be unraveled with the help of some great books.

The Bible. "Today students send letters to know the extent to which issues have been debated, what the outcome of the discussions was, what solution is in store and when the new handouts will be available." Thus wrote Heidegger to Husserl's daughter in 1919. Who knows what he would have said today. And who knows what he would have thought if Elizabeth Husserl had replied with a text full of CU, DUNNO, GOOD4U, and so on. To be honest, those abbreviations bother me as well: I hate writing *x* instead of *per*, and I waste a lot of time, losing my patience, whenever I have to write a text message. But that is another story; it concerns older generations, who grew up with the cult of orthography, and therefore are still capable of indignation in front of a mistake (*you're* instead of *your*). To me it seems like a mortal sin, but I can understand that others might not care one bit. If people spoke as they write, I would not find it scandalous at all. Why should writing imitate speaking and not vice versa? What would be wrong with it? And is this not exactly what happens now and has always happened,[11] at least in phonetic alphabets?[12] The only limit is that of practicability: if in theory the imperative "speak as you write" might seem easier to practice than "speak as you eat,"[13] then it is truly harder to practice, because we speak with the mouth, and the mouth needs vowels. Now, it is not clear how one could say "thx" instead of "thanks." Still, there are illustrious examples of apocope as such; think of the Jewish name for God: the tetragram JHVH for "Jahveh" is a little like THX for "thanks." Did the Almighty

express himself via texts? Why not? He always revealed a predilection for written communication: think of the Bible, or the Ten Commandments. It is at this point that the mobile phone might become a mo-bible, a Mobile Bible, a Bible on your mobile phone; and in fact it is not a matter of imagination, given that services exist that will text you daily with biblical verses.

Once again, notwithstanding all the prophecies on orality, we are on a path that leads to writing. In order to notice this, it suffices to free ourselves from the prejudice in favor of orality that, by means of false pieces of evidence, stubbornly claims the opposite: that is, the prevalence of the oral over the written in a world that, in reality, is getting closer and closer to the Library of Babel. I could speak or write about this a lot more, but I will limit myself to a very simple example. It consists of two long quotes that are to be read like the antinomies of the *Critique of Pure Reason*. Only, the latter looks true, whereas the first is blatantly false.

The Library of Babel. Here is the antinomy. Take the reflections of a web enthusiast and compare them to Borges's *The Library of Babel* (1941). Who is right, in the end?

Thesis: Hypertext

The hypertext therefore questions: (1) prefixed sequence, (2) the definition of principle and end, (3) the 'greatness' of a short story and (4) the idea of unity or a 'whole' associated with these concepts. One can therefore expect that, in a hypertextual short story, the single forms, like for instance the plot, the characterization and the setting, would change exactly like the literary genres produced by the melting of these techniques. The text, i.e., the hypertext, is a largely unknown object in continuous redefinition. . . .

It is necessary to free ourselves form the prejudice that keeps seeing the hypertext and hypermedia as evolutions or the extensions of textual technology, and consider the hypertext rather as an autonomous reality that, through its characteristics, allows the electronic text to express its potential in the best way. . . .

The relations regulating the electronic text and, as we will see, the hypertext are of an associative kind, very close to the functioning of human mind. The links between thoughts happen instantly and in a paradigmatic way: two concepts, in mind, get in contact either because they express different aspects of the same problem, or because they evoke similar contexts that facilitate their placement in reciprocal relation. . . .

Electronic writing inherits a great part of the prerogatives of oral speech, precisely thanks to the efficiency and fastness of informatics. The most blatant case in which this orality manifests itself is that of e-mail, a very agile means of communication that keeps both the informality of oral speech and the freshness of immediate communication.[14]

Antithesis: The Library of Babel

The universe (which others call the Library) is composed of an indefinite and perhaps infinite number of hexagonal galleries, with vast air shafts between, surrounded by very low railings. From any of the hexagons one can see, interminably, the upper and lower floors. The distribution of the galleries is invariable. Twenty shelves, five long shelves per side, cover all the sides except two; their height, which is the distance from floor to ceiling, scarcely exceeds that of a normal bookcase. One of the free sides leads to a narrow hallway, which opens onto another gallery, identical to the first and to all the rest. . . .

This much is already known: for every sensible line of straightforward statement, there are leagues of senseless cacophonies, verbal jumbles and incoherences. (I know of an uncouth region whose librarians repudiate the vain and superstitious custom of finding a meaning in books and equate it with that of finding a meaning in dreams or in the chaotic lines of one's palm. . . .) . . .

The Library is total, and its shelves register all the possible combinations of the twenty-odd orthographical symbols (a number which, though extremely vast, is not infinite): Everything: the minutely detailed history of the future, the archangels' autobiographies, the faithful catalogues of the Library, thousands and thousands of false catalogues, the demonstration of the fallacy of those catalogues, the demonstration of the fallacy of the true catalogue, the Gnostic gospel of Basilides, the commentary on that gospel, the commentary on the commentary on that gospel, the true story of your death, the translation of every book in all languages, the interpolations of every book in all books. . . .

I cannot combine some characters

dhcmrlchtdj

which the divine Library has not foreseen and which in one of its secret tongues do not contain a terrible meaning. No one can articulate a syllable which is not filled with tenderness and fear, which is not, in one of these languages, the powerful name of a god. To speak is to fall into tautology. This wordy and useless epistle already exists in one of the thirty volumes of the five shelves of one of the innumerable hexagons— and its refutation as well. (An n number of possible languages use the same vocabulary; in some of them, the symbol library allows the correct definition a ubiquitous and lasting system of hexagonal galleries, but library is bread or pyramid or anything else, and these seven words which define it have another value. You who read me, are You sure of understanding my language?)[15]

The moral of the story is simple. We have seen it many times: sails, cannons, gunpowder, locomotives, cars, telephones, radio, atomic bombs, televisions, and obviously computers (but also other devices, like, for example, the Neapolitan flip coffee pot and sticky notes that have been unfairly neglected) have become the symbol of epochal revolutions—modes of "setting-itself-to-work of truth," as Heidegger (1935–36) would put it (Taylor and Francis 1977, 184). Now, rather curiously, this attitude, while pretending to be respectful and solicitous with regard to technology, turns out to be typically neglectful as for technology's proper character. Technology, in fact, is by definition always equal to itself—that is, it consists of a possibility of retention ensuring iterability, and is thereby able to potentiate resources that (rather confusedly, since the dividing line is far from clear) are called "natural" (Gehien 1957).

In this sense, the praise of the Web would merely repeat, as has happened so many times before, Solon's naïve attitude (*Timaeus* 22b SS)—he claimed to narrate the Great Flood to the priests of Sais, who objected that that was not the *only* flood but merely the *last* one, and that it destroyed the Greeks' archives (so that the Greeks were destined to be forever young), but not the Egyptians' archives.

Bouvard and Pécuchet. In Egypt all is written, and in Western cultures as well. Yet with all this, we have not entered a more literate and literary society. On the contrary, there is no doubt that, since McLuhan's times, the indifference toward book culture has increased, instead of diminished. On one hand, it might even be a good thing: the value of notes, photocopies, and "materials" gathered for a book decreases. In the same way, empty erudition diminishes in the age of Google, which is nothing but an acephalous erudite, an enormous Bouvard and Pécuchet who remembers everything and understands nothing, like Zeno Cosini in Svevo's novel,[16] and like writing in Plato.[17]

The increase of writing is developed also where once there would have been only spoken words. Think of the boom of written forums on scientific matters, or of blogs on everyday issues. Where people would have once met to discuss a book, now they write one another—and these posts, as long as the discussion lasts, fill up your computer.

As often happens, we are dealing with a twofold phenomenon. On one side, it seems like writing is infiltrated and threatened by oral speech, because these letters (written in a hurry and in great number) do not seem to reveal much literacy. On the other, though, the fact remains that what would once have been (mostly or only) orally expressed—after all, the *Objections and Answers* at the end of the *Metaphysical Meditations* by Descartes are like a huge blog and an enormous eighteenth-century forum—is now *written*.

A cantor of orality, so as to defend coherently his thesis of the prevalence of oral speech, would be forced to claim that Plato's dialogues, literary and hyper-written works, represent an invasion of orality into writing.

La Comédie Humaine. Still, the stuff that mostly invades our e-mail archives, and that could hardly be defined as a triumph of orality, reveals a character that, in principle, only belongs to written culture. That is, what we might call "ungrammaticality": mistakes, negligence, and mostly a lack of consideration for orthography, grammar, and syntax. Take e-mails and compare them to old letters: in e-mails you will find plenty of mistakes, sloppiness, and so on, not only in the form but also in the content.

It does not only depend on haste: orthographic errors, in e-mails, can be *deliberate*. A very high percentage of the e-mails we receive consists of spam—advertisements for pills and moisturizers, generally with the aim of improving sexual performances; or of e-mails by supposed descendants of African dictators asking for your bank account number so they can deposit money (which they claim they will take back later after leaving you a generous portion of it). The interesting part of this is that, as the experts say, 1 percent of these messages actually work: someone actually does fall for that scam. The remaining 99 percent of customers try to get rid of them, and usually there is the junk mail feature, recording the subject of the message and preventing it from being received again. Does it work? Yes, most of the time. Yet, if you check your junk mail folder, you will still find spammers promising you to lose weight while sleeping, writing in the subject line: Loose Weıght Whıle you Sleeeepe. The same goes for offers of Valium, Viagra, and Xanax, that might pop up as Best Source V|@gra, Vali(u)m, X(a)n@x. At times, you find some gibberish in the end, like Create a new income with eBay . . . bnrcrnqmad (maybe the final "mad" really means something).

Among the e-mails—signed with names that would suffice to fill seven thousand *Comédies humaines*: "Dana," "Tracy," "Gonzalo," "Juana," and "Mabel"—some are e-mails promising filters to avoid junk e-mails, and yet they jam up your account and keep changing sender aliases and subject lines. In all this, though, the outcome is that the degree of writing has increased, not decreased: what can be more rigorously written than those cryptographies?[18]

And now access the Internet. You will truly enter the Library of Babel; recall Borges' passage: "This much is already known: for every sensible line of straightforward statement, there are leagues of senseless cacophonies, verbal jumbles and incoherencies." Of course, one could point out that, in the library, nonsense will always prevail, given that it contains all that is writable. Yet on the Web, while there are many false statements, everything is still oriented toward a meaning: there are no absolutely meaningless texts or, if there are, they have been written with that precise intention. I admit it: it is not the Library of Babel, but it is close. The Web is a *degraded* version of the book, and at times it can seem like a book written by an idiot,[19] an exploded book, in which, though, we have to deal with *emphasized* writing.[20]

The unexpected: the boom in writing. The end of the book and the boom of writing: that is what Derrida announced in 1967, in his *Grammatology*. Nonetheless, once again, I invite you to consider that in the spaceship in *2001: A Space Odyssey*, dated 1968, we find normal typewriters, far from personal computers. A mobile phone (in the proto-form of a watch with TV and two-way radio) appeared in *Dick Tracy*, but that, strangely, seemed like utter science fiction. In short, no one (apart from Derrida) was expecting this, and we can verify it with a little experiment.

Arriving in Turin by car, from Milan, one encounters relics of past futures: the factories on the left and right of the highway. The same happens when leaving the city to the south (there is the Lingotto, the area where Fiat used to thrive). The hangars next to the highway where Fiat used to built cars once represented the future. Then, for a long period, they were a real and actual present, and now they are the vestiges of a past that is no more.

But things are not always this linear. Shortly before the Lingotto, in fact, we find a strange chronological excrescence: a future that was never realized and yet seemed to be at hand when we imagined it. I am alluding to the odd relics of "Italia '61," the expo dating back to more than half a century ago that was meant to celebrate the hundredth anniversary of Italy's Unification. A pavilion was named "Turin in the year 2000," a little like *Part en l'an 2000* by Jules Verne. To refer once again to Leopardi's poem, "the magnificent and progressive fate" of humankind is depicted on those shores (of the Po river, to be precise), that is: A monorail falling off that, we must assume, should have constituted the normal means for urban transport in the future Turin (today, famously, the metro is not finished yet, and it was only started in 2006). Ruins of great pavilions that were made of glass and steel and supermodern in '61 are now reduced to undecipherable functions, arcane like druidic cults, and today empty, broken, and taken over by rust and wild plants. And there are other weird contraptions and rusted spikes reminiscent of highways left unfinished for lack of funding. Had there been a channel, we can be certain they would have built a bridge. But there is just the Po, and not far from there you can see the initiatives of the fiftieth anniversary (1911), looking much better—at least because, instead of prophesizing the future, they re-evoked a medieval past (a burg, a castle).

Anyone who was a dedicated reader of the *Mickey Mouse* comic strip around 1961 (I was one myself) would have considered it all, from the monorail to the supermodern pavilions, as part of an imminent future, made of flying scooters, monorails, and even flying carpets (all that survived the Darwinian selection are *tapis roulants*, generally in airports). Certain highway stops are in fact close to the buildings in Mouseton in the year 2000; these ghostly edifices are scattered around Italy (in particular, one on the way from Como to Milan, the other going from Milan to Genoa, a short distance past Serravalle).

This phenomenon is not exclusively Italian, of course. One of the most intense activities in the former East Germany after the reunification consisted in demolishing the futuristic buildings that were built in the sixties to celebrate conquests and cosmonauts. Not much is left of them. I am thinking in particular of a glass skyscraper in the shape of a rocket in Leipzig (not to be missed), whereas in Berlin they tore down almost the entire Alexanderplatz. The effect is vaguely Pompeian: frozen moments in life. Yet that life never existed in the first place, it was only prophesized: a virtual place that never turned real. The ironic part is that many other realities that came along a little later were not even included in the most hazardous virtualities. Following "Italia '61" there was "Italia '68," with other virtualities, not technical but moral and social, that did not stick (communes, open relationships), while other, unexpected, things grew and flourished, like the growing number of single people. And no one ever thought that the future would bring increasingly transportable writing machines in the form of computers and mobile phones. Certainly, McLuhan did not.

A modest counter-proof comes from this cover image of the 1999 reprint of the Italian edition of one of the most famous works by McLuhan. For this reprint, the publisher used as a dust jacket the image of the Statue of Liberty holding a computer in one hand and a mobile phone in the other (the one with the torch). The cover changed in the 2002 edition, not because computers and mobile phones were in regress, but on the basis of the wise and obvious consideration that in 1964, McLuhan, like anyone else, did not have a clue about them.

The future behind us. The reason for this unpredictability is obvious: *one cannot predict what is already there.* New writing machines draw their capability of being absolute tools and marvelous machines not from something else, such as a surprise or an event changing the course of history, but from the most ancient and remote of technical resources: the possibility to leave traces and to record in written form.

When we tried to guess the future, writing was already there. It was in the traces with which animals mark their territory, in the paintings of Neolithic caves, in Egyptian tombs, in rolls, books, libraries, newsagents. It was in the very pages in which prophets prophesized and science-fiction authors fictionalized, offering the modest and immense possibility of *recording.* Upon closer inspection, this is not only the common denominator of e-mail, the Web, and the mobile phone but also television, radio and letters.

THE MOBILE PHONE

The prevalence of the mobile phone. If all I have said so far is true, then the prevalence of the mobile phone should come as no surprise, as it unifies in a limited space *all* of the functions listed so far, thus constituting the *absolute device*, and because it is mobile, it also presents itself as the effect of writing and teleportation. It is a gigantic and yet pocket-size archive that one day will incorporate all kinds of the data about us: maybe the day will come when we will be buried with our SIM card, in future memory. For now, there are testimonials of mobile-shaped tombs in Ghana.

The absolute device should make us think. So far, philosophers have reasoned a lot about artificial intelligence and not much about the mobile phone, with a prejudice that is antithetic to that of web fanatics. They regard it with disdain, as if it were something for madmen or idiots. The computer

seems much more noble. Yet—and we are starting to notice it—it is not so at all. The debate on artificial intelligence went more or less along these lines: computers are images of the human mind, traditionally depicted as a *tabula* to write on. And the fundamental question is: Can the work done by computers be called "thought"? And, inversely, can what we call "thought" be explained by analogy with the computer? The conclusion of the debate has been more or less that the analogy holds true only to a certain extent, both because the human mind turns out to be extraordinarily more complicated than a computer and because, for instance, a computer does not

laugh or cry, get bored or entertained, nor does it have intentions (as they say, in my opinion, problematically).[21] End of story. The computer does not think: the marvel disappears.

At this point, though, a guy passes by with a mobile phone, talking to who knows who, texting at full speed and maybe (if he has ear buds) looking like he is talking to himself. Call him stupid. This guy is doing something even more sophisticated than simulating human thought: he can be (within the limits I tried to describe) connected to everything and be found anywhere. The marvelous machine is his, the mobile phone, not the computer. More precisely—as the system teaches us—the destiny of the cunning machine seems much more tied to the silly machine than we might be willing to admit.[22] The reasoning is more or less the following.

For the past twenty years or so, the computer has entered not only laboratories but also our homes, where it is mostly used for recording and archiving purposes, not just calculations. But when did the machine become something more than a mere writing tool? When it allied itself with the phone. Through e-mails, the computer turned into the possibility of reaching everyone with a quick and almost infallible post (to be honest, with the spam and antispam it is getting worse). And, through the Web, it became the key to the world that, I proposed (with no claim to originality), we call the Library of Babel, containing everything and more.

But if this is, so to speak, the essence of the computer, then we are dealing with a variant of the mobile phone, given that its fundamental resource ultimately depends on delocalization.[23] So much so that mobile phones and computers now coincide in the same physical object—the smartphone or tablet. Yet, above all this, there is the boom of writing, manifesting itself in the fact that, on one hand, you can call people via the Internet using Skype on a computer, for example,[24] and on the other, you can access the Internet via your mobile phone (in which case the phone becomes a computer).[25]

The invisible man. Note that everything I have said about e-mails can be said about text messages, another instance of the boom of writing—with the crucial feature of traveling through machines that were originally designed for oral speech, given that they looked like a modification of the oral medium *par excellence*: the phone.

A penitent of the confraternity of the Santisimo Cristo de los Alabaderos was once photographed while sending a text message during the procession of the holy week in the Royal Palace in Madrid. Was he perhaps getting even with JHVH? Whatever the reason for his action, it certainly represents a situation that, not long ago, was hard to imagine: writing on the phone, writing while walking (*pace* Flaubert, who claimed that *on ne peut écrire qu'assisi!*) and, maybe, even sending images.

Now, when were texts born? For what I know, the first message was sent in 1992 from a computer to a mobile phone (and the allegiance was slowly taking shape).[26] Initially, they were conceived as tools for technicians, destined to the transmission of information on the phone traffic. It was therefore an ascetic and aseptic function, while today texts have a completely different purpose: they are used not only by technicians but almost by everyone and, mostly, the vast majority of them has some *emotional* content.

The first Morse message sent via telegraph in 1844 was: "what hath God wrought." Maybe the penitent in Madrid would have been pleased by it, maybe God wrought also his text, but note the difference. The Morse message, like the telegram, was public and read by a vast number of people; the text message (at least in principle) is private and secret, realizing the dream of the invisible man: to communicate with others without being seen or heard.

The reason for all this is, as usual, very simple: the absolute tool, the mobile phone, is handy and palm-sized, easy to transport and hide—apart from when they take a picture of you sending texts during a procession.

One could object that this is all well and good, but the mobile phone still is an inert contraption, like any other tool. I do not deny this, but there is a sense in which quantity becomes quality.

Mms. Think of the hundreds of people photographing the last public appearance of John Paul II in the Piazza San Pietro. A few days later, while the pope's body was being carried out of the church, the crowd gathering on the side of the streets had difficulty seeing him, with all those people around. There was someone who, therefore, stretching out his or her arm equipped with a mobile phone, tried to capture at least the picture of the pope—a bit like a submarine sailor at the periscope.

All this photographing, once again, constitutes an extra power incorporated in the absolute tool, given that not long ago no one, if not a tourist with the tourist look, would have been carrying around a camera all day.[27] Most times this superpower is, like text messages, meant for affective functions (Doring et al. 2005)—even though, taking one's cue from James Bond's Minox, one can also photograph texts. In a blander way, our relationship with the image also changed, thanks to the instant impressionism stemming from the possibility of always having a camera or a video camera on us. Hence the mobile cinema (very popular in Korea [see Ok 2005]), which does not mean watching films on the phone, but actually making them using the device.

The Chinese room. Read this: "Now you can 'talk' to a medium via SMS. £1.50 per answer (o2/ Voda/ Orange)." Here is an interesting advertisement, which one can, obviously, receive via SMS. For the modest price of a pound and a half, it is possible to access the paranormal, which is surely not bad at all. Again, call it a stupid machine.[28] Besides, it also solves in one shot—in a little Draconian but efficacious way—the old dispute on artificial intelligence. Do computers think? Do machines in general think? Those were, as I mentioned, big questions that, for instance, Searle answered negatively, by way of the famous thought experiment of the Chinese room.

Searle's (1980) argument goes like this: Imagine shutting a person who speaks no Chinese in a room. The person is given two sheets of paper: the first sheet shows a series of Chinese characters, the other the English instructions on how to use them. She has to produce—only by following the instructions—sets of ideograms that would answer to other Chinese characters she receives from outside the room, which are the questions. The fundamental point of the experiment is that the Chinese person asking the questions and reading the answers might conclude that the person in the room speaks Chinese, while, in reality, she is merely manipulating symbols of which she ignores the meaning. Moral of the story: computers do not think, and the program of "strong" artificial intelligence is wrong.

All well and good, but how do people think? Consider the experiment invented in 1886 by a French novelist, Villiers de l'Isle-Adam. He imagines, in *Tomorrow's Eve*, a mechanic android fabricated by Thomas Alva Edison in the basement of Menlo Park, with a gramophone guiding its gestures and words. This android, according to Villiers, surpasses humanity in the sense of the spirit. Lord Ewald, a baffled visitor, asks Edison how the robot can reply, and Edison answers, "The man who loves, doesn't he repeat at every instant to his beloved the three little words, so exquisite and so holy, that he has already said a thousand times over? And what does he ask for, if not the repetition of those three words, or some moment of grave and joyous silence?" (Villiers 1886, 137).[29] That is to say: in fact, when we speak we do not act very differently from the person in the Chinese room. We surely possess lexical competence, but this is far from enough to prove that our intentions are "originary."

Predictive text systems incorporated in mobile phones know this, foreseeing the banal sentences we want to write in our texts. The curious thing is that, in Italy, this system of writing is also called "intuitive": it is not intuitive for us (as I said, I have big problems with it, and prefer to do without it, like many other people), but it is assumed that *it*, the phone, performs a kind of mind reading on us, intuiting our intentions.

Serendipity and concentration. Also in this case, the mobile phone is the center of everything: intentions and intuitions, writing and images, affects, instrumental communication, and so on. In a way, it is a case of serendipity: the incredible luck in bumping into very important things while looking for others, like Columbus looking for India and ending up in America, to his pleasant surprise. Here, we were looking for a wireless phone and found instead the absolute tool, absolute because it is handy and hand-sized.

We have more modest testimonials of this serendipity mixed with ecologic size. Think of the fact that, for instance, credit cards are issued by financial institutions with different pasts (American Express used to be in the traveler's checks business, Diner's was mainly used in restaurants) and then were unified into a piece of plastic of the right dimension, which was then used also by debit cards for the immediate request of money, and later on became the standard size for all documents (driver's license, ID card, phone cards and so on). Elsewhere credit cards themselves turned into phone cards, IDs and so on. The phone, so to speak, gives a soul—namely a processor of sorts (the SIM card) and a battery—to functions that used to require an external support, with the result of producing a gigantic monopolist concentration, even more impressive as it is concentrated in a hand-sized object.

THEORY OF CRAFT

The human and the hand. In order to define what I call (perhaps a bit pompously) a "system," advertisements are more than suitable: that is, as strange as it may seem, they are not misleading at all. A lady wrapped in a very long phone wire ending with a mouse; a mobile phone looking like a computer; an ancient code on a bookstand connected to a keyboard and, of course, a mouse; a book popping out of a mobile phone; book designs increasingly inspired by the graphic design of web pages. Here is, in our hands, at hand (*Zuhandenheit*), the absolute device: handy, as we have seen.

To tell the truth, philosophers (from Anaxagoras[30] and Aristotle[31] to Hegel[32]) claim that the marvelous machine is the hand itself, the "tool of all tools," because, by grasping, the hand permits the use of scissors, pens, doors, chairs, stools, and obviously computers—it makes even agreement possible (There we'll be hand in hand, dear, / There you will say, "yes."[33]). We even have exaggerations, like the one we find (as often happens) by Heidegger, who is responsible for the following passage, which is slightly permeated by folly:

> We are trying to learn thinking. Perhaps thinking, too, is just something like building a cabinet. At any rate, it is a craft, a "handicraft" (*Hand-Werk*). "Craft" literally means the strength and skill in our hands. The hand is a peculiar thing. In the common view, the hand is part of our bodily organism. But the hand's essence can never be determined, or explained by being an organ which can grasp. *Apes, too, have organs that can grasp, but they do not have hands.* The hand is infinitely different from all grasping organs—paws, claws, or fangs—different by an abyss of essence. Only a being who can speak, that is, think, can have hands and can be handy in achieving works of handicraft. But the craft

of the hand is richer than we commonly imagine. The hand does not only grasp and catch, or push and pull. The hand reaches and extends, receives and welcomes—and not just things: the hand extends itself, and receives its own welcome in the hands of others. The hand holds. The hand carries. The hand designs and signs, presumably because man is a sign. (2004, 16; emphasis added).

Man is a sign and an ape could not buy a mobile phone, not because it is devoid of money and language, but because it does not have hands—or, at least, *one* hand. Only man is endowed with a *Hand*, therefore only man has the right to a *Handy*. Who knows if Heidegger would have been pleased by this proof of the German language's philosophic character. And who knows if, vice versa, he would have been pleased to find out that in Thailand the mobile phone is called *mue tue*, "hand extension" (Ukritwiriya 2005), which has the same meaning it has in Finland, where the mobile phone is called *kanny* (Nyìri 2005a, 259).[34] Speaking of ethnocentrism and anthropocentrism, it is unclear how Heidegger, residing in the Black Forest, ever could have run into apes that would allow him to proclaim that apes have no hands. In this regard, Claire Brétecher's deduction comes to mind (see picture).

In short, being human counts only to a certain extent: the greatest merit goes to the hand and a fistful of devices, internal and external, on which craft is based. In fact, in the half-serious system proposed in this chapter, there is also a slight reformation of Hegel's dialectic, *à la* Gentile. What makes it work is not, in fact, a movement of the spirit (as Hegel thought), but a transformation of craft, that is, what Heidegger would have called the *Gestell*, the imposition or disposition: namely everything that objects allow us to do, given that we can use a screwdriver to open a can of beer, but not to clean our ears. It is not like the spirit falls somewhere and is embodied in the subject who creates the objects. On the contrary, there are objects that rule over subjects, although not unconditionally (because the subjects, in turn, possess determined characteristics, given that they are not pure spirit).

If you think about it, at this point it all works. There is no difficulty in thinking that first there was the club, then the lever, then the wheel, then the car, and so on—whereas the confused explanation we find in the *Phenomenology of Spirit* always seems a little bizarre and arbitrary. It was noticed early on that Hegel was describing, in the language of theology and history, a transformation that took place in matter and craft. Hence the

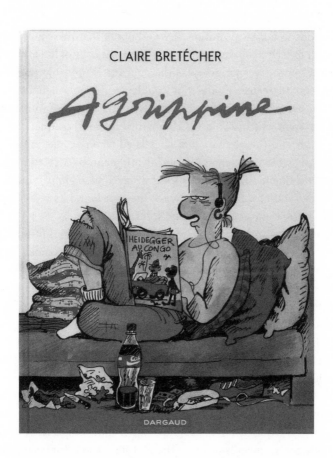

thousands of pages on craft written in the nineteenth and twentieth centuries, which we could dwell on for years. What I tried to propose with my little system is a particular test, with the aim of illustrating the essence of craft: that is, iterability, which finds its best realization in writing.

The tabula. So, how is iterability realized and what is its condition of possibility? We have seen that the advent of writing could not be foreseen because it was already there, behind us, since the dawn of time. Furthermore, and this seems even more important, *writing was not only outside us, it was also inside us.* That is to say, *Perì mail* has already been written, long ago: it is Aristotle's *Perì psyches* or, even before that, Plato's *Philebus* or *Phaedrus.* Our soul is similar to a book in which thoughts and sensations are written down, and this is the real book because everything else (wax, papyrus, paper, or electronic devices) is nothing but the imitation of the writing inside us.

Now, due to a typical illusion, it was thought that these external writings, inert or technical, were only a surrogate or a copy of the *logos* written in the soul of the learner, whereas the opposite is probably true: namely that, without these devices, the soul would have never thought of itself as a book. It is not excluded that we would have never had the dominating image of the soul, which would have remained *anemos*, an uncertain spirit wrapped around the body or that is exhaled when we die, but of which there is no "scientific" representation (while neurobiology thinks of the brain as a writable surface, and speaks of cerebral *engrams*). But indeed, since some kind of support was found, the soul found its representation, and the interpretation succeeded and stuck.[35]

Libraries, newspapers, the Web: all these are expansions of this *tabula*, and it is inevitable that the recent reflections on the "extended mind"—namely the fact that thought lies not only in the mind but also in the body and in external devices—far from contradicting the *tabula* hypothesis, confirm it (Clark-Chalmers 1998). With all this, I do not want to abuse the extended mind (see Marconi 2005): it is not really our mind that extends itself—the proof of this lies in the fact that someone caught cheating during an exam with a mobile phone cannot defend himself by asserting that he was just peering into his own mind. In another sense, of course, the extended mind exists, but we call it different names: "societies" or, if you like, "objective spirit." But no one would ever think that a post office is a part of one's mind. What I wish to highlight is rather the omnipresence of the *tabula*, both inside and outside us, in the computer and the mobile phone, in libraries and the Web.

One might even think that, in the face of globalization, there are two worlds—one online and the other on paper—with different celebrities and scoundrels and therefore also two different spheres of advertising and secrecy, maybe even different religions (JHVH on paper and online) so that a thing unknown in paper is famous online and vice versa.[36] The two worlds, through complicated legitimating processes, might brush against each other without ever truly touching; or maybe they could give way to strange experiences so that the Leibnizian hypothesis could actually occur (for instance, by turning on a computer or, inversely, going to the library, one could encounter the other world, finding different customs and values).

The phone and the car. None of the above is excluded, we will see what happens. But after all, if I am not convinced that the changes will be quite as radical and grand, it is because of what I call the argument of the phone and the car. With the phone, there was no longer a need to see people in order to communicate with them synchronically. But one does not see people only to communicate, nor does communication only happen through words: therefore, one takes the car, the train, or the bus and goes to see one's friends. Also, it is not only about seeing people but also, for instance, about seeing the sea or the mountains, about being in a dry climate or getting some fresh air and so on. This circumstance, if we pay attention to it, is the proof of rather complex philosophical arguments, and lies largely at the basis of the fact that Kant did not only write *Critique of Pure Reason,* but also the *Critique of Practical Reason* and the *Critique of Judgment.* He did not merely analyze our power of knowledge. In fact, if life were all about knowledge only, having a mobile phone would be more than enough to live (at least in many cases). This is not the case, though. We also have aesthetic needs: we are not only interested in whether something is true or false but, frequently, we want to see it or touch it. Then there are moral duties and social obligations, and replacing your presence at a wedding or a funeral with a phone call is usually a fallback option.

This is what I wish to underline after my cautious apology of humanity. The implicit assumption of the praise of the Internet is that the core of what happens and will happen is communication, and that communication is everything. But is it really so? We have just seen that communication is not enough. And as for writing, why not wonder whether the essence of writing, its *eidos*, lies rather in recording, in accordance with the intertwine between iteration and the *tabula* I sketched earlier in this chapter?

The umbrella. Before moving on to this theme, which I will develop in the next chapter, I wish to draw (although in a slightly schematic and dogmatic way) conclusions from what I have said so far.

1. Craft—any craft—needs a hand and a *tabula.* The hand inscribes, the *tabula* records and thus permits iteration, which is the essence of every craft.
2. The hand can use prostheses, for example, clubs, daggers, pens, keyboards, a mouse, or a *mobile phone.*
3. The *tabula* also needs prostheses: all the writing surfaces in this world, like cave walls, papyrus, paper, computer memory, or *mobile phones.*

The mobile phone, unique among these tools regarding the hand and the *tabula*, manages to guarantee both conditions. A pen, a mouse, a memory stick (shaped like a pen but equipped with the function of a memory device) perform these functions only partially: they are either on the hand's side or on the *tabula*'s side. The mobile phone, by contrast, is hand *and* tabula at once, at least when put in perspective. It is furthermore much more resistant than the computer, almost like a human body (even if it is more sensitive to water than a cat). It is also much smaller and has therefore a technical advantage that anyone can appreciate, even just by considering that small umbrellas caused the long and bulky ones to disappear.[37]

After demonstrating that the mobile phone is the best writing machine on the market, one should ask oneself what it means to *write* and, mostly, if writing essentially means *communicating*.

3

RECORDING

Bruce Willis. Action? On the mobile phone. "In this violent action thriller, instead of moving around, all the characters (policemen, criminals, even a six-year-old child) perpetually speak on the mobile [phone], with their hand scrunched up on their ear."[1] Here is a whole theory of language: the spoken word is the surrogate for action, and when one can talk—if at a distance, with a mobile phone, even better—action can go to hell.

The word surrogates action because it is communication. All this seems to go against what I said in the previous chapter, namely that the mobile phone is for writing just as much as it is for speaking. It also goes, even more strongly, against what I am about to say: namely that the essence of writing is not essentially communication, but recording. So how can we make this add up?

First, it is necessary to look at several counterexamples. At the 2001 G8 conference in Genoa, for security reasons the organizers jammed the cellular signal, starting from the obvious consideration that nothing can help coordinate a military or protest *action* better than a phone.[2] And, probably, the fact that phones are not distributed to soldiers along with uniforms and weapons only depends on this: to interfere with the signal is child's play.

More generally, though, I need to clarify three arguments. First I will elucidate in what sense the *eidos* of writing is tied to recording rather than communication. Second, I will try to explain what recording consists of and what it entails. Third, further developing my theory of objects, I will show that recording has much to do with truth.

Here is the first task: To clarify that the essence of writing cannot be reduced to communication. My thesis is that believing that the essence of writing is mainly communication is a bit like thinking that tables are essentially made for blocking doors: one of its functions, perhaps a showy and picturesque one, is mistaken for its essence. This can be verified by comparing two texts.

Sumerians, 3500 BC. Imagine someone tells or writes us: "The most ancient writing known and interpreted so far—the Sumer one, dating back to around 3500 BC—seems to have been invented for functional reasons, namely to preserve the memory of certain data: the most ancient texts are about cereals and sheep. For a long time what we call literature was orally transmitted; then, after the invention of writing, religious poems and others, like the Homeric ones, were written down." This quotation, seemingly reporting a solid truth, hides a prejudice that is revealed through a strange slip: "Writing was invented for functional reasons." And for what other reason should it have been invented? To pass the time? What the author wants to say is different. Those dumb Sumerians might have invented writing, but they did not understand that its essence lies not in recording but in communication. Or at least, this is what is believed. First you record, then you find out you can also communicate, and you become really clever. But is this how things really are?

Hanover 2005 AC. Consider an article referring to the 2005 Hanover fair, whose title is worthy of Derrida: "Beyond the voice, the cellular revolution." Here are a few passages from the article in question:

> The mobile phone . . . will no longer be just an instrument for making calls or for being reached wherever you are. It will be something else, something more: It will become the means for connecting to the television and to the Internet wherever you are, for downloading music from MP3 portals . . . with the new wireless lines you will be able to have broadband connections to the Internet. . . . Even while traveling for work or leisure, we shall be able to look for whatever we need online. . . . The extended memories of the new minimobile allow us to see our favorite television programs online. . . . The new mobile phone replaces the music lover's walkman. . . . And it is also in direct competition

with handheld Gameboy and PlayStation: if you use the mobile phone to access any site, you can download or play any videogame in real time. . . . Last but not least, the mobile phone is becoming a portable videophone. It doesn't merely take photographs, but it also shoots films with a resolution of three million pixels.

The Hanover mobile phones are just like the Sumerians: they write to record rather than to communicate. Also, the small pieces the Sumerians used in their counting system to record calculations were portable and *handy*, just like the slightly bigger mobile phones that are called phablets.

The alpha and the omega meet: writing is not *essentially* for communication, but rather (and the Sumerians were right about this) for recording.[3] This is understood even better thanks to the mobile phone, which is used also for transactions (to pay bills, for instance); for finding addresses and getting to one's destination thanks to GPS systems; for buying cinema tickets or watching a film on television; for dealing with one's identity (which is not that far-fetched, as I will show shortly), and even for the exact opposite of communication: isolation. Because a person who is listening to Beethoven on the train, watching a film or a football match, reading *War and Peace* by episodes, or playing a videogame (all of this on his or her mobile phone) does not want to communicate, but to interrupt the connection ("all around you") and be in holy peace forgetting about the rest of the world (Okabe et al. 2005, 66–67).

Robinson and the shopping list. Obviously, that writing is for recording rather than for communication is not a thesis that can be applied only to mobile phones or to the Sumerians, it also holds true for all that lies in between.

Imagine Robinson Crusoe on his island. As we know, at a certain point he starts cutting notches in the wood so as not to lose the sense of time. Considering that before Friday's arrival he has no one to talk to, he is indeed writing not to communicate, but to record. He might have been trying to communicate if, like Tom Hanks in the movie *Cast Away* (2000), he had drawn a smiley face on a ball, baptized it "Wilson" (the ball's brand), and started talking to it so as to keep himself company. This would only have been an attempt at communication, though, more or less like the case of people who talk to cats.

Now imagine someone going to the supermarket with a list in her pocket. The list, in my hypothesis, was not given to them by someone else: this person is single. In this case, therefore, the writing was, once again, meant to record. Imagine then a detective following the first person and taking note of what she buys: there would be another list that, again, is not for the purpose of communication but for recording.

Now imagine opening a letter from your bank. It might consist of two parts: One contains real communication (for instance, changes in the interest rate and costs, a subscription, and so on). The other, namely the list of transactions, does not communicate anything at all (it is all about things you did, at least the payments) but, instead, only simple records, just like during Sumerian times; or, better yet, in the age of the mobile phone, given that, with the phone, we can make bank transactions that are everything but an act of communication (it is one thing to do a bank transfer, to communicate that you have done it is another thing).

There are several such examples. Someone who is calculating on paper or with the computer, or even mentally, is hardly communicating something. The same goes for someone who is following the rules of a game (from this point of view, a solitaire player and a poker player are the same). Or again, someone who is conferring, through a performative, a title or a status is, at least partly, not communicating but producing something. Obviously we still can (and sometimes have to) communicate something: we can utter the result of a calculation, if someone asks for it; or say "checkmate" or "royal flush" when playing a game. But it is still possible to distinguish, in principle, recording from communication, even in the same sentence: "I pronounce you doctor in Philosophy" is a production, an act (the conferring of a title that was not there before), and a message that is given to the interested person—and possibly her relatives—about the outcome of her graduation.[4]

Note this: To realize a performative, communication alone is not enough. One needs an act and also what I will analyze as *registration*, another form of recording. It might happen that, at the end of an exam, I say to the candidate, "I can only give you eighteen."[5] The moment I utter this sentence, though, I have not given her eighteen, I only said I could do so. I will have given her eighteen only after the candidate accepts it, I write the grade on the register, and she signs the papers—that, in turn, will be valid only if countersigned.[6]

Logocentrism. To neglect these circumstances means to enact a removal dictated by what Derrida defined as "logocentrism." I will quickly verify this, by supporting my thesis with canonical (i.e., banal) examples.

As I mentioned in the previous chapter, Plato is also famous for his condemnation of writing, seen not as a remedy for memory but as a poison, given that people, reassured by the external writing, will cease to use the internal one. At least two aspects are interesting in this condemnation.[7] The first and most evident is that external writing is condemned in the name of another type of writing: an internal one. It is worth to quote the passage, because it manifests an attitude we often encounter.

> *Socrates*. I cannot help feeling, Phaedrus, that writing is unfortunately like painting; for the creations of the painter have the attitude of life, and yet if you ask them a question they preserve a solemn silence. And the same may be said of speeches. You would imagine that they had intelligence, but if you want to know anything and put a question to one of them, the speaker always gives one unvarying answer. And when they have been once written down they are tumbled about anywhere among those who may or may not understand them, and know not to whom they should reply, to whom not: and, if they are maltreated or abused, they have no parent to protect them; and they cannot protect or defend themselves. . . . Is there not another kind of word or speech far better than this, and having far greater power—a son of the same family, but lawfully begotten? . . . I mean an intelligent word graven in the soul of the learner, which can defend itself, and knows when to speak and when to be silent.
>
> *Phaedrus*. You mean the living word of knowledge which has a soul, and of which written word is properly no more than an image? (*Phaedrus* 275c–276b)

Plato is one of the biggest supporters of the image of the soul as a writing board (*Thaetetus*, 194e), therefore his condemnation of writing seems no less than bizarre. And here I come to the second aspect, a little less manifest: the communicative function, in both external and internal writing, appears to be secondary with respect to the recording one. In our soul we have an internal scribe, a *homunculus* annotating feelings and thoughts (*Philebus*, 38e–39a); after all, the condemnation of writing as a poison for *memory* lies within this very horizon. Then, it is true, the written logos is also accused of neither being able to defend itself nor to attack, because it can only say one thing, and is devoid of the father's help, that is, of the help of he who formulates the discourse—which seems like a difficulty to communicate but, note, it communicates a *recording* that is already there, in the soul or in the writing.

Aristotle, another great theoretician of the *tabula rasa*,[8] seems more unbalanced on the side of communication, at least in the *Perì hermeneias*— yet, one could say, *pour cause*, as it is a treatise on expression (Derrida 1967a, 29; 1968b, 91–98). Aristotle's theory is that the ideas present in the soul manifest themselves through symbols—words—which in turn are symbolized through writing (*Perì hermeneias*, 16a 3). The result is that writing appears, so to speak, as the imitation of an imitation: a second order reproduction. Yet, writing is reduced to this subaltern state only under the condition that one shares the presupposition that communication is what matters most. If one looked instead at recording, one would notice that the ideas impressed in the soul, that is, the *tabula*, are writing, and that therefore writing is not only at the end of the process (as a copy of the word in a communicative function) but also at the start of it, as the recording of ideas. What in the theory of expression lies at the end is instead at the start in the theory of recording.

Rousseau, in his *Essay on the Origin of Languages*, also manifests a significant contradiction.[9] He does not possess a theory of the *tabula* and he does not speak of recording, because his analysis takes place (like the *Perì hermeneias*) at a communicational level, given that languages undoubtedly are first of all for communicating. Yet, there is a problem. On the one hand, Rousseau admits that the gesture is prior to the word, which equals recognizing that a writing function lies at the very origin of communication: the gesture, as Bacon put it, is a "transitory hieroglyph," requiring no words—so much so that people speaking different languages can understand one another through gestures or ideograms. Nonetheless, Rousseau recovers the logos at another level, which is axiological. The gesture, common to humans and animals, is the expression of a need. The word, instead, is the vehicle of a feeling, and is only human. Therefore, from the point of view of right and merit (if not from the point of view of facts and time), the spoken word precedes writing and communication prevails over recording.

Hegel, in his *Encyclopaedia*, claims that alphabetic writing is in and for itself the most intelligent: a logocentric statement if there ever was one, which assumes that writing is the more intelligent the more it serves a servile function with respect to the spoken word.[10] It is interesting to see how he reaches this conclusion, because he does it in a completely antithetical way with respect to Rousseau. The latter claimed that the word is superior to the gesture because the first is noble and human, the second is functional and animalistic. Hegel, instead, declares that alphabetic writing is superior to the ideogram (that is, to the gesture, in Rousseau's system): in fact, although it seems to be intellectually developed, it is so for *practical reasons* (that is, after all, animalistic ones).[11] Hegel's idea, in fact, is that ideography can only work in an immobile system like the Chinese one, where few things are invented, given that ideograms stay more or less the same. However, Hegel observes, in a society in constant evolution like the Western one, where new techniques, ideas, and objects are constantly created, it is impossible to forge new ideograms at great speed: it is enough to have a few letters in a phonetic alphabet and it is a piece of cake. Nonetheless, Hegel seems to forget the circumstance for which a really strong ideographic element—numbers—serves the same function as the alphabet, but does *not depend on speech*.

The least we could ask Lévi-Strauss, with respect to Hegel, is to be a little less ethnocentric. If Hegel, while proclaiming the superiority of the alphabet over the ideogram, is really affirming the greater dynamicity of the West over the East[12] (times long gone!), we might expect a broader outlook from an ethnologist, who by his own profession is required to silence the prejudices of the Western tribe. Yet, in a chapter of *Tristes Tropiques* (1955, 281–82), he tells this story.[13] On a trip, he is studying an Amazonian population that never moved beyond the Neolithic: the Nambikiwara. He records their uses and customs on a notebook, and this intrigues the indigenous people, who try to write themselves. The problem is that—the ethnologist observes—*because they are primitive* they do not understand that the essence of writing is communication. They merely trace lines (it is the name they give to writing) and only the leader, a little cleverer than the others, shows to have a glimpse of understanding about the communicative role of writing. Which is like saying that the leader sticks out of the tribe only when he associates writing with communication—one could conclude that every time we draw a diagram to foresee the behavior of gases we regress to the Neolithic.

Finally, Ignace J. Gelb, author of a book entitled *Foundations of Grammatology* (1952), should at least be sensitive to the qualities of writing, and yet he is not. Gelb's book, in fact, presents itself like a doctrine of writing consisting of the tale of its evolution, from the image to the ideogram (where the image is also a sign), then to syllabic writings, and finally to the alphabet, the most clever of them all, because it is the closest to speech.[14] It is therefore an apparent praise of writing hiding a powerful praise of speech.

What is the moral of all these stories? More or less, that sometimes we like to deny the obvious, namely the fact that the *eidos* of writing is recording. We pay attention to the most evident function, communication, so that writing becomes a merely secondary function with respect to the spoken word. Claiming that one can still delete a text message, or use the shopping list of one of (illiterate) Charlemagne's literate vassals so as to learn something about the Middle Ages does not change this fact.

Paradoxically, in this logocentric group, the greatest critic of logocentrism is McLuhan (1964, 16), who claims that the content of writing is the word, the written word is the content of press and press is the content of the telegraph; but if we wonder what the content of the word is we discover that it is thought, *which in turn is nonverbal.* In other words, here he contests precisely the Hegelian assumption according to which "we think in names." Of course, McLuhan does this in order to give way to his praise of the image and, *jointly* (which is bizarre), of the spoken word,[15] but we could still bend his reasoning to an apology of writing and reread the passage of *Perì hermeneias* that echoes *Understanding Media* precisely in the light of this intuition.

SIM card. Another, more interesting conclusion that can be drawn from this suggests distinguishing two types of writing: a derived one (writing as a support of the word in a communicative function) and an essential one (writing as recording) that should be called, following Derrida, "archiwriting." It is the system of inscriptions that comes to the fore, for instance, with the evolution of mobile phones, lying neither in the letters and buttons nor in the text messages (that are writing), but in that *tabula* that we call SIM card, and then in the more and more powerful and capacious memory that we find in mobile phones in their gradual transformation into computers (and this is archi-writing).

It is important to pay attention to this distinction. Given that communication is a really beautiful thing (in this very moment I am trying to do so with all my might), I conclude that there is *only* communication. At a certain point I have even proclaimed that we have entered the age of communication (which is apparently everywhere but between partners and between parents and children), and so there are graduate courses in communication studies, in which we read books communicating things on communication and so on.

This is all well and good. Only—like when a guy passes with a mobile phone in front of a philosopher who is reasoning about artificial intelligence—one could receive the bank statement I referred to earlier. Without those recordings, the bank could not exist, while it could go on very well without communicating with me—I often do not even read the communications I receive. If we consider that the first function of writing was the recording of the king's income, debts, and credits, we find another obvious truth denied by logocentrism.

Here is, in short, what we try to remove when we insist on communication: an archi-writing is recording our perceptions, thought, acts, memories, and functioning even if we do not keep a diary (which, after all, is usually secret, that is, not destined to be shared).

Simplicio. Obviously, one—I will call this person, with all due respect, Simplicio, as he will put forward the arguments of holy common sense that the Aristotelian *Dialogue Concerning the Two Chief World Systems* sets against the Copernican ones defended by Salviati—could object that pontificating upon the boom of writing is absurd, for at least three reasons.

First, people affected by the so-called relapse into illiteracy watch television, just like the originary illiterates in the Middle Ages read the *Biblia pauperum* painted on the church walls because they could not read the written Bible, that is, the Bible for the clerics and the rich. How to deny, therefore, the overriding role of images both in the past and today?

Second, Simplicio would have every right to note, referring to his own and other people's experience, that one first learns to speak, then goes to nursery school, and only around the age of six learns to write, through some effort. How could we claim that writing precedes oral speech? Can there be a more ludicrous idea?

The third and most insidious move by Simplicio might be this: even if we denied the obvious and claimed that television and chess are also writing and that illiterate people also write, it would still remain to be seen what can be done with this fantastic metaphysics.

Here is how I would respond to Simplicio. On one hand, I would invite him to reread the cases presented above, about Robinson, the bank, and graduation: in none of these cases writing is essentially communication. Once we are freed from this prejudice, it will be easier to see that recording is not only done on paper or through the computer but, indeed, also by means of the *tabula* of our mind, which certainly exists before we learn to speak and go to school—actions that are futile and vain in the absence of a *tabula*. And once we distinguish writing from archi-writing, it also will be easier to understand what the appeal to inscription is for and in what terms it represents something more than a baroque metaphysics. To use a philosophical jargon, the *tabula* is a transcendental: something constituting the possibility of something else.[16] In other words, if Kant claimed that our experience of the world is made possible by two pure forms of the intuition (space and time) and by twelve categories, I limit myself to affirming that the world has its rules and imposes them, but that these laws could not be known or structured by us if we did not dispose of a recording system, which in the case of social objects becomes also, as I will show, a construction system. Now, what does it really *mean* to record? The example of writing provides a good thread to follow.

RECORDING SCIENCES

Memory stick. Now that I contested the essence-identity between communication and writing (in short: writing is not essentially communication, although it can be, contingently) I have to show why we write. One could, in fact, object and rightly so: "when I write an e-mail to you I first of all and essentially want you to read it and I do not care that I *record* what I have to say to you." Of course. But note, to begin with, that you want me to read the message, that is, you want me to *record* it. Furthermore, the day might come when that e-mail turns out to be decisive and the very possibility of recording offered by e-mail archives makes this possibility more and more concrete: think of the stolen letter in Poe's short story, no longer important for what the minister wished to tell the queen, but crucial as a proof of the fact that the minister wrote to the queen. After all, it is a story we witness everyday. In the beginning, computers had little memory and when we bought new computers we did not keep the archive: it was not clear, yet, that the decisive matter was to save what we had written; all this became progressively evident and even obvious in time. So much so that the archive function has long ago overcome the communication function, as is proved by a device that is *only* for recording and that has been around for a while. It is a good transactional object, something in between physical presence and remote backup: the memory stick (or USB stick, pen drive, flash drive). From an ontological point of view it is a very interesting object because—worth reflecting upon—it is called *pen* drive and yet it has the perfectly antithetic function of an enormous writing surface: a never-ending piece of paper or an unlimited wax board.

Some pen drives are produced by Victorinox, the company producing Swiss army knives. The company incorporates them into the knives themselves (which probably causes problems at the airport, as you will hardly pass security with them). Some people keep their pen drives on their key rings, but thus expose themselves to the risk of losing access to both their homes and their archives (luckily there are remote backup services). The function of the memory stick was also subsumed by the mobile phone. Now, what is it for, if it is not for communication?

It is obviously for recording. Just like the mobile phone is already an archive (how many things you can learn from someone else's phone, if only you are indiscrete!). This seems to be suggested with macabre peremptoriness by a mobile phone–shaped tombstone in an Israel cemetery (Google it). On one side, of course, it manifests a hope to communicate, the wish to keep the contact, given that the phone is open. On the other, though, it bears the name of the deceased: it is a recording, just like any other tombstone.

To come back to what I suggested at the end of the previous chapter. Where does the greater power of the evolved *Handy* (the memory stick and the mobile phone) derive from, compared to the weaker one of the primitive *Handy* (the mouse, which rather belongs to the category of knives and hammers)? Essentially it derives from the fact that the former are endowed with memory. This is why, as I have shown, the mobile phone plays, in our system, the role of the Absolute.

One might perhaps be tempted to see in the "mobile phone epopee" the confluence of two separate stories—a recording system and a communication system—that happened to cross ways by accident. Perhaps: credit cards, as I have shown, also have heterogeneous origins. In short, it is difficult to separate completely communication and recording (think of an animal marking its territory: is it communicating or recording? Probably both). Yet, this is not a sufficient reason to make recording disappear behind communication. To surface it, it is necessary to understand, what does recording entail? At least three elements:

1. The possibility of accumulation, that is, *capitalization*.
2. The possibility of *saving* (the primary function of computers), that is, preservation, beyond caducity.
3. The possibility of *idealization*, that is, a process of indefinite repetition.

Capitalization. I will tackle this matter by starting with a quote by the Peruvian economist Hernando De Soto (whom I will return to in chapters 7 and 8):

> Capital is born by *representing in writing*—in a title, a security, a contract, and other such records—the most economically and socially useful qualities about the asset as opposed to the visually more striking aspects of the asset. This is where potential value is first described and registered. The moment you focus your attention on the title of a house, for example, and not on the house itself, you have automatically stepped from the material world into the conceptual universe where capital lives. (2001, xvii; emphasis added)[17]

And it is far from being an exaggeration. De Soto underlines a crucial aspect connected to the property of estates and terrains. This property, if not adequately documented (that is, in the terms I am suggesting, *recorded*) cannot be easily and quickly converted into capital: real estates and terrains cannot be sold outside local circles where people know and trust one another and, without assuming an impersonal character, they cannot function as a warranty for a loan or as a share in an investment. In advanced economies, vice versa, every aspect connected to goods is accompanied by some kind of "writing," a document attesting and asseverating the ownership, giving birth to a system of representations: a visible dimension parallel to the hidden and mute life of things. In the Unites States, real estate mortgage loans offer the basis to generate riches. Ex-communist countries and what used to be called the Third World are devoid of this formal system of representation of property, so that many of them have an undercapitalized economic system. Businesses in the so-called emerging economies therefore look similar to those societies that, in developed countries, cannot issue new securities to obtain new investments. And so, without recordings—without writing—these patrimonial activities are "dead capital."

This is the theory. But capitalization can turn out to be literal. Again at the Hanover trade fair we learn that "the mobile phone becomes a wallet. A chip inserted into the device functions as an electronic moneybag for trains, parking spaces, and shops." How? Thanks to "rather simple silicon plates (containing only a few encrypted codes) integrated in a small electromagnetic antenna. If these chips are placed close to a reader, it will give them enough energy to be activated, sending data and payment information in response. The outcome is a phone that, even when switched off, can be placed near a parking meter or a metro turnstile and will pay the small sum, automatically detracting it from the credit in the chip." As a consequence, mobile phone companies became (virtual or real) credit institutions, presenting themselves as not only mobile phone companies but also public funds managers.[18]

Nonetheless, capitalization does not represent only an economic function: it applies to everything. A monkey noticing that potatoes washed in seawater are tastier and transmitting her discovery is capitalizing on this discovery. Ways to build houses or furnishings, to hunt moles or breed chicken, to educate children or cook food constitute forms of capitalization (imagine a man who discovered everything, from hot water to the fact that eggs are edible: one can presume he would not go too far). And, at the basis of capitalization, there is always writing, that is, recording, that might not appear in a literary or literal form but that remains a kind of writing. After all, it is what Rousseau posited: before the invention of writing, time went by and mankind stayed young, because it had to rediscover everything, generation after generation.[19] Time is money, as the saying goes, also because money is time (possibility of performance), and the boom of writing I tackled in the previous chapter is not only an expansion of communication (which is the most noticeable aspect) but mostly of the possibility of registration and accumulation that are immanent to writing.

Saving. Writing in the most ordinary sense of the term is, in fact, saving. How does one save? This is a relatively new question. Once upon a time, there was no need to save; the problem was not to lose what there was. A long, long time ago humans made carbon copies. And then along came the photocopier. But the idea remained that the original was one thing and the copy—less perfect, less exact—was another. And there was an outcry when photocopies came to be so good that the copy was no longer distinguishable from the original: parliamentary questions and philosophical essays were launched on the issue. But now things are different. The page you have laid out before you on the computer (assuming that it is a page; it resembles a page with its letters and pictures, but is unlike a page in not being there when the computer is turned off) or on the table (if the worst comes to the worst) is indeed the original; but it is also something that needs to be saved. Immediately. Otherwise, even though it is there in front of your eyes, it will disappear.

What is set in motion is what one might call an anxious ontology: the things you have in your head have to be saved onto paper or in a file. And this is the old system, as ancient as the invention of writing. But then the file or the paper are not enough, the computer is not enough. You need a backup on the computer, on an external hard drive, in the cloud, a site so distant that you have no idea where it is—here is the genuine "where are you?" of our time—but that seems pretty damn safe. Certainly the "true writing" takes place less and less on paper (unlike what it used to be till not long ago) but instead on another medium, more volatile and yet more resistant. So, to save things online will be more and more like *being saved* by the Internet, entrusting our memory (what we remember and what others remember about us) to an arcane medium that is not afraid of fire and floods but is threatened by magnetic storms, blackouts, a pipsqueak in computer calendars (remember the millennium bug?),[20] and mostly (and this was the same with paper) by itself and its productiveness as well as (and this was not the case with paper) its continuous evolution (we can read incunables and even Dead Sea manuscripts, but we cannot read fifteen-year-old computer programs).

Now, at the basis of this proliferation of prostheses, phantoms, and websites lies the principle of the immanent capitalization of registration. This necessity of recording cannot be considered accidental. Today you get asked (and I am talking about philosophers): "Do you have a website?" It is the first thing people want to know about you, the first thing you are expected to do—or rather, to construct. On your website you will put everything you wrote, so whoever wants to quote you, finding you courtesy of Google, will be spoilt for choice.

Well, for others the website is the last thing one wants. Timothy Leary, quite a long time ago, tried to ensure his immortality online by building a website with his images, texts, and recordings of his voice. He has not quite succeeded, I am afraid, since I am one of the few (or maybe the only one) to remember this detail, and maybe if you looked for the site online you would get "page not found" or even (in a sinister or ironic way) "page *expired*."

Again, this saving is obviously also the presupposition of capitalization, both the Sumerians' and the one we have in our minds, in the writing board of our memory, which, not by accident, is at times compared with a casket[21]—and this is maybe the only alternative image to the writing surface, but alternative only to an extent, given that inscription is the condition of possibility of capitalization. From this point of view, modern prostheses are simply (and it matters) more ductile than the ancient ones: they are more capacious and allow us to write and delete more easily. Not so long ago, computers were soberly defined as "text editing machines"; which meant, more or less, that the computer could be used to write and to modify what had been written. This hits the nail on the head and gets to the essence of what writing is. In effect, writing consists of two basic functions: that of *marking* and that of *canceling*. These were the two functions that Freud attributes to the mind in his *Project for a Scientific Psychology* (1895).[22] He illustrates it many years later with the image of the "mystic pad" (1924, 64–65), a wax tablet covered with a sheet of cellophane, on which one can easily write with a stylus (the letters appear where the cellophane is in contact with the wax) and very easily erase (taking the cellophane off the wax). These two mental functions are not found together when one uses paper, because on paper, while it is easy to leave a mark, it is not so easy to cancel it without leaving some trace. On the computer and on the mobile phone, on the other hand, this is just how it works: writing on an external surface at last becomes as malleable as writing on the *tabula rasa* of our memory. As Hamlet vowed to Claudius: "And thy commandment all alone shall live / Within the book and volume of my brain / Unmix'd with baser matter" (Shakespeare, *Hamlet*, 1.5.98). If he vowed, it is because, at times, memory can be deleted.

Idealization. What this process tells us about is the complete history of idealization. The aim of saving texts to distant locations, making them independent of any accident or incident, is to be able to recover them when needed by use of the appropriate tools. If this is not immortality, and alas it certainly is not, it is at least an approximation to it: philosophers have long called it idealization. The computer can break, the house or the archive can burn down, yet all is not lost: way out there, in some remote place, it is all saved and subtracted from what one might pompously call the *transitoriness of things*. That is a scant consolation. Had the Egyptians been able to back up the Great Library of Alexandria, we would not have lost all those manuscripts. It is a sad story, like the one that happened to the English writer Aldous Huxley, whose archive burnt down ("now I am a man with no memory," he said), which would not have happened today, at least not in such painful terms.

The real theoretical point, here, is the close connection between idealization and iterability suggested by Derrida (1967b, 86). The reasoning goes like this: what is an idea? It is, in principle, independent from its thinker, such that it can exist even after its thinker stopped thinking about it (for the moment or for good). Now, for such a condition to be realized it is not enough to assert that the idea is "spiritual," precisely because thus it could seem exclusively dependent on the psychic acts of the individual.

Instead of focusing on the spiritual character of the idea, Derrida invites us to consider the circumstance that an idea, in order to be such, must be indefinitely *iterable*; also, he notices that the possibility of repetition starts when a code is instituted whose archetypal form is offered precisely by the written sign, the trace that can be iterated also (although not necessarily) in the absence of the writer. So a piece of writing, be it the shopping list or the launderette receipt, best represents the condition of ideality, because (unlike psychological processes) it can access an existence separated from its author.

How? Derrida explains this in his comment on Husserl's *Origin of Geometry* (1962, 131). Thales discovered theorems. Now, suppose Thales immediately forgot about his discovery. In that case, everything would have vanished into oblivion in the wait for another discoverer, who might also have never been born. So, for the idea to be saved, it was necessary that the protogeometrician (a determined individual) fixed it in himself, formulated it by linguistically transmitting it to others and, finally, wrote it down. Notice the three phases of the process: the protogeometrician knows some geometrical truth; this truth must be written in order to be remembered and iterated; the idea is therefore saved—as human knowledge—by being inscribed. Now—and this is an aspect I underlined in chapter 1 and that, as I will show in chapter 6, Derrida has not considered enough—for him, the idea as an ontological being would have subsisted also without a corresponding inscription. Things are different for social objects, where an unrecorded promise does not properly exist. But after all this talk about *inscriptions* there is another point that needs clarification: *truth cannot do without objects.* It is an issue that is misunderstood and that I would like to clarify before continuing with the issue of the construction of social objects through recording. In order to do so, I wish to consider a conflict between theories of truth: one by an intelligent forefather of postmodernism, William James (1842–1910), and the other prevailing in the environment where Alexius Meinong's theory of objects was formed.

THEORY OF TRUTH

Indiana James. Russell (1908, 119) charged James with the invention of the "transatlantic truth"—a truth that turned the question "Have Popes always been infallible?" into the question "Are the effects of thinking them infallible on the whole good?" Russell's imputations did not fall short of a certain malevolence, since he maliciously noted that Le Roy, a pragmatist, suffered papal condemnation for writing on the problem of God (116). Here is how James (1909, 273) replied: "We affirm nothing of so silly as Mr. Russell supposes. Good consequences are not proposed by us as a sure sign, mark, or criterion, by which truth's presence is habitually ascertained, tho they may indeed serve on occasion as such a sign."

Were Russell and James talking about the same thing? No, and I will try to demonstrate it, by pontificating myself on God, but also on James's dark object of desire—namely the "automatic sweetheart." First, I will examine the characteristics of the transatlantic truth: the pragmatic theory of truth. Second, I will compare it with an ontological perspective, namely what I propose we call the "Pacific truth"; not just because it reflects common sense (that is, it is obvious) but also because it points to an example by Davidson (1973, 274): if language organizes experience, does it organize the Pacific Ocean too? Third, I will test the two theories of truth on the automatic sweetheart case. Lastly, I will unravel the mystery and argue that the theory of truth by James—a William James who at times looks like Indiana Jones, an "Indiana James," so to speak—is in fact a theory of scientific research. And at least *for a while*, a theory of scientific research can hope to be separated from ontology. On the contrary, Russell's theory is indeed a theory of truth, and as such it can *never* do without ontology.

Transatlantic truth. In order to illustrate what the transatlantic truth is, I will start with a passage that Putnam borrowed from James (1999, 119). It can be found in a note from a well-known 1908 conference, "The Pragmatist Account of Truth and Its Misunderstanders," subsequently published as chapter 8 of *The Meaning of Truth* (1909).

Here is how James answers to his objectors: pragmatism is not a new edition of positivism, it does not stress the action only, nor (and this is the paragraph where we find the note) is it unable to acknowledge those truths that fall out of the range of our experience—be they those about our best friend's headache or those about God. God is necessary for a pragmatist, since a universe of pure matter would be unsatisfactory, and only God can make the universe meaningful. By the same token, James goes on, we want a "real sweetheart," an "automatic sweetheart" would not make us happy.

I see here a chance to forestall a criticism which some one may make on Lecture III of my *Pragmatism*, where, on pp. 96–100, I said that "God" and "Matter" might be regarded as synonymous terms, so long as no different future consequences were deducible from the two conceptions. The passage was transcribed from my address at the California Philosophical Union, reprinted in the *Journal of Philosophy*, vol. i, p. 673. I had no sooner given the address than I perceived a flaw in that part of it; but I have left the passage unaltered ever since, because the flaw did not spoil its illustrative value. The flaw was evident when, as a case analogous to that of a godless universe, I thought of what I called an "automatic sweetheart," meaning a soulless body which should be absolutely indistinguishable from a spiritually animated maiden, laughing, talking, blushing, nursing us, and performing all feminine offices as tactfully and sweetly as if a soul were in her. Would any one regard her as a full equivalent? Certainly not, and why? Because, framed as we are, our egoism craves above all things inward sympathy and recognition, love and admiration. The outward treatment is valued mainly as an expression, as a manifestation of the accompanying consciousness believed in. Pragmatically, then, belief in the automatic sweetheart would not *work*, and in point of fact no one treats it as a serious hypothesis. The godless universe would be exactly similar. Even if matter could do every outward thing that God does, the idea of it would not work as satisfactory, because the chief call for God on modern men's part is for a being who will inwardly recognize them and judge them sympathetically. Matter disappoints this craving of our ego, so God remains for most men the truer hypothesis, and indeed remains so for definite pragmatic reasons. (James 1909, 189–90)

The same thought is to be found in Daniel Paul Schreber, president of the Court of Dresden and famous patient of Freud and Jung, who was convinced that God was taking care of each and every moment of his life. During the same lapse of years he published *Denkwürdigkeiten eines Nervenkranken* (1903), where he shows his weird personal intimacy with God and, in the last pages, celebrates the order of the world. Thus, as far as God is concerned, if we consider Schreber 1903 and James 1909, there is no difference between the *Memories of a Nerves-sick Man* and *The Meaning of Truth*.

If we cannot help pick one of two crazy hypotheses, then, would it not be more convenient for us to believe in the automatic sweetheart? Is it not a more corroborating and funnier idea than the idea of a God who teleologically organizes the universe? Note the flaw that James does not seem to perceive here: it is one thing to acknowledge the teleological ordain of the world and to maintain that a clock has to have a clockmaker (there is no need for the clockmaker still to be around, or to care about us: what if there is an assembly line in China?). Another thing is to have a machine pretending to be a person, who, again, cares for us. In the first case, we have the clock on one side and the clockmaker on the other. In the second case, we have the clock pretending to be the caring clockmaker as well. This is quite a bit too much of transatlantic truth, and indeed James acknowledges this: he admits God, but not the automatic sweetheart. However, *according to his theory*, if he admits the first one, he ought to admit the second one too.

In fact, James's theory of truth, if rigorously applied, should allow us to believe in the caring feelings of the automatic sweetheart: "*True ideas are those that we can assimilate, validate, corroborate and verify. False ideas are those that we cannot*" (James 1907, 97). The sweetheart corroborates us and we are not in a position to verify whether she is mechanic any more than we can do so for any other being in the world (could we not all be automata?). Moreover, we cannot verify that hypothesis more than we can verify that God exists. Therefore, everything should be all right with her feelings being true. But than why does James reject this hypothesis?

It is likely that James considers, wisely, that the things we meet in the world are not necessarily made to corroborate us. He assumes it, as a common sense rule, but he does not say it, and this is a flaw or, better, a "sin." Troubles began as soon as James (1907, 28) explained the etymology of "pragmatism": "The term is derived from the same Greek word *pragma*, meaning action, from which our terms 'practice' and 'practical' come." That is true, but it is only one of the many meanings the word has. Others are "state of affair," "real fact": a real thing that may be good or bad, since among the meaning of *pragma* there is both "good business, usefulness, profit" and "annoyance, trouble, worry, difficulty." The fact that there are troubles is troublesome, but it is a fact that there are troubles. Still, if James's definition of truth—which James absurdly refuses to apply to the automatic sweetheart—held true, there should not be any troubles at all.

On one hand, then, there is the theory, the transatlantic truth. On the other hand, there are common sense and honesty complaining and protesting. And they cannot help protesting against the transatlantic truth, because James overall admits the traditional notion of truth as correspondence of the proposition to the thing. He only objects (rightly) that it is a rather trivial and vague theory, since it is not exactly clear what this correspondence would consist of. Still, the correspondence theory of truth says roughly how things actually go. And these considerations clash badly with the other side of James's theory of truth—the corroborating truth.[23]

The copresence of a theory of truth as *adaequatio* and a theory of truth as happiness raises a serious problem, precisely because it is not always the case that the world smiles at us. Pondering this, hermeneutic philosophers (who are less honest than James) have come directly to a theory of truth as openness, as project (see Heidegger 1935–36). In fact, I had better believe that the world makes sense, that a text makes sense, that humanity is going to better itself, and that I will not die in twenty seconds. Otherwise the range of the things I can do with truth would be rather limited; for instance, I would not start studying physics or the history of the Sumerians, I would not write a constitution or a project for the reformation of social public healthcare in Apulia. Here, actually, the link between truth and happiness looks tighter, as whoever has conceived dreams of glory knows.[24] The solution is a good one, but again it clashes with common sense.

For instance, this solution does not pass a polygraph test. Indeed, is the truth revealed by the lie detector a project or a correspondence, that is, *adaequatio*? When, in detective movies, we see people submitted to the polygraph test, whoever was not trained by the KGB reacts in terms of correspondence of the proposition to the thing. Tom, who has not been trained by the KGB, answers "No" when asked, "Have you ever seen Mr. Brown?" If he really has never seen him, then the machine does not jolt. If, on the other hand, he has seen him and he is lying, then the machine starts tracing long irregular lines. Dick, who has been trained by the KGB, answers "No," even though he has seen him, but the machine does not uncover any emotion in him. Tom follows a theory of truth as *adaequatio*, Dick a theory of truth as project, *but Dick is lying because he is not formulating a higher-order truth.*

It is difficult to avoid *adaequatio*, and James knows it.[25] He has never thought of being a novelist, as his brother Henry, who by writing *The Turn of the Screw* told us a story where the truth crumbles into different standpoints. Henry adhered implicitly to a theory of truth even more radical than the hermeneutic one: the postmodern theory of truth as nontruth. Maintaining that truth is violent, whereas nontruth is kind, postmodernists are not liable in any way to the objections that James (who preserves *adaequatio*) and hermeneutic philosophers (whose truth as project has to come to terms, sooner or later, with truth as conformity) are liable to. On the contrary, according to postmodern thinkers, there is downright nothing to verify. Having arrived that far, they can give free rein to happiness entirely: the era of the theory of knowledge is over and we can replace objectivity with solidarity (see Rorty 1982).

Is James's contradiction solved by the postmodern thesis of truth as nontruth? Obviously it is not. Postmodernists have simply come to a skeptical upshot, the well-known fortress that is very easy to step into but extremely difficult to get out of. And the refutations are utterly obvious. First, someone who says that man is measure of all things cannot explain why it should be so.[26] Why not the pig?[27] Second, if someone says that there is no truth, then either he is right, and then there is truth (his own), or he is wrong, and again there is truth (the others' truth). Third, and more aptly for this kind of controversy: It is not possible to deny seriously a truth if not in the name of another truth—that is, in the name of a "true truth," and not of a half-truth or a nontruth. And a "true truth" is an objective truth, namely something concerning objects.[28]

Pacific truth. Now, what is the true truth: the transatlantic or the Pacific truth? The Pacific one. The Pacific truth causes trouble for James, because an honest philosopher as he is sticks to truth as *adaequatio*. Therefore, he can enjoy neither the secondary advantages of truth as half-truth nor the extraordinary (and useless) benefits of truth as nontruth. If he holds on to *adaequatio*, then he cannot do without accepting a sphere that is indispensable to truth, that is, the world of objects: the proposition "snow is white" is true if and only if there is snow, and it is white.

James does not feel like denying that. On the contrary, hermeneutic philosophers would say that maybe, in the future, snow could turn black; postmodernists would claim that snow is already black, white, and colored as you like, and maybe that there is not even anything like snow. This is very good for James's consciousness and honesty, but it is quite bad for his theory of truth, since the impassivity of the objects makes it difficult to claim that "good consequences are not proposed by us as a sure sign, mark, or criterion, by which truth's presence is habitually ascertained, tho they may indeed serve on occasion as such a sign" (James 1970, 273).

This is an important point. The idea that the last word goes to truth rather than nontruth and that a thesis such as "truth does not exist" may be seriously maintained only on the assumption that truth exists, has a lot to do with the evidence of sensible experience and the experience of objects. Its genesis, in fact, is right there in sensible experience: I can doubt an optical or tactile illusion just in so far as I have sensible certainty. And I can think that there is truth only in so far as I assume that there are subjects that meet objects that are separated from the first, and that confirm or dismiss the expectations about them. So, *the last word goes to the object, not to the subject*, since experience is called to verify, and then to falsify, and then to verify again, against the clash with the object.

It is hard to find better words than Husserl's: "the un-true, the non-existing goes away by itself already in the passivity."[29] How? It is easy: snow is white if and only if snow is white. And if there is no snow, there is nothing you can do about it, not even for the most Stakhanovite among the pragmatists. And if I saw it pink before, but now I realize that it is white, two things—the snow and my eyes—will inform me. Here is Husserl (1918–26, 164) again: "'I now *see* that it is an illusion' is a mode of evidence too."

This is just what James could not stand, because at the end it points to a passive and contemplative notion of truth. This is the point I would like you to focus on. Pragmatists, hermeneutic thinkers, postmodernists: they all lack a theory of objects—an ancient and metaphysical theory. Quite a lazy and passive theory indeed, which (as I have shown in chapter 2) was developed during James's times not in the lively America, but in the quiescent Kakania—the same region of the Moravian Husserl and close to that of the Polish Tarski, the guy with the white snow. This theory of objects was thought and written in Gratz, in 1904, by Alexius von Meinong. It is true that Meinong exaggerated, by denouncing the prejudice toward the real and admitting in his repertory nonexistent objects as well (hence turning into another victim under the arrows of Russell [1905], the critic of the two worlds). Still, as a matter of fact, a good theory of objects yields the only way to take the object away from the theories that dissolve it and turn it into something else. In the same way—following Kazimierz Twardowski (1894), born in Vienna and died in Poland—a good distinction between the act of thinking something and the object being thought of is the only way not to lose the world. I will come back to Twardowski in chapter 4, but for now I want to stick with James.

Does James have a theory of objects? No, clearly and necessarily no, at least according to his explicit theory of truth. In *Does consciousness exist?*, the conference held in Rome in 1905, James (1904, 19) maintained that the dualism between subject and object is fake, and that *"thoughts in the concrete are made of the same stuff as things are"* that is, objects are absorbed into thoughts, or at least thoughts and objects do not differ from each other. A theory as robust as it is bewildering, because I cannot believe that a cultivated man such as James, by writing that "thoughts in the concrete are made of the same stuff as things are" did not have in mind Shakespeare's *The Tempest* (4.1.156–57): "We are such stuff / As dreams are made on and our little life / Is rounded with a sleep." The gist of James's words is the same.

Prospero or not Prospero, this annihilation of the object was not to the liking of an eminent Austro-Hungarian, Franz Brentano—the master of Husserl, Meinong, and Twardowski. Here is another note, this time from the *Untersuchungen zur Sinnespsychologie*. Brentano (1907, 96–97) upholds the difference between sentient activity (the subject) and what the activity is directed to (the object), between the sensing and what is sensed, between my hatred against an enemy and the enemy. They should not be mixed up; still, lately—Brentano complains—more and more people do so.

Among others, William James has endorsed [this point of view] and argued for it extensively in a long presentation he gave at the International

Congress of Psychology in Rome in 1905. When I cast a glance in a room, my very act of seeing appears to me together with the room; moreover, the fantastic images of sense objects are distinct but by degrees from sense images with an objective cause; and lastly, we say that bodies are beautiful, but the difference between beauty and ugliness depends on the moods of the soul. For those reasons the psychic phenomenon and the physical one are not to be considered as two classes of distinct phenomena. To me it is difficult to understand how the orator could not see the weakness of those arguments.

To appear together does not mean to appear as the same thing, as much as appearing at the same time does not amount to being the very same thing. This is why Descartes, without undergoing any contradiction, could first deny that the room I see exists, and deny only afterwards that my seeing the room exists. But . . . if a fantasy were distinguished from a perception only by its intensity, as soon as the difference vanishes, what would hinder (for what has just been said) the full identity of fancying and seeing meaning nothing else than their being identical with a single psychic phenomenon? In the third argument, he talks about beauty. . . . Now, it is a strange logic indeed the one according to which, from the psychic character of the "pleasure arising from beauty," we should also infer the psychic character of the appearance of what this pleasure depends on. Were this true, then every sorrow would be identical with that for which someone feels sorrow, and one should refrain from repenting for one's mistakes, because by repenting one would repeat the mistakes one has made.

We cannot annihilate the object into the subject, the sensed into the sensing, what is thought into the thinking. This is the basic request of the struggle against psychologism: thoughts are objects. If thoughts were not separated from who thinks them, we would not be able to understand each other, and logic would turn into a branch of psychology.[30] And if there were no physical objects separated from the subjects—objects that not always coddle us and make us happy—then speaking of truth would be meaningless.

Here is another important point. By absorbing the object into the subject—exactly as Giovanni Gentile absorbed historical events into the history that tells and comprehends them, and the *Divina Commedia* into the commentary to it[31]—James's theory reminds one of a scene from the first Indiana Jones film I referenced earlier. In *Raiders of the lost Ark*, Indiana Jones is about to face a duel with a bully wielding a scimitar, but then it occurs to him he is carrying a gun, and the confrontation is resolved quickly. All right; still, had he been carrying a water gun, he would not have found the same easy way out: the gun solves the problem because it is a real gun, namely because of features immanent to that very object, and not because of the subject who needed it and who is corroborated by it. Inversely (to use again an example I mentioned in chapter 2), if in Hitchcock's *The Birds* the protagonists' house had been equipped with shutters made of steel, they would have all enjoyed their stay at the home. That is to say that the thing constraints, it is not just a resource: it may be a limit or a hindrance. Still, it never ceases to be a real thing.

This fact holds true already in the scientific enterprise: things are at the interpreter's disposal only to an extent; otherwise there would not be any difference between knowing and believing to know. And we can be certain that if the empirical research had rebuffed the theory of relativity, Einstein would not have been happy with that; his theory then would have been false, and the denial of it true.

Even more so, in our experience things are not at the interpreter's disposal: try to clean your ears with a screwdriver and you will know what I mean. I can hold a doorknob to open the door, but only if it is solid enough, if it is not a painted doorknob, for example. I can use a Mont Blanc pen as a filter to observe a solar eclipse, but I could not do the same with a silver Sheaffer pen: my room to maneuver is not unlimited, since the material conditions of the object have to be such to allow the performance of its function. Now, the properties that can induce me to make use of higher-order performances are based on lower-order properties, which are *exclusively* possessed by the object, and this also holds for beings that do not have the faintest idea of what a door knob (or a pen, or an eclipse) is; for example, a worm crawling on my Mont Blanc is using it as a ground for moving. It is simply not true that any object can be used as any instrument, since a spade may be used as a club, but not the other way around.

Moreover, by overthrowing the natural stance, pragmatism assumes that we spend most of our time grasping objects, people, or theories, namely in intentional and conscious activities; all the rest being roughly an indistinct, irrelevant, and almost inexistent mass. As a matter of fact, though, we do not often stretch toward the objects around us, we rather *shun* flies, trams, and annoying people; and we cannot accomplish that simply by considering flies, trams, or whatever else as *eide* possessing no existence, or *sense data* aggregated by a daemon who hates us.

The automatic sweetheart. Now, to come back to the automatic sweetheart test that I was talking about earlier. A hundred years ago, in Rome, James (1904, 18) claimed (shocking Brentano) that "sometimes the adjective wanders as if uncertain where to fix itself. Shall we speak of seductive visions or of visions of seductive things?" Now, since "thoughts in the concrete are made of the same stuff as things are" (19), and *"true ideas are those that we can assimilate, validate, corroborate and verify"* (ibid.), what hinders the automatic sweetheart from making us happy? Moreover: is it not more convenient for us to believe that she is true? Would she not make us happier than a God who orders the universe? Are we not downright masochist not to believe in her? Is it so difficult to please us? No, we cannot accept the doll, for at least three reasons.

First, we would not be happy. This is James's argument: Our ego would not be satisfied, because we would not feel like our affections and love would be returned in kind. This is sacrosanct, but just because, *pace* James, thoughts and things are *not* made of the same stuff. Even our internal states, in many cases, are determined by the fact of whether they grounded in objects or not; quite a different thing from the blurring of "seductive visions" and "visions of seducing objects." For instance, we are happy, as often as we are unhappy, due to something or someone; otherwise it is "euphoria" or "depression," which are not exactly feelings. Antidepressants alert us to the fact that they can cause euphoria; they do not tell us that they could provoke happiness (see Ferraris 2004c; 2004d). Now, it is obvious that, as a thought experiment, the doll does not satisfy us, exactly because there is *no thought experiment that can satisfy us*, and exactly for the same reason for which happiness is different from euphoria. Still, if James's theory that there is no distinction between subject and object were true, she should satisfy us instead.

Second, she would not be happy either. Because *if* the doll existed for real, *if* from the thought experiment we shifted from the actual construction of a doll in the real world, *then* sooner or later the automatic sweetheart could tell us, quite rightly: "don't call me baby." In fact, we would deal with Leibniz's dream, with an "automate spirituel ou formel, mais libre" (1695, §15), namely with a person. And we would have no right to be unhappy with it; at worst we could start wondering if we are not automatons too, in accordance with what I said about Searle's Chinese room.

Third, willy-nilly, the doll does not exist, it is an object that is *not* there: James deals with a thought experiment and Villiers with a *feuilleton*. God is not a hypothesis verifiable in the world, whereas the automatic sweetheart, within certain limits, is: I look for her, but I do not find her; I may find her only in my mind, during a thought experiment or while reading a French novel. Thus, when it comes to the act of verifying, we realize that the automaton does not satisfy the New Yorker James, not more than—to stick to American literature—it could satisfy a true Bostonian such as Edgar Allan Poe, who in *Von Kempelen and His Discovery* (1849) comes across an automaton as well. It was the Turkish chess player, invented in 1770 by a Hungarian nobleman: an automaton who defied Franklin and Napoleon, and whom Poe saw in 1835 in Richmond. Yet, the truth was that the automaton hid a real chess player inside. That is to say that ultimately, put to the test, automata are a fake, whereas there could never be a similar test for God's existence. The flaw, hence, is in the object, which not even Indiana James manages to avoid, exactly because he does not despise—wisely, generally speaking, but disastrously for his theory—the doctrine of truth as *adaequatio*.

Here is the point: we cannot escape from *adaequatio*. Thus the sentence *"true ideas are those that we can assimilate, validate, corroborate and verify"* is problematic: it is one thing to assimilate, corroborate, and validate, as those are active functions of the subject; another thing is to "verify"—a function in which the subject largely depends on the object.

The sun and the moon. Thus, James, an adventuring but honest philosopher, has never retreated from the idea that truth needs objects and *adaequatio*. This clashes with his other idea, that truth has to corroborate us and makes us happy. To come back to my starting point—the face-off between James and Russell—it seems clear, so far, that Russell and James do not talk about the same thing when they talk about "truth."

Russell refers to truth, James to the well-being of a scientific enterprise. Russell talks about ontology, about what there is, and James talks about epistemology, about what we know and what we have to do to know it. Those two tiers, although James does not realize it, do not coincide at all, even if sooner or later they meet. It is a good hypothesis to prospect therapies against cancer, but once we have cancer it is there for real, and it is true that we have it even though this does not enhance our good mood.

Otherwise we would be like the crazy man in *Penal Colony* who rejoices when the harrow scratches his condemnation on his back.

Pragmatists do not distinguish between *criterion* and *meaning*, between the way of doing research and the objects we are referring to (Russell 1908, 120). Had they done that, Russell would have had much less to object. Their stance, he adds, is a rough generalization of the method of inductive sciences (126)—the method of proceeding by advantageous hypotheses. That said, it is still the case that once we assume that the catalog made by the British Museum is faultless it does not follow that the catalog could do without the books listed in it (121). Which is another way of saying that truth cannot do without objects.

James is not the only one in making this mistake, since—even if he criticizes the neo-Kantians (they were the polemic target of the conference)—he bequests from Kant precisely the confusion between ontology and epistemology (see Ferraris 2000, 89; 2004b, 65–72). More exactly, he inherits an entire Kantian package. First, this package includes the Copernican revolution—the idea that we should not ask how things are in themselves, but how they have to be made in order to be known by us (even worse, according to James we have to ask how they have to be made in order to make us happy). Second, and as a consequence, the collapse between ontology and epistemology: encountering something and knowing it is one and the same. Note that only from this perspective the idea that happiness is a sign for truth might look likely (I may be happy for having discovered a virus, not for having caught it). Happiness can be a sign of truth only if we melt truth and reality, swallowing reality into truth, just like, before, we had swallowed the object into the subject.

Hilary Putnam, in his however sympathetic review of the pragmatist theory of truth (1997, 182–83), signals the deadly *cul de sac* where James ends up. Once he acknowledges the difficulty he is in (in particular, about the irrevocability of the past), he insists that we have to distinguish between *realities*, which cannot be changed (or amended), and *truths*, which can be changed. Is that true? A judge may say, on ground of proof he or she has at disposal, that Amanda Knox is a murderer. According to a different assessment she may be considered innocent. Nevertheless, the confrontation here is not between two truths, but rather between a false judicial truth and a true judicial truth—in short, a nontruth and a truth. Otherwise we would not see why the court should revise the first verdict (see Van

Caenegem 1973, ch. 2). Truth is to be found in reality, namely a sphere of objects.

Yet James was probably thinking about something different, something like the following: the truth of the sun does not change, it is just that Ptolemy could say the sun revolves around the earth and Copernicus that the earth revolves around the sun. Therefore, reality does not change, truth does. All right, but it changes exactly in the sense that Ptolemy's theory turns out to be wrong, while Copernicus's is right. It is quite difficult that two truths can reign together at the same time. The only example I heard of, which is often quoted as a proof that this may be possible, is the complementarity of the wave theories of light and the corpuscular ones. At any rate, the theories of Copernicus and Ptolemy never touched the nature of objects and the experience thereof, not even at a nonscientific level—otherwise we would have to conclude that because of his wrong theory Ptolemy has never really seen the sun during his whole life.

Now, if things are like that, then the theory is epistemology, and the sun is ontology. Epistemology is the moon, because, if it is true and in order to be true, it always shines by virtue of reflected sunlight. I do not know whether this theory of the sun and the moon, with its Dantesque and Mediaeval flavor, can help us solve the question whether popes or emperors are infallible, possibly on ground of the *Führerprinzip*. In my opinion, it can help us dismiss papal infallibility on ground of the obvious assumption that we apply it to the doctrine and not to the objects—that is, to God and not to the world. However, leaving aside the Pope (lest I end up like Le Roy), I believe that acknowledging the primacy of ontology over epistemology is the only way to get rid of Heidegger's idea that, if truth is openness, "the action that founds a state" too is "a way in which the truth is present" (1935–36, 46). Which is a slightly mystic but unequivocal way to justify the *Führerprinzip*, and a very sad middle-German application of the transatlantic truth.

I conclude with one last example. Every two years, many Italian professors are involved in the editorial board of PRIN, Programs of Relevant National Interest, applying for funding for scientific programs. The pragmatist theory of truth is what we use when we are trying to have a project of ours accepted by the ministry. Once the project is accepted, however, we have to report its accomplishment, and in order to do that we must deal with the old conformity of the proposition to the thing. When reporting, we have to show not only that we had been in Paris for study reasons (by way of experiences, through tickets, bills, and so on) but, again on ground of *adaequatio*, that we have found *something* (and this is science). That is why, unfortunately, the certain sign of truth is not happiness, but very often unhappiness, since we can realize too late that we have had it all wrong—or at least, they will not accept our report. So, epistemology too, sooner or later, has to face ontology, for the same reason that promises have to be kept, sooner or later. It is sad: *for the same reason that things have certain characteristics, and are not reducible to our purposes, truth—or something like it—does exist.* Once this is clear, we can get rid of our "constructionist" anxieties and enter the world of social objects.

4

CONSTRUCTING

I turn off the mobile phone and walk into a library. I take a book and fill out a form obliging me to give it back within thirty days (note that I *sign* the form; it is a point I will dwell on at length shortly). My commitment does not necessarily have to be put in writing: I could also borrow a book from a friend and promise him to give it back next week. The agreement might even take place without a single word being uttered, as when we shake hands for a deal (it is not advisable, though, to use this method with books, as the other party might think that I am not committing to returning the book, but am thanking him for the present instead). The essential point is not the writing, but the archi-writing, the inscription in a figurative sense: it is necessary for both parties to register the commitment in some way, even just in the memory.

Is there *an object* here? One could say there is one: the book. But it is clearly not so, since the book will stay the same regardless whether I promise to return it, take it as a present, or steal it. If there is an object it is not a physical one, and not even an ideal one (as anyone who ever tried to return an idea will know: ideas can only be stolen, unless they are under copyright). One could also oppose that there is no need for an object: the promise or the present are simply manifestations of the subject's will. But figures still do not add up, because one's will can be changed: I can choose not to return the book, or to ask for a present I made to be returned (even though I would give a bad impression). I can also decide (changing my will) not to go to the cinema: if I did not promise anyone to go with him or her, no one can reproach me for it.

Why? Because, in fact, when I make a promise (even if only to myself, like the famous "tomorrow I'll quit smoking") I leave the sphere of my individual psychic life and build a mini-society—a society that might become enormous (like when politicians on TV enter into contracts with all Italians) and that does not imply only one will: it requires at least two of them, a promisor and a promisee (which, in the case of the promise to quit smoking, can coincide).

This *act* produces an *object*, different from the physical object it possibly refers to or an ideal object. The act requires an *inscription* (the memory of the people involved, a written voucher, a magnetic trace): what, in the case of promises, is so rightly called the *given word*, as it belongs no longer to me but to the promisee. It implies constraints, like any other object: just like there can be no colorless physical object or an ideal object without given properties (a triangle cannot have four sides, five is an odd number), so the "I promise" or the "I promise that," *per se*, are not a promise. Only something like "I promise I will return the book in thirty days" is one, as it entails a promisor, a promisee, an object of the promise, and a deadline. Promisor and promisee are finite (human beings) and so are the object and the deadline: if I promised to return an infinite sum, I would not be really promising (as the commitment would never end). This is why, when Christ guarantees eternal life to one of his companions on the cross, he is not making a real promise, as the promisee will never be able to verify its content.

Construction. To sum up the steps taken so far. In chapter 1, "Speaking," I described the transformations of presence entailed by a small but powerful object: the mobile phone. These transformations, though, do not invest physical reality, unlike what postmodern thinkers believe: they merely modify a certain way of being in the world. In chapter 2, "Writing," I pointed out that these speaking machines, in reality, are writing machines. One could respond: So what? What does this matter? As I explained in chapter 3, "Recording," it matters indeed: writing is not *only* a form of communication but also—and mostly—a form of recording (Derrida's archi-writing) that, in the sphere of social objects, I suggest we call *inscription*. Inscription allows many things: archiving, capitalizing, and idealizing. That is, nothing less than the constitution of social objects.

This is the sense in which to inscribe equals to construct. Through an inscription—on paper (in the usual case of the library), on the computer, or in the mind—and through an agreement between at least two people, a social object is constructed. This object does not add a single molecule to the book, yet something physical subsists, elsewhere: in the place (text, mind or both) where the inscription lies. This circumstance must not be underestimated, as it determines the difference—or, rather, the differences—between the world of physical (and ideal) objects and that of social objects. I wish to point out at least two of those.

The first has to do with *existence*. Physical objects are as big as the sum of their molecules and change only if the latter change. Ideal objects exist without molecules and would be such also in the supposed absence of all intelligent life on earth, independently from any recording. On the contrary, social objects exist if there is an *act*, even if a mute one, tying up at least two people, and if there is an *inscription*, entailing a (small) quantity of molecules that can change without altering the nature of the object. I can take a mental note of an appointment, I can write it down on my agenda or in my mobile phone: the appointment is still the same, unlike the physical objects. It is the same with memos: I can use Mount Blanc or a pin to remind me of something, but the *memorandum* stays the same.

The second difference has to do with objectivity. The marvelous character of social objects—what makes them different from, for instance, tastes and imagination—lies in the fact that *while depending on subjects, they are not subjective*. This point is obvious, yet it is often misunderstood, given that one of the most banal and false assumptions on this is that social objects are subjective. There is clearly some confusion about the meaning of *subjective*. I can *find* a picture ugly even if everyone else loves it, and this is what we call subjective: *de gustibus non disputandum est*. I can also *say* that that picture is valued at thirty, three hundred, or three thousand euros, and the valuation certainly depends on the subjects (for a beaver it would be another story), but here we already have to do with an element that is surely not subjective in the sense, as it presupposes social sharing. Finally, I have no difficulty in *imagining* that the value of the euro depends on a deliberation in which subjects intervene; but if, in my room and with no authority, I decided that a euro is worth twenty dollars I would be, at the very least, a solipsist.[1]

Acts, objects, inscriptions. The material we are dealing with is therefore made up of three elements: acts, objects, and inscriptions.

Acts are deliberations regarding at least two people, and presupposing (at least phenomenally) *intentions*. In reality, what intentions are is neither very clear nor is it certain they truly exist, given that we do not know whether we are free or mechanically necessitated. Furthermore, also at a superficial level, it is unclear whether an action produced by envy, on the rebound, or due to social imitation is really intentional. Still, the social system (for instance, the system of punishments and rewards or contracts) postulates, as an axiom, the existence of an individual intentionality.

Acts produce objects, which are always tokens of types presupposed at the moment of the act.[2] I do not invent the promise, I formulate it so that it is compliant with requisites that do not depend on me, whereas what I promise, the fact that I promise it, and so on depend on me. The same goes for a law, a contract, or a bet. Types, instead, are not properly created: either they are already there (as in the case of the promise), or they are tokens turned into examples (models; see Ferraris [1995]) for other tokens (a law with many applications, a book printed in many copies, translated into many languages and so on). It is entirely plausible that social objects known *so far* constitute a modest or minimal portion of an ontology that includes *all* possible social objects (not to mention formerly existing social objects we have lost memory of). Nevertheless, the types of that virtual ontology become relevant only the minute they occur as tokens in a real ontology, although, once discovered, the characters of social objects manifest a full necessity (in the sense that, usually, from its very first occurrence a promise has certain features: promisor, promisee, object, obligation, claim).

Each of these objects requires as its *necessary* condition an idiomatic recording. In general, the phenomenon of inscription belongs to a sphere of increasing social specificity, and under this profile we can distinguish four elements. *Traces*: anything that might count as a sign, from the traces of an animal to a bent piece of iron (a sign that it was bent), to natural codes, like the DNA. *Recordings*: any form of inscription, in the mind, on paper, on the mobile phone; these recordings are also (or, rather, mostly) individual and not social, like our memories, for instance. *Inscriptions* (proper): recordings endowed with a social value, like receipts, cheques, banknotes, contracts. *Idioms or signatures*, namely those individualizing processes that determine the validity of a social object (a check with an amount but without a signature is incomplete, a check with a counterfeit signature is false). Obviously, traces can also assume a social value (for instance, the DNA in a police investigation), but here I wish to outline the big picture. I will develop in detail the problems connected to inscription in chapter 8.

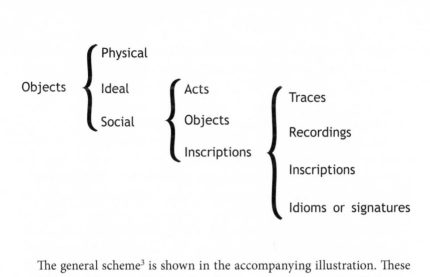

The general scheme[3] is shown in the accompanying illustration. These problems might seem obvious, but they are not, since—as I will show—their discovery was long and laborious, in accordance with the (perhaps surprising) principle that the reasons for the most familiar things often turn out to be the most difficult to explain.

ACTS

"Mister Mario Rossi, by the power vested in me, I pronounce you doctor in Philosophy." This is something I often happened to do as the president of a graduation committee. After those words, Mario Rossi acquired a new property, becoming *doctor* Mario Rossi. It is neither the first nor the last property he gathered throughout his life: the object "Mario Rossi" was long before baptized "Mario," maybe a few years before he married, perhaps he got a driver's license. Here is a series of social objects placed upon a person 6 feet tall and weighing about 176 pounds: an Italian citizen named Mario Rossi, a doctor of Philosophy, a conjugated person, the bearer of a driver's license and maybe, in time, also of a mortgage, a penal conviction, a permanent infirmity, a Nobel Prize for Literature. It seems hard to deny that, in these cases, words *do* things, they constitute social objects. These acts do not merely *describe* something, they *construct* it, like in the examples of performative utterances by John L. Austin (1911–60), who discovered them.[4]

"I do" (I take this woman as my legitimate wife). "I christen this boat *Queen Elizabeth*." "I leave my watch to my brother." Now, why did it take so long to reach such an obvious conclusion? It is worth to ask *why*, both so as to clarify the nature of the acts I am talking about, and to shed light on the ontology of social reality as a whole.

Idols. Social acts impose new properties so that a preexisting object becomes a new one, a social object. "Dal dì che nozze, tribunali ed are / dier l'umane belve l'esser pietose / di sè e d'altrui."[5] Here is the concise version of the basic concept of Giambattista Vico's "Idea of the Work," which he places at the start of the *New Science* (1744, 255–58). Humans pass from the state of nature to the civil state by means of *acts*. So as to clarify this point, a certain intellectual audacity is required. We admit with no difficulty that there are physical objects and, with a little effort, that there are also ideal ones. Instead, it is very hard for us to even consider things like military grades, the municipality of Florence and the ban from walking over the grass as "objects." In certain cases, we are tempted to classify them as physical objects or as ideal objects; in other cases we do not even think about it—which is bizarre, as they are many and far from irrelevant.[6]

Many idols, in Bacon's sense (that is, many blunders and prejudices), tend to blur this class of objects (see Smith 1997; Gilbert 1989 and 1993; Johnasson 1989). Take the sentence "I promise you a book." The idea I wish to suggest is that here the social object is not the book, but rather what ensues from the act of promising it and its inscription. Still, it is possible to read this sentence in many ways, concealing the object behind others, that is, with idols:

> I promise you a *book.*
> *I* promise you a book.
> I *promise* you a book.
> I promise *you* a book.

Here is the list of idols:

1. I will start with the *idola tribus,* those of the tribe we belong to. Considering that, for our mind, the paradigm of the object is offered by the physical object (see chapter 1), and since *a social objects is a higher-order object* (that is, it is built upon another object), the inferior one—through a reductionist strategy—takes the place of the superior one: a smoking ban consists of the sign, a prime minister is a man (or woman).

2. Next up, the *idola specus,* the idols of the cave, coming from education and especially from the fortuitous situations one happens to be in. If social objects require social acts, and these need subjects, then social objects seem like simple offshoots of subjectivities (and are thus reduced to

nothing or almost nothing: a *flatus vocis* or an act of the mind that cannot be distinguished from a will or a fantasy). Now, this is clearly not so. To test it again on the case of the promise: "I want to get married" and "I want to marry XY" are the manifestations of an intention; "I want to marry you" is a promise with no legal value, but it is already a social act; "I do" in response to a legal representative asking, "Do you want to take XY as your wife/husband?" is a social act endowed with a legal value; the same answer given on a theater stage or at the cinema is the simulation of a real legal act, but it is still a social act as it belongs to the social functions of art.

3. Now to the *idola fori*, namely the idols of the marketplace, generated by language, which is reluctant to classify social objects as "objects," because they are often (if not always) accompanied by an expression. At this point there are no objects but only words, occasionally stirred by an action.[7]

4. Thus we get to the *idola theatri*, the idols of the theater: the philosophical prejudices that contribute to dissipating social objects before the more respectable (or substantial) physical ones and ideal ones. The crucial prejudices, in my view, are: First, the Cartesian perspective for which everything that lies outside *episteme* (that is, for Descartes, essentially physics) must be ascribed to the *doxa*, that is, opinion and interpretation. Second, the Kantian assumption that the sphere of actions and reasons belongs to subjectivity as a purely intelligible world, entirely separated from the sensible world.

Autonomy from the subjects. The problem is not only with social objects being slightly vague: rather, if they look so evanescent it is also because of the subjects, of the I, that is, what Gadda rightly defined as the "most obscene of all pronouns," the most cumbersome and noisy.

The second stage of my quest for the Holy Grail of social objects is the recognition of the *autonomy* of social acts with respect to individual subjects. Imagine that someone (it once happened to me) receives an invitation of this kind: "X and Y are thinking about getting married," followed by date, place, and time of the merry event. Now, of course, the invitation is ironic, because it is not enough to think of marrying someone to actually do it, just like thinking about scoring a penalty will not produce a goal. *Thoughts in people's minds* that undoubtedly have a lot to do with social objects like weddings and football matches *are different from social objects, which are public.*

The hero of this part is the Scottish philosopher Thomas Reid (1710–96),[8] who recognized the specificities of acts or social operations that, unlike judgments, are not individual and entail the intervention of at least two people constituting what Reid (1827) calls a miniature society. Reid's approach presents the advantage of defining social acts without referring to history or the spirit, as well as that of differentiating them from acts referred to ideal objects (that look like the closest candidates to assimilation). Furthermore, Reid's proposal is characterized by a solid realism. Against empiricism—which resolves the external world into the I and then reduces the I itself to a mere set of feelings—Reid supports a "natural realism." There is a brutal physical reality, untouched by social or institutional facts, and perception is referred to an object that is different from the act of perceiving.[9] Over this independent reality there lies a world of social operations that has no constitutive role with respect to the physical world, but possesses its own autonomy.

Take, once again, the case of the promise. Its traditional interpretation conceived it as a mere manifestation of will (and, as such, subjective); for Reid, instead, it consists of the construction of an objective social act. There are two fundamental theses.

First, the promise is an action, not the simple expression of an internal state: it is a *praxis*.

> A man may see, and hear, and remember, and judge, and reason; he may deliberate and form purposes, and execute them, without the intervention of any other intelligent being. They are solitary acts. But when he asks a question for information, when he testifies a fact, when he gives a command to his servant, when he makes a promise, or enters into a contract, these are social acts of mind, and can have no existence without the intervention of some other intelligent being, who acts a part in them. (Reid 1827, 654)

Here is the crucial difference between a purely mental act and a social act. Think again of the cinema example: if I choose to go to the cinema alone and then change my mind, nothing happens. Yet if I choose to go with someone, I made a promise, and if I do not keep it I must at least let that person know. Between the two situations there is an essential difference: in the second case, through my promise I performed a social act; in the first case I simply formulated a proposition wholly dependent on me.

Second, a social act needs essentially an expression:

> Between the operations of the mind, which, for want of a more proper name, I have called solitary, and those I have called social, there is this

very remarkable distinction, that, in the solitary, the expression of them by words, or any other sensible sign, is accidental. They may exist, and be complete, without being expressed, without being known to any other person. But, in the social operations, the expression is essential. They cannot exist without being expressed by words or signs, and known to the other party. (Ibid.)

Note the element of signs (that I have just differentiated into traces, recordings, inscriptions, and idioms): in certain contexts even a hand-shake, blink, or look can count—like the *taliata* in Camilleri's novels—that is, the gestures of functional nature that Rousseau subordinated to voice as the expression of feelings. Here, too, the role of inscription turns out to be decisive: if expression is not recorded, it goes unnoticed as if it were never uttered.

Praxis. The third part of our path is the theory of performative utterances. Its importance lies in the fact that it identifies a sphere of utterances that do not just describe states of things (that would exist independently from them) but produce them. In this case, it is recognized that these acts are in fact such—that is, they are a *praxis*: just like brushing your teeth or driving a car, which is different from the *description* of brushing your teeth or driving a car. The hero of this part is John L. Austin, who developed the problem of social acts by speaking of "speech acts."[10] Austin's idea directly attacks one of the *idola theatri* mentioned earlier in this chapter: Aristotle's assumption that discourses that, like prayer, speak neither the truth nor the untruth, must be ascribed to rhetoric and poetics. Austin does so under the influence of Wittgenstein's thesis[11] according to which referring to something is only *one* of the functions of language (otherwise the theory of the academy of Lagado in *Gulliver's Travels*[12] would work smoothly).

In particular, Austin wants to confer full philosophical dignity to utterances that do not ascertain or describe something, but *perform* it, like for instance, a bet, a promise, a christening, or a wedding, which Austin calls "performative." What are they? If I buy a potato, or if I order chips at a restaurant, the transferring of property requires an encoded act, that is not a simple description since it determines a disposal, a change not of physical state but of the juridical one. Coming back to the wedding example: again, it is not a simple description ("it was a nice ceremony, the groom was really moved, the bride a little less"), it is not a prescription ("at this point you can only go for a shotgun wedding"), nor is it a ban ("this marriage is not to be performed").[13] It is an *act*.

Nonetheless, as for the problem discussed here, the analysis of speech acts—later systematized by Searle in the late 1960s and early 1970s[14]— provides a necessary but not sufficient contribution. The formulation of social acts in Austin is centered on the *linguistic* expression, and therefore does not account for all the operations that can happen tacitly—like for those who are "used to silently obey,"[15] in the case of a so-called "mute law" (see Sacco 1993), or in that of someone undergoing violence (which is undoubtedly a social act (see Salice 2004), differently encoded, and that does not necessarily require words).[16]

Also, the fact that social acts are conceived as essentially linguistic throws a decisive point into the shade, namely the role of what I called *inscription* in the construction of social reality: typically, a will can hardly be considered a speech act, because it becomes operative when the owner can no longer speak.[17] The next step—following a logical order, after the recognition of the autonomy of social acts and of the peculiarity of the performative with respect to other functions of language—is the recognition of the fact that social acts give life, indeed, to social objects: not only do they constitute a *praxis*, they are also a *poiesis*.

OBJECTS

Consider the following sentence:

I am going for a walk.

Once the walk is over, there is nothing left. The walk ceases to exist the minute I stop walking, becoming at most a formerly existing object. Now consider the following sentence:

I make a vow to Virgin Mary.

Making a vow requires a few seconds. Keeping it may take a whole life. The difference between the two sentences lies essentially in the fact that the first has no object outside of itself, while the other does.

Poiesis. Here is therefore the third step. An act does not simply mean doing something; beyond itself, it produces an object, constituting an entity that can outlast it, just like a marriage hopefully lasts longer than the wedding. In the terminology valorized by Aristotle, it would be called (as I said above) a *poiesis*. If I promise something, I perform an act that goes beyond mere description (and it is, indeed, a *praxis*) but, also, I constitute an object: the promise (and it is therefore a *poiesis*). The hero of the last part, which is logical and not chronological (since it comes *before* the discovery of speech acts), is the German philosopher Adolf Reinach (1883–1917).[18]

> Through the act of promising something new enters the world. A claim arises in the one party and an obligation in the other. What are these curious entities (*Gebilde*)? They are surely not *nothing*. How could one eliminate a nothing by waiving or by retracting or by fulfilling? (Reinach 1913, 8–9)

Starting from this consideration, Reinach develops a theory of juridical beings as peculiar kinds of objects, not situated in space (unlike physical objects) but located in time (unlike ideal objects), because a promise or an obligation starts at a given moment and sooner or later should come to an end. It is at this point that acts started to be recognized as producers of objects.[19] It is important to note from the very start that Reinach insists on types rather than tokens, on the apriorical principles of social objects rather than actual social objects, and this is why his proposal will require a few adjustments, as I will show in the second part of the book.

Realism. Note that the stress on *poiesis* entails in no way the arbitrary character of social objects. Rather, for Reinach the very opposite holds true. Social objects require, for their existence, a bearer (*Träger*) and content (*Inhalt*) as well as a counterpart (*Gegner*). These elements turn it into something "as solid as trees and houses."

This circumstance is a priority. The minimal requirement for the constitution of an ontology of social objects is the adoption of an underlying realism. Realism, here, is not a scientific theory supported by physics, but the obvious presupposition of a research that can be developed both in the direction of a study of nature and toward an inquiry of the social world, as they constitute *one* world and not two distinct and irreducible entities. I will show later how such a request might turn out to be demanding, but for now I will focus on the two central points that constitute the condition of possibility of social objects: first, not everything is socially constructed and second, what is socially constructed is not consequently subjective, because it concerns at least two people.

INSCRIPTIONS

We have acts and we have objects. Is that all we need? No, we still need inscriptions, and no one, apart from Derrida, realized this. And yet, in retrospect, it does not seem so hard to recognize. What did Reid write again? "[Solitary acts] may exist, and be complete, without being expressed, without being known to any other person. But, in the social operations, the expression is essential. They cannot exist without being expressed by *words or signs*, and *known* to the other party." Yes, that is right; but it is not enough for them to be known for an instant: they must be kept and recorded. This is what all the theories presented so far have not sufficiently valorized: for social objects to exist, inscriptions are necessary and they must be idiomatic. I will now briefly explain these points, which I then will extensively consider in chapter 8.

Documents. How can we solve the alternative between a construction by the subject and a law found in the physical world or in the hyperuranium, as if it were a mushroom or a theorem? I think that what I said earlier on mobile phones with regard to recording-construction could come in handy here and show us the way to follow. What is wrong with the act? The fact that it might seem subject dependent. What is missing in the object? The fact that it appears rooted in the world, in accordance with the privilege of physical objects. And, as a third problem, it is unclear how objects could come out of acts.

From this vantage point, I believe, it is much easier to understand the point I am trying to make. Not objects, but subjects are rooted in the world: their possibilities are determined by the nature of their physical objects, the length of their life, the resources of their bodies. Subjects are, at least legally, responsible for acts producing objects. How? Through inscription, which is the aspect that Reid only hinted at, Austin underestimated (since, in his theory of speech acts, he focused his attention on the word only) and Reinach neglected concentrating on the apriorical form of objects.

Inscription, transforming an act into an object, does not account for the genesis of social objects (for inscriptions to be possible, instead of mere traces, a society must exist), but it provides a necessary condition (without inscriptions there are no objects) confirmed by the obvious observation that the social world is a world of receipts, checks, banknotes, and other vouchers.

We are truly dealing, once again, with the purloined letter that in Poe's short story could not be found, not because it was hidden like a needle in the haystack but, on the contrary, because it was too evident. Acts create objects through writings and papers. Think of the frequency of these terms—from the papers on our desks that now host mainly our computes, to legal writings, to rescripts, to ID cards, credit cards, and playing cards.[20] Obviously, these inscriptions can be simply *blips* in the computer or traces on the *tabula* of our mind, but without them there would not be something like an *object*, capable of surviving the transitory character of acts.

Scripta manent, that is all. In short, it is hard to underestimate the role of *documents* in real society, from the minimal case of receipts filling our pockets to the very relevant one of the *omissis* online in the Calipari case, up to the Nibelungen representation we could see in the film *The Downfall* (2004), with mountains of documents thrown out the window during the Berlin battle and the ensuing fires, in the attempt at making a whole world of objects disappear. Had they truly all disappeared, evil would have added up to evil. In particular, the wish formulated at 58 Am Grossen Wannsee on January 20, 1942, would have been realized, namely that the final solution would have been "a historical decision no one will know about"; and this is a very serious reason why we can say that, in social ontology, paper truly matters.

Idiomaticness. One could say: once it is registered, we have the object (a marriage, a promise, and so on). Yes, but what differentiates *this* marriage from another, *that* promise from another? What defines the identity of that specific object? The fact that it crossed the mind of those two social agents and not others. Then, an often neglected element turns out to be decisive, namely the *individual mode of presentation* of the act, and its *specific form of recording*. This idiomaticness is relevant, and this is the point I wish to underline.

I will start with an example that has nothing to do with social objects. Imagine someone asks me to think of a winged horse. Done. And now? I thought of a winged horse, you will say. Of course, but now we need to distinguish: the mental element of an *act* (my thinking of a winged horse); the *mode of presentation* of the act (the winged horse as I picture it, white and moving); and the *object* to which the act refers (what you and I understand when we speak of "winged horses," regardless of their being white or black, standing or moving). This is a fairly recent philosophical discovery, at least if we consider philosophy's slow speed. At the end of the nineteenth century, distinguishing the act from its mode of presentation and from the object was a necessary move in order to reply to psychologism, that is, the reduction of logics to psychology (Costa 1996).

From this perspective, there is a famous distinction proposed by Frege (1892) between sense and reference: the descriptions "the morning star" and "the evening star" are two senses with the same reference, Venus; they offer two peculiar ways to reach the same object (see Dummett 1993). In the accompanying formulation, proposed by Twardowski (1894), we are dealing with act, content, and object. This distinction—which is also present in Meinong (1899; 1904) and, in different terms, in Husserl (1900–1)—insists precisely on the essential difference between *act* (the fact that I think of something), *content* (the specific mode of presentation of the object in my mind), and *object* (the ideal and common sphere of reference, the content shared, for instance, by everyone who thinks of the object designated by the word *horse—cheval, cavallo, Pferd*—and independently from the fact that their mode of presentation, that is, the content, may vary).

Act	Psychic process
Content	Idiomatic inscription
Object	Common idea

Reforming Twardowski. Obviously, Frege (interested in ideal objects) considered content as a superfluous element, almost a pathology of language. For me it is far from superfluous, as it is decisive for social objects. Furthermore, for the theory I am proposing, it is necessary to reform Twardowski. He spoke of processes taking place only in people's minds; I speak of objects that are given in the social world, even though in some cases their inscription can indeed be only mental. His content was a small physical object in the subject's brain, mine can be an object with a higher physical value, like a signature on a document, or even a full manuscript—as still happens in certain legal systems, like the French one, where warranties for tenancy agreements must be handwritten and reproducing a form, submitting the unlucky warrantor to a torture that is reminiscent of Kafka's in *In the Penal Colony.*

Therefore, with respect to Twardowski, some things will change but the essential stays the same: the inscription, which *can* but does not necessarily *have to* be external (think of tacit agreements), is idiomatic—typically, it must have a given calligraphy or it must happen in the mind of *that* person and not another.

Is it possible to assimilate internal content to external inscription? Of course: style is precisely this, hence the saying *le style c'est l'homme*. I can look at the *Rouen Cathedral* painted by Monet: it is *content* (the specific mode of presentation of that object in Monet's style) which neither corresponds to Monet's *act* (he has been dead for a long time and, likely, has not been thinking about it for a while before dying), nor to the *object* (given that I can say "Rouen Cathedral" and you will understand me without necessarily thinking of Monet; so much so that the cathedral is there even if I do not think about it). Yet, if I decide to go to a museum to see Monet's *Rouen Cathedral*, then what I want to see is precisely the *content*, or I would be happy with my memories, or a picture. For the same reason, if I want to listen to *The Marriage of Figaro*, it is precisely to enjoy its written content, which is undoubtedly related to the contents that went through Mozart's mind.

Now take the example of a real wedding: as Derrida (1971) noticed (it is an open secret, but charged with consequences), it is not sufficient to perform it, one's signature is necessary, together with that of the partner and the witnesses on a register, otherwise there would be no object (would there be weddings in a society where *everyone* suffered from Alzheimer's? If this was also a society without writing, I doubt it).[21]

All this, though, in conformity to a (written) rite and an (idiomatic) formulation. Notice that the idiom also has its rules: if one wrote one's name with a writing stencil, or changing it every time, that would not be one's signature. And this is not the only case. The decisive act of a wedding, notoriously, is the "I do." Now, if one said "of course" instead of "I do," the marriage would not be valid (as not compliant with the inscription). Accordingly, it would not be valid if one pronounced the vow in falsetto, or in another language, or mimicking a different dialect (as not compliant with the idiom). Moral: *for a social act to exist,* be it an order in a bar or the ordination of a priest, *there must be an inscription and it must be idiomatic, that is, it must conform both to a ritual and to an identity.*

As far as I know, and I will explore this further in Part II, the attention to the content—that is, in my formulation, to the idiomatic inscription—has been scarce in the sphere of social objects, even though, as I noted earlier, it is precisely in that sphere that it appears urgent and decisive. In short, if now no one would affirm that the law of noncontradiction depends on how our brain is made, many are still willing to claim that the form of a social object depends on people's free will. But even among those who recognized the independence of social objects with respect to acts, the attention to the idiomatic inscription was vastly neglected, almost as if social objects were ideal objects. Not even Twardowski thought of a different application of psychology. A massive gap, I believe, but in retrospect things can be fixed. So here is the result of my reformation of Twardowski.

Act	Minisociety
Inscription	Idiomatic content
Object	Reference of the inscription

THE CONSTRUCTION OF SOCIAL REALITY

At this point I am able to formulate a theory of the construction of social reality. As I have shown, for a social reality to exist three ingredients are necessary: acts, objects, and inscriptions. And given that the point I was more interested in was to know what kind of being a social object is, I believe its nature can be summed up in the following formula:

Object = Inscribed act

The *object* is a promise, a debt, a wedding, a war. The *act* is what happens between at least two subjects, in a minisociety (for instance, a promisor and a promisee: the last man on Earth would not be the world's owner, he would simply have *no* possession). The *inscription* is the idiomatic recording of the act, on a piece of paper, through a handshake, with a meaningful look, even simply in the *tabula* that lies in the two contracting parties' minds.

To follow Manzoni (1834, 68), or, more precisely, Agnese, Lucy's mother:

There must be two witnesses, nimble and cunning. You go to the curate; the point is to catch him unexpectedly, that he may have no time to escape. You say, "Signor Curate, this is my wife"; Lucy says, "Signor Curate, this is my husband"; you must speak so distinctly that the curate and the witnesses hear you, and the marriage is as inviolable as if the pope himself had celebrated it. When the words are once uttered, the curate may fret, and fume, and scold; it will be of no use, you are man and wife.

In this excerpt, "hear you" stands for "inscription," "say" for "act," and "marriage" for object—and intentionality, at least the curate's, does not count one bit.

Whether this theory is true is the topic of Part II.

THE BOTTLE IMP

At this point, I invite you, dear reader, to turn off your mobile phone, and recall a story by Robert Louis Stevenson, the author of *Treasure Island*. The story I want to focus on is a disquieting one: *The Bottle Imp* (1891). It tells the adventures of a magic bottle with an imp in it, capable of giving its owner all the goods in the world, in exchange for the owner's soul. Compared with other Faustian deals of this kind, the bottle offered an escape route. It was enough for the owner, once achieved his goals, to sell the bottle and the work is done: it is the new owner's problem now.

So, is everything all right? Only to an extent. Because the bottle has to be sold at half the original price. At the start, it is very easy. In the age of Napoleon—who got everything he did thanks to the bottle, only he got rid of it too quickly—the bottle was worth a fortune. But in time, in the end it came to be worth only, say, a euro.

Now, the chances of selling it are reduced to two: 50 cents, 25 cents, and that is it, because there are no coins worth 0.5 cent. Whoever buys the bottle is warned. The only possibility of getting rid of it is to find first a dupe, and then a masochist looking for eternal damnation.

Something similar happened in philosophy in the past decades. Whoever proclaimed that "the real world has turned into a fairy tale"—that is, only science holds the truth or not even science holds it and we must turn to fantasy—bought the bottle for a euro. Applauded and worshipped in life, in his last days he started thinking about what would come next, and found someone, the dupe, who bought it for 50 cents. Now this person, going even further, claimed that truth does not exist. Great effect and commotion, also because truth can hurt and be unpleasant. So once again symposiums, applauses, and conferences, until the denier of truth had to think of saving his soul. He unfortunately had to find someone entirely masochistic, because even a dupe knows that there is no 0.5 cent coin. Incredible but true: he found one. It was he who claimed that there are no facts, only interpretations.

I do not know how he managed to save himself at the last minute; perhaps he convinced the devil that there are no facts, only interpretations, and therefore there was no deal between them. I really do not know. But maybe there is something we can learn from all this: it is not true that the world is at our disposal; it is not true that it is a simple representation in the subject's mind.

Kind readers, I hope to have demonstrated this in Part I. We opened up our mobile phones, looked inside and, as you have seen, there was a lot in them indeed. It took us a while, but we made it and (count the pages) we are at two thirds of the book.

I will now ask for one more effort from you: read Part II. It is shorter but, developing what I said so far, promises you much more: an ontology of the social world. A world in which there are assumptions, revolutions, conferences, layoffs, trade unions, parliaments, companies, laws, restaurants, money, properties, governments, weddings, elections, games, receptions, tribunals, lawyers, wars, votes, promises, exchanges, procurators, doctors, cathedrals, culprits, taxes, holidays, medieval knights, presidents. The world in which the mobile phone exists but which, rather paradoxically, seems also to exist *in* the mobile phone, just like the mind is in the world and the world is in the mind.

Part II

SOCIAL OBJECTS: REALISM AND TEXTUALISM

A classification. Now I have all I need for my theory. To test it, I will compare it with existing theories,[1] which I classify into four fundamental categories, as shown in the accompanying diagram.

Strong realism
Social objects are as solid as physical objects.

Strong textualism
Physical objects are socially constructed.

Weak realism
Social objects are constructed upon physical objects.

Weak textualism
Social objects are constructed by idiomatic inscriptions (small physical objects).

The terms *realism* and *textualism* indicate, following Rorty's (1982, 149–66) suggestion, the contraposition between philosophers who believe that objects exist independently from the subjects and those who think that objects depend on the subjects just like texts depend on authors. The adjectives *strong* and *weak* indicate, obviously, the narrow or broad character of such assumptions. Although there are various versions of these positions, I deem we can find serious thinkers that exemplify them at their purest.

Strong realism was supported, in open opposition to juridical positivism, by Reinach.

Strong textualism was professed by postmodern thinkers, whose forerunner is Foucault.

Weak realism was set against postmodernists by Searle.

Weak textualism was proposed by Derrida, who, as I will show, is falsely mistaken for a postmodern thinker.

And here is, in synthesis, my strategy. I will start by rejecting strong realism and strong textualism; I will examine weak realism and indicate its aporias; and then I will show how, from my perspective, all these difficulties can be solved by weak textualism, which is the only theory capable of valorizing the element of idiomatic inscription as a decisive ingredient for the construction of social objects.

5

STRONG REALISM

A chimpanzee uses a stick to extract ants from an anthill and eat them (he loves them), and then puts the stick down. Along comes another chimpanzee, picks up the stick, and then uses it for the same purpose. When the first chimpanzee returns, the other fellow hands the stick back to him. I do not know for sure if this is always the case (after all, chimpanzees seem like rather litigious subjects), but it happens. Moral: Property exists without any explicit codification in a very primitive society.

THE STICK AND THE CHIMPANZEE

As suggested by Rodolfo Sacco, who valorized and theorized this example, we are dealing with "cryptotypes,"[2] that is, hidden but objective typologies. It is hard to imagine that some positive law might have ever informed the two chimpanzees about its properties and norms. And here we are dealing with a consideration that touches upon deeply rooted intuitions: There is a way in which to bump into a social object is like discovering a continent or a theorem. Laws were not created by us, and the legislator himself, in formulating them, had to submit to formal and material constraints, those that lead to induce the (fallacious) conviction that there is a natural law. These laws, *de facto*, simply present constraints that are hard to avoid: just as it is impossible that color exists without a wavelength, it is impossible that a promise exists without a promisor, a promisee, an object, a commitment, and a claim. Without these requisites, we do not have a promise, just like without legs we do not have a chair and without a back, instead of a chair, we have a stool.

Nevertheless, the fact that property seems (at least in certain circumstances) subjected to laws before any positive codification does not imply that the norms of property, or even the concept of what can be regarded as a property, come out of nothing, without the intervention of history or society. Property exists more or less in the same way as progress, craft, and a number of other things. Among things that exist, though, there is also a very primary writing: memory. If the deutero-chimpanzee had not remembered that the stick had been used by the proto-chimpanzee, a fuss would have ensued—unless the proto-chimpanzee had forgotten about it as well (that is, unless he had no inscription of it). In my terminology, this is a recording: the preform of social inscription.

Hence the resources, but also the limits, for a stronger claim than Sacco's, namely Reinach's theory. According to Reinach (1982, 3:6),

> If there are legal entities and structures which in this way exist in themselves, then a new realm opens here for philosophy. Insofar as philosophy is ontology or the a priori theory of objects, it has to do with the analysis of all possible kinds of object as such. . . . [P]hilosophy here comes across objects of quite a new kind, objects which do not belong to nature in the proper sense, which are neither physical nor psychical and which are at the same time different from all ideal objects in virtue of their temporality.

Reinach illustrates the prenormative a priori nature of juridical entities by means of a comparison with physical entities. A rose, which is a physical object, is the basis for objects of higher order, which are founded on the rose and which Reinach calls "states of affairs" (*Sachverhalten*): the existence of the rose, its being a flower, its being red, its being fragrant, and its being in the garden. These states of affairs depend on the rose but are not identified with it, since, for instance, the "being fragrant" of a rose (the state of affairs corresponding to a propositional content) is *not* itself fragrant, and its "being in the garden" is not in the garden.

As the rose supports the state of affairs of being red and being in the garden, so, every time I make a promise, such as "I'll give you ten euros tomorrow," a *claim* and an *obligation* are activated. Given that, in order to make the promise disappear from the world, there has to be a revocation, a renunciation, or its fulfillment, the claim and the obligation cannot be considered nothing or merely arbitrary but must be granted an objective existence distinct from that of the other objects listed by Reinach—physical, psychic (thoughts in someone's head), and ideal. Unlike physical objects, juridical entities cannot be seen or heard; at most, the things to which they refer can be perceived: I see a stick or a house and not the property in them.[3]

Furthermore, unlike mere thoughts, juridical entities persist even when no one is thinking about them: I have a mortgage even when I manage not to think about it. And, unlike ideal objects, they have a determinate existence in time; in a certain sense, their ambition is the opposite of that of ideal entities: if ideal entities aim at existing forever, promises and bets wish to come to an end, sooner or later.

The world has its laws and imposes them. Reinach's perspective derives directly from Husserl's idea that the world is not made up of a disorderly mass of sense data, but rather of objects that are already endowed with their own law-likeness and that display the same binding character as the laws of logic. It is possible to find in every object a nonrelative and nontransitory essence, an a priori necessary type, even if discovering it (the first formulation of a token) can come about contingently and a posteriori. Emboldened by this principle, Reinach mounts a frontal attack on the presuppositions of juridical positivism, according to which the law produces its own concepts autonomously. On the contrary, these are principles that exist independently from any juridical doctrine and that possess properties as constraining as those of physical objects. The discovery and formalization of these laws thus becomes the task of ontology, which Reinach, following Husserl, understands as the a priori doctrine of the objects.[4]

The advantage of Reinach's perspective, with respect to Reid-Austin's, lies in the fact that it does not make objects depend on a contractual dimension (the social act is an expression, but not the constitution, of a social object) and therefore explains why we immediately and intuitively grasp the absurdity of certain laws. The social world also has its laws, and imposes them; categories lie in objects, as Aristotle thought, and not in the subjects' minds, as posited by Kant. We had better leave the initiative to the object, given that it is about making a discourse on being as independent from the cognitive relationship with the subject.[5]

Strong realism, as embodied by Reinach, has three main points. The first is that *reality* incorporates within it not only physical objects (maybe constructed by the subject, as in the hypothesis of Kantian transcendentalism) but also higher-order objects.[6] The second is that these entities constitute a material a priori and possess the same powers of necessitation that the tradition attributes to logic.[7] The third and most audacious point—but with regard to which, unlike others (see, for example, Scheler 1916), Reinach was very cautious—is that these entities include *values*, which are in the objects before they are in the minds of those who contemplate them; that is to say, not only am I able to recognize the essence of a chair on the basis of a chair and not on that of an idea of a chair, but I am also able to recognize the good or evil of an action or line of behavior irrespective of the dispositions of my subjectivity.[8]

To what extent is this a supportable view?

REALISM: PROS AND CONS

Pros. Against the idea that individuals can do what they want with themselves, and that society and its objects are the infinitely malleable product of this omnipotence, realism catches a very solid consideration: wherever we are in the world, we find objective connections that are not products of chance: a greenish red is impossible. Things are the same for social objects. These structures are not merely in the heads of the people who form a community or, worse, in the heads of interpreters, but they are endowed with properties that belong to objects, before the subjects who contemplate them.

Strong realism thus suggests an important point: it is not the structures of human thought that are necessary, but rather the states of affairs and this applies even in the realm of law. In an obligation or a property right, the element that is juridical is closely connected to the way—in the actual world—the promise, the cattle, and the appreciation of land values *are*. Social objects are states of affairs that can be encountered in the world: *peccatum meum contra me est semper*. In turn, states of affairs are determined by the objects that constitute them.

The paradigm of the object in Roman law is enlightening from this point of view.[9] Juridical objects such as obligation, inheritance, and usufruct are originated by states of affairs, and from this very genesis they derive their exactness—which is diametrically opposed to Hume's idea that there is no necessity in a material sense, but only in a logical sense. Therefore, it is the thing that imposes its rights, and precisely in this sense we can fully appreciate the value of the saying that "names are a consequence of things."[10]

Table manners are also instructive in this respect. Apparently, a many etiquette issues are conventional: you can eat with your hands, with cutlery, or with sticks. Nonetheless, within these possibilities—which presuppose different ways of cooking food and presenting it—the use opportunities prevail that are suggested by the objects and the material constraints of the subjects, so that not even one single act of etiquette has radically conventional origins.[11]

This noncontingency becomes necessity when from the tokens of social objects we go back to the types of obligation, claim, and promise. Now, what do these constraints and their constancy depend on? Undoubtedly, there is a physics of the social world, but it is largely a naïve physics:[12] there are not only pieces of perceptive evidence but also higher-order ones, which constitute an encountered reality, that is, they impose themselves as something intuitively given and not conceptually elaborated (see Metzger 1941, 22). In turn, processes, prices, and debt exist, that is, they cannot be resolved neither into the subjects nor into atomic units,[13] and this also holds for terms like *innocence, guilt, murderous intentions,* and *nervous*.[14] In fact, a good part of our lives deals with common sense issues, and we have to deal not only with protons and viruses but also with laws, contracts, obligations, software, weddings, homes, and so on, all of which we must account for, in many cases, independently from physics. Furthermore, the reality captured by physics has progressively moved away from ordinary reality that still has to be accounted for within the frame of an ontology of common sense.[15]

In this conception, therefore, there is an implicit ecological horizon[16] coherent with what I suggested in the theory of objects in chapter 1: the basic idea is that in the approach to social objects we deal with spatial and temporal dimensions that orientate and limit the importance of convention. Contracts, laws, rent, and money are more deeply influenced by the immanent form of the social object and by space-time coordinates related to the surrounding environment rather than by the will of the contracting parties.[17]

Cons. So far, so good. Yet, realism shows its difficulties when we try to clarify it beyond the boundaries of a descriptive metaphysics (aimed at retracing the constraints and invariants of human thought and its environment) and of a general theory of states of affairs submitted to social objects.[18] In fact, if we descend into the details and want to assign a necessity to social objects not as types but as tokens, we find ourselves having to regard the tax rates for any given fiscal year as necessary, when on the contrary it is obvious that the laws are enacted on the basis of contingent principles. Now, it is precisely contingency that is determining for the concrete occurrence of social objects. This can easily be seen by considering the variety of states of affairs that, in different juridical traditions, fall under the notion of a *contract*, and even more significantly, by bearing in mind the deliberate use in law of vague notions that allow a high level of flexibility in handling relatively homogeneous states of affairs (see Ajani 2003). The variability is not only geographical and related to juridical traditions, but also historical, as can be verified through the comparison of two impossibilities: an eidetic one (relative to the form of the law) and a hyletic one (relative to the material submitted to the law) illustrated by Marx and easily falsifiable.[19]

Eidetic impossibility: "No one is forced to contract marriage, but everyone who has done so must be compelled to obey the laws of marriage. A person who contracts marriage does not *create* marriage, does not *invent* it, any more than a swimmer creates or invents the nature and laws of water and gravity. Hence marriage cannot be subordinated to his arbitrary wishes; on the contrary, his arbitrary wishes must be subordinated to marriage" (Marx 1975a, 308). Much could be said about this reasoning today, but certainly not that it is indisputable.

Hyletic impossibility: "The gathering of fallen wood [is compared with] the most composite wood theft! They both have a common definition. The appropriation of wood from someone else. Therefore both are theft. That is the sum and substance of the farsighted logic which has just issued laws. First of all, therefore, we call attention to the *difference* between them, and if it must be admitted that the two actions are *essentially* different, it can hardly be maintained that they are identical *from the legal standpoint*" (Marx 1975b, 224–25). Now, Marx goes on, "There exist objects of property which, by their very nature, can never acquire the character of predetermined private property, objects which, by their elemental nature and their accidental mode of existence, belong to the sphere of occupation rights, and therefore of the occupation right of that class which precisely because of these occupation rights, is excluded from all other property and which has the same position in civil society as these objects have in nature" (232). Now, this is falsified as well, given that multinationals can even patent natural species.

Most likely, the conclusion to be drawn is this: We possess determinate social objects that we have *discovered* in the course of our history. These objects are carriers of laws of essence that are configured in a certain way. But that does not mean that we have discovered *the only* possible social objects either in space or time. As regards space, because of their history, the Chinese, for instance, have discovered some social objects different from those we have discovered—as well as many that are identical—each endowed with its own necessity (and thus we avoid inferring that the *variety* of objects implies that they are *random*). As regards time, we might notice that even an institution like the family, as such essentially biologically influenced, has undergone huge changes in many societies in recent memory. Nevertheless, these transformations are never presented as the upshot of simple decisions, but have always had to negotiate with states of affairs and laws of essence.

ARISTOTLE'S POKER

To sum up what I have mentioned so far. Reinach does not put ethics and social ontology on the same level. His social ontology wants to be independent from any ethical consideration, because ethicality constitutes, so to speak, an extra value typical of certain states of affairs and not others. Social ontology and ethics are therefore two spheres that touch on each other, but are not identical. We may infer Reinach's position with regard to ethics, but this is a *bona fide* reconstruction, given that he wrote too little on this topic. Furthermore, Reinach's social ontology is overall too poor, since it addresses uniquely a priori juridical issues. He writes that his conclusions are useful for social sciences, but he never truly elaborated a theory of other social objects that are not juridical entities.

Reinach recognizes the variability of positive law in front of the invariability of his a priori law. Positive law is constituted by things that must be done.[20] Maybe it is possible to correct only this part of his theory without discarding the rest, and thus have strong and impenetrable objects on one side and more penetrable and variable objects on the other. Once this is clarified, one can conclude that—as exciting as it might be from an intellectual point of view, since it firmly rejects the subjectivistic paradigm that undoes social objects—Reinach's model presents at least two major flaws.

First, the project of an "a priori doctrine of civil law" seems very implausible. Civil law is *analytically* something historical. Reinach is well aware of this, but now the problem becomes clear: Reinach's proposal seems in the first instance to be a maxim ("do not think that the laws are mere fruit of subjectivity") rather than a positive instrument for the construction of a theory of social objects. Second, Reinach maintains that juridical objects possess their own "independent being." Again, this claim poses another problem. In fact, Reinach himself posits that it is immanent to their nature that social objects have a beginning and an end in time, as can be seen from the a priori falsity of the following sentences:

Aristotle wanted an ace-high poker.
Plotinus thought he had scored a goal.
Proclus supported Panathinaikos.
Antithenes took out a mortgage.

In the end, Reinach devoted all his attention to the *object* (and only afterward to the *act*), overlooking the circumstance that what seems crucial, for a social object as such (unlike a physical or an ideal object)—as I have shown and will extensively argue in the following chapters—is *inscription*. His approach can be schematized as follows:

Act
~~Inscription~~
Object

The result, therefore, is that strong realism does not work if not as a maxim. I will cross it out (see accompanying diagram).

~~Strong~~ realism

Social ob~~jects are~~ as solid as ~~physical~~ objects.

Strong textualism

Physical objects are socially constructed.

Weak realism

Social objects are constructed upon physical objects.

Weak textualism

Social objects are constructed by idiomatic inscriptions (small physical objects).

Can its failure mean the success of postmodern strong textualism? Luckily, it cannot.

6

STRONG TEXTUALISM

I once heard a famous ethnomethodologist argue that astronomers create astronomical reality. "Look," I said, "When you and I go for a walk in the moonlight and I point at the moon and say 'nice moon tonight' are we creating the moon?" "Yes," he responded.

—SEARLE 2001/2002

GEERTZ'S MOON

Metabasis eis allo genos. I imagine you will ask me who, apart from the fearless postmodern thinker attacked by Searle (1998, 20), could have ever professed such a bizarre doctrine, but the answer is easy and the records are vast. In general, the ingredients are a Cartesian subjectivism, a Kantian confusion between ontology and epistemology, and a Nietzschean theory of the will to power. They take from Descartes the notion that ideas are uncertain, and that the only thing one should not doubt is the subject; from Kant they take the thesis according to which the only way to give the world some stability is to submit it to science's conceptual schemes; from Nietzsche they take the hypothesis that science is nothing but the manifestation of the subjects' will to power. At this point, the recipe consists of a systematic conversion into another genus *metabasis eis allo genos*: I begin with a claim that has a very restricted application and then I generalize and apply it to fields where it becomes controversial (see Ferraris 1998, 17–20).

Consider the position of Foucault (1966, 400–14), who claims that perhaps when the human sciences disappear humans will also disappear. What has gone wrong here is the generalizing of the particular case from which his enquiry started, which was the assumption that madness is a result of psychiatry (Foucault 1961). Which, in one sense, is banal: our specific way of dealing with behaviors that we call "mad" is psychiatry, which talks about things like schizophrenia and paranoia where once the vocabulary included that of possession, demons, or gods. Furthermore, madness is certainly an epistemological object, since to call something "madness" instead of "divine possession" is certainly a choice that has to do with what we know.

This absurdity becomes quite plain when it is applied to humanity whose disappearance is prophesied. Featherless bipeds existed before and presumably will continue to exist after the human sciences will have ceased to exist. And to think, or to write with apparent lyrical enthusiasm, the contrary is simply to mistake ontology for epistemology and the social for the individual, and to consider the individual as the realm of an absolute subjectivism that, on the kindest reading, can be ascribed to solipsism—so much so that a conference of postmodern thinkers would end up generating an association of solipsists, that is, a square circle.[1]

The most serious problem with strong textualism is that, by excluding from the start the possibility of an *adaequatio* between intellect and thing (given that there is nothing outside the text), it turns out to be *ex hypothesi* immune to any possibility of falsification. The situation is literally psychoanalytic: if the analyst asks you whether you have ever felt homicidal urges toward members of your family, you can answer "yes" and confirm his hypothesis; but this is not falsified even if you answer "no," given that in that case the analyst would argue that it is a case of resistance.[2]

HOW TO MAKE THE WORLD DISAPPEAR INTO THE TEXT

In all this there is some irony. The discovery of social objects takes place in the historicist tradition (the one that originated postmodernism) and in the frame of the contraposition between natural science, dealing with physical objects, and science of the spirit, in charge of tackling social objects (Ferraris 1988, 177–79). Apparently, it is the opening of a huge dominion of objects. Yet, the idea of delegating them to history and the spirit first has made social objects evanescent, and then it annihilated physical objects as well, in a twentieth century nihilism with respect to which Fichte, in comparison, seems moderate. Rather paradoxically, the discovery of social objects therefore coincides with their erasure in two moves, ending with a blindfold chess game for who started the match.

First move. The historicist idea of social objects is that they are the manifestation of a freedom with no objective constraints that manifests itself in time and is made of spirit, which can be embodied by institutions. In this framework, objects turn out to be conventional and modifiable at will. In other words, if there is an ontology of social objects, then it is a historical ontology (Hacking 2002), given that it entails such a strong relativism that it impedes any classification.

From this point of view, the position held by Wilhelm Dilthey (1833–1911) seems exemplary. He formulated a general theory of science of the spirit (that he sets against natural science, *tertium non datur*) and qualified social objects as "objective spirit" that is realized in institutions. Apparently, we have objects recognized in their autonomy with respect to the natural sphere, but they are such only in theory. For Dilthey, the only possible relationship with the institutions of objective spirit is, in fact, that of a historical interpretation, whose task is to reawaken the meaning of decisions made in the past and to explain their genetic reasons, up to the *psychological* act from which they stemmed. Dilthey conceives this transformation in terms of a criticism of historical reason: if Kant's Copernican revolution teaches to ask not how things themselves are but how they have to be made in order to be known by us, then it is a matter of making an extra effort and show that the categories through which we know did not fall from the sky, but possess their own historical origin and contingent interests.

At this point, objects become rather shadowy. Natural sciences possess real objects, and their task is to *explain* causal links. Sciences of the spirit, instead, do not have them, since their aim is *understanding*, which, according to Dilthey, consists of a form of identification in which a subject is transferred into another subject (understanding the object "Julius Caesar" is to be transposed into the subject "Julius Caesar"). Like a time bomb, the paradigm of biography and autobiography as the model for understanding in sciences of the spirit triggers the dissolution of social objects that are born in a subject and live again in another subject (see Ferraris 1992).

Second move. The second move involves Heidegger, who tackled social ontology starting from the analysis of the individual subject (see Heidegger 1927), and christening it as "existential analytics" and "hermeneutics of facticity," among other names. Here ontology does not count as a theory of objects, but as the search for a being that transcends them. Here, too, there is a grounded intuition: that is, the idea that social objects would not exist in the absence of people who believe in their existence. Heidegger posits, however, that the dependence on subjects is a dependence on the monadic individualities (so that social objects are assimilated to the moods of the single subjects) and assumes that what depends on subjects is subjective, and therefore infinitely interpretable.[3]

Hermeneutics and postmodernism merely radicalize this fallacy. For Gadamer (1960, 542), with a complete assimilation of the natural with the social, being is reduced to language. For Foucault (1966) the social, even when it is applied to the study of nature, is a pure manifestation of the will to power. With this move, relativism exists in the sphere of the sciences of the spirit and enters natural science. Everything is socially constituted; objectivity is revealed as subject dependent; therefore, everything is infinitely interpretable, and, in the final analysis, nothing is. Typically, in order to mitigate the morally unacceptable consequences of such an outcome (had Hitler won, would he have been in the right?), Richard Rorty committed to an apology of democracy.[4]

Blindfold chess. Because the presupposition is that of an annihilation of objectivity, nothing, in this position, can offer some kind of serious argument to distinguish true and false or good and evil. Suppose that, instead of Rorty, we meet another American, someone a little meaner: "I have been assured by a very knowing American of my acquaintance in London, that a young healthy child well nursed is at a year old a most delicious, nourishing, and wholesome food, whether stewed, roasted, baked, or boiled." It is a passage from Jonathan Swift's *A Modest Proposal* (1729), suggesting, with grim irony, to eat Irish children as a remedy for famine in Ireland (see Swift 2004, 90).

A coherent relativist—say the ethnomethodologist of Searle's story—would have to say that the modest proposal is far from indecent. For the sake of theory, he should highlight (drawing from ethnography, history, and psychoanalysis) that anthropophagy is attested in many cultures, that when we order a steak it is not only for lack of proteins, that mourning itself constitutes a form of anthropophagy (you introject the other), that Hitler was a vegetarian and—if he is an imaginative relativist—that communists eat children.

Faced with the absurdity of his statements (it is a bit like saying that the moon is a theoretical construct, but morally much worse), the relativist could perhaps evoke a counterexample. Imagine, in keeping with the theme of violence, that, instead of Cortés, an ethnologist had arrived in Tenochtitlan. So many advantages: no imposed Christianity, no destruction of idols. But in this example, the relativist exposes himself to an obvious objection. Had an ethnologist arrived in Tenochtitlan, there would not have been the end of human sacrifices (in some cases, twenty thousand people were killed in one celebration, which explains the conquistadores' easy military success—they encountered an exasperated population riotous toward the Aztecs). And now, imagine the same ethnologist in Auschwitz: would he have dared invoke tolerance toward the Nazi customs?

The only outcome of this *Merry Widow*–like relativism is to lead to *Te Deum*–like antirelativism, and this, after all, is its greatest historical responsibility. Now, relativism, used case by case and with a lot of common sense, is the only practicable theory in ethics, as long as one has a theory of objects. But postmodern thinkers reached the hyperbolic and false conclusion that, in order to found relativism, it is necessary to claim that *everything*, from scientific theories to ordinary perception, is socially constructed. And they corroborated their nihilism with the fallacy according to which what is socially constructed is purely relative and rather subjective, so that the alternative between sticks and knife and fork or that between heliocentrism and geocentrism are two cases of cultural variety. Thus, they expose themselves to the no less hyperbolic objection that, since there are nonrelative truths (2 + 2=4, Caesar crossed the Rubicon, atoms exist, the Earth orbits around the Sun), *then* we must not be relativist in ethics either.

One learns from one's mistakes, or at least others do: *in order to be a relativist in ethics, it is necessary to be a realist in ontology.* The fundamental mistake in strong textualism is not relativism (which, by the way, was not invented by it), but the criticism of objectivity, strangely considered as the premise for absolutism, whereas the contrary is true. It is only with a good theory of objects that we can be relativists, and in a nonarbitrary way, because we will be able to know which objects we are referring to. Banally, it is necessary to assume that there is an external world, independent from our constructions and conceptual schemes in order to give meaning to our vocabulary, even the moral one. "Thou shalt not kill" is an imperative that makes sense only if killing someone is different from thinking about killing someone. This does not entail that what is in the external world necessarily influences our decisions. One can choose, at the restaurant, thanks to the menu and, in more serious issues, thanks to criteria that do not depend on ontology. And, in order to keep freedom of choice and the following responsibilities, it is not necessary to invoke the "socially constructed" character of reality as a whole.[5]

THE MORAL OF THE STORY

Our ethnomethodologist's adventures suggest a moral: strong textualism is false. In its literal formulation—the one claiming that physical objects themselves are socially constructed—the doctrine appears manifestly absurd, and stems from the confusion between the theories and their objects, ontology and epistemology, what there is (e.g., the moon) and what we know (or do not know) about what there is.

One could object that there is nothing wrong with claiming that social objects are socially constructed, but in that case we would not really have a theory, but a solid tautology. The claim would become interesting again, or at least not tautological, if it were suggested that "socially constructed" meant "subjectively constructed," except that, in that case, we would be faced with a clear falsehood, as we would see if someone decided subjectively that theft is no longer a crime or that money has no value. This blatant nonsense can be hidden behind the big statement that "there are no facts, only interpretations" (Nietzsche 1885–87, 7 [60]); but it becomes very clear thanks to a simple thought experiment, consisting in picturing a court where, instead of "all are equal above the law," there was, indeed, the sentence "there are no facts, only interpretations."

If the thesis of strong textualism seeks to be less than a tautology (social reality is socially constructed), then it must be a claim that social reality is subjectively constructed. Therefore, in the act-inscription-object tripartition we have an exclusive valorization of the act, which is tantamount to a psychologizing of the entire social world.

Act
~~Inscription~~
~~Object~~

~~Strong~~ realism	**~~Strong~~ textualism**
Social ~~objects are~~ as solid as ~~physical~~ objects.	Physical ~~objects~~ are socially ~~constructed~~.

Weak realism	**Weak textualism**
Social objects are constructed upon physical objects.	Social objects are constructed by idiomatic inscriptions (small physical objects).

So, the strong textualist is also wasting his time, since his doctrine—just like the strong realist's—does not work. Once again, it should be crossed out (see diagram).

"THERE IS NOTHING OUTSIDE THE TEXT": THE CORRECT READING

One more observation, before I move on. How should we read Derrida's (1967a) statement, "There is nothing outside the text," if we want to keep Derrida in our social ontology?[6] The claim can easily be interpreted as an assertion declaring the nonexistence of a reality independent from our interpretations, the language we use, and the theories through which we refer to it. Now, in these terms the saying is clearly false given that, literally, it would coincide with the countersense for which there would only be texts and not the world they refer to.

And this is how, for instance, Searle (1995, 153–56, 189–93) interprets it, when he commits to showing the essential difference between the parts of reality that depend on language (for instance, the sentence "There is snow and ice on the top of Mount Everest") and the parts of reality fully independent from language (like the *fact* that there is snow and ice on the top of Mount Everest). Or when he unmasks the hidden countersense for which reality is mistaken for the instruments used to define it (for instance, the world is mistaken for the physical theories we can formulate about it), by means of the evident countersense that Searle weighing 73 kilograms and Searle weighing 160 pounds would then constitute two distinct beings (ibid., 165).

The point is that Derrida (1988, 136) made clear that the sentence had to be understood as "there is nothing outside the context," meaning that, for instance, it is one thing to see a meadow during a walk but to see it through a botanist's lens is another thing. Searle finds Derrida's clarification simply banal,[7] which is not necessarily true, if one considers that in ontology—at least with regard to physical and ideal objects—*everything* exists outside the text, if it is true that there is snow and ice on the top of Mount Everest and $2 + 2 = 4$ independently from our language, interpretations, and conceptual schemes.

That Derrida's assertion referred to epistemology (the way in which we know things) and not ontology (the way things are) seems to be easily demonstrated by a simple consideration. Starting from Husserl, Derrida never believed that physical reality is constructed. It possesses by definition an existence distinct from the knowing subject and the theories that possibly swirl in his mind. The principle that "there is nothing outside the text," therefore, can only be applied as regards the *socialization* of ideal objects (which, once discovered as independent, must be shared) and the *construction* of social objects (which, instead, require a recording for their very existence).

Here lies Derrida's mistake, which is not the same as the strong textualists' mistakes (believing that physical objects are socially constructed), but rather the more sophisticated one of mistaking ideal objects for social objects, and mistaking knowledge for its socialization. In short, triangles exist even without an inscription, but contracts do not, and Derrida confused triangles and contracts. From all this, though, we can draw a positive principle for social ontology even though—I admit—it is less powerful and sexy than "there is nothing outside the text": namely, *inscription is the necessary but not sufficient condition for social objects.* That is all. And it is on this basis that I will develop, in the two remaining chapters, first a critique of Searle and then the apology of Derrida.

7

WEAK REALISM

I am on the train and the inspector asks for my ticket. When I show it to him, I notice an unpleasant omission on my part: I only had stamped the receipt, not the actual ticket. While the inspector is looking at my ticket, pondering, I start preparing my argument: the two tickets are really the same, because at the ticket office they stapled them together; also, they refer to the same event on a certain day—Turin-Milan on the morning of May 9, 2005—as is indisputably demonstrated by the receipt. So, it was enough to stamp only one of them.

Luckily, the inspector does not force me to such a long demonstration and lets it be. But had we started to argue and to present reasons in support of my theses (for instance, the inspector could have highlighted that by saying "the tickets were stapled together" I was admitting that there were precisely two tickets, one of which, namely the real ticket, was not stamped) we would have been dealing with ontology. That is to say, we would have been asking questions on what an object is (the ticket), what an event is (the journey), and finally what Searle called the "huge invisible ontology" that makes up the texture of rules, obligations, and duties constituting the thread of our lives.

SEARLE'S BEER

Imagine that the inspector had fined me (all the ontologies in the world notwithstanding, the law was on his side). At this point, I would have had to pay, taking a piece of paper (or a credit card or a piece of metal) out of my wallet. Whatever the object, it would surely have been a physical object, certainly not socially constructed, given that the molecules constituting it were not created by the Governor of the Bank of Italy. Only, an object like a banknote possesses a social value, allowing me to buy things; and this does not simply depend on me, because money counts as such also for someone with completely different ideas and moods from my own, just as it counts for me in exactly the same way regardless of my beliefs and feelings. How is this possible? How can these physical objects acquire a social value?

Searle explains this miracle this way: "I go into a café in Paris and sit in a chair at a table. The waiter comes and I utter a fragment of a French sentence. I say, 'un Demi, Munich, à pression, s'il vous plaît.' The waiter brings me the beer and I drink it. I leave some money on the table and leave" (Searle 1995, 3). Apparently, everything is visible: the beers, the tables, the waiters, the money, and so on. Not really: the scene is far from simple and, most of all, it is not entirely visible.

Searle goes on to say, "Notice that we cannot capture the features of the description I have just given in the language of physics and chemistry. There is no physical chemistry description adequate to define 'restaurant,' 'waiter,' 'sentence of French,' 'money' or even 'chair' and 'table,' even though all restaurants, waiters, sentences in French, money, and chairs and tables are physical phenomena" (ibid.). Indisputably, all the things in Searle's list are physical objects (even the sentences in French). However, as Searle points out, the language of physics does not exhaust their possible definitions, since, for instance, a sentence in French cannot be reduced to the vibrations in the air and in the tympanum.

Here, in fact, is where the invisible comes into play: "[Notice] that the scene as described has a huge, invisible ontology: the waiter did not actually own the beer he gave me, but he is employed by the restaurant which owned it. The restaurant is required to post a list of the prices of all the *boissons*, and even if I never see such a list, I am required to pay only the listed price. The owner of the restaurant is licensed by the French government to operate it. As such, he is subject to a thousand rules and regulations I know nothing about. I am entitled to be there in the first place only because I am a citizen of the United States, the bearer of a valid passport, and I have entered France legally" (ibid.).

So where exactly is this legion of invisible objects? Here it is: owner, employed by, required to post a list of the prices, operate, government, rules, regulations, entitled, citizen, United States, valid passport, France, and so on. All these are instances of social objects. It looks as if Searle's aim was that of writing an appendix to Meinong's *Theory of Objects*, combining it with Reinach's *A Priori Foundations of Civil Law*.

On one hand, in fact, Searle seems to suggest with Meinong that we had better get rid of our stubborn prejudice in favor of the real: the physical existence of tables and chairs is not the only possible kind of existence. If Pegasus and the round square may count as objects, then why not count "the citizens of the United States" as objects as well? Given that when we refer to a round square we are not referring to a "wooden iron" and when we think of Pegasus we are not thinking of Bucephalus, analogously when we talk of the "citizens of the United States" we are not referring (at least, for the moment) to the "citizens of Iraq."

On the other hand—following Reinach—such invisible objects are not chimeras or visions, for they can have quite tangible consequences. The invisible ontology of social reality is not some kind of imaginary zoology *à la* Borges, nor a classification of some hierarchy of angels. Rather, it is a world of laws, institutions, obligations that exist independently from—and cannot be identified with—our individual acts of volition and imagination. They are not the same as our will and are not made of the same stuff that dreams are made of, since a promise made, say, on Monday is still the same promise on the next Friday, and it still counts as such even when I am asleep and dreaming.

How, then, can we reconcile *invisibility* with *solidity*? Searle's answer is that social objects are higher-order objects whose *inferiora* are constituted by physical objects which accounts for their apparent concreteness. The price, for instance, is that of twenty-five centiliters of a particular kind of liquid, namely beer; the citizen of the United States in question weighs roughly 160 pounds (and the waiter has a weight too, even if we do not know it); money typically consists of pieces of metal and paper. When we enter the social world, we are not entering some sort of spiritual sphere, but rather a mixture of physical objects and psychological acts often associated with speech acts (but this is not always required, given that sometimes a simple handshake may suffice, for instance, to come to an agreement).

Searle's view presents two promising features. On one hand, it gets the social sphere out of postmodernists' clutches, whose accounts typically make such a sphere a friable, vague, and infinitely interpretable matter. On the other hand, Searle goes well beyond the traditional conflict between sciences of nature and sciences of the spirit, by emphasizing the absence of a real hiatus between the physical and the social.

A vast design indeed, and I say this with no irony, because this is exactly what I wish to do through my hypotheses of reification in which, if you like, instead of the beer I have laid my mobile phone on the table. And Searle certainly has the merit of having reawakened within analytic philosophy the importance of the issue of social ontology, without merely analyzing, for instance, the intentionality of social objects, transferring those objects from people's minds to the stage of the world.[1]

HOW TO MAKE WORDS WITH THINGS

Searle's idea is genius in its simplicity. Austin, with his analysis of the performative, wondered "how to do things with words" and found the answer precisely in those acts that, as I have shown, do not merely prescribe a state of affairs but actively produce it, creating christenings, marriages, bets, promises and so on. Austin's view was a bright example of *strong textualism*, precisely the theory whose weaknesses I showed in the previous chapter. In situations like the ones considered by Austin, there is truly nothing outside the text.

But Austin knew what he was doing, and he especially understood very well (which is the presupposition of his reasoning) that the performative is only *one* of the possible uses of language, which very often merely describes a reality existing independently from words. This is exactly what I tried to underline by marking the difference between social objects on one hand, and physical and ideal objects on the other. If we neglect this difference and turn the world into a product of language, then we have two options: If we are lucky, we are God, who through a famous performative ("Let there be light") created the world (or, at least, light, since *Genesis* narrates that, prior to the divine performative, the spirit wandered on the waters, which therefore were already there). If we are less lucky, we become like the ethnomethodologist who claims to be creating the moon with his theories.

Now, the advance of strong textualism must have awakened in Searle— who in the meantime had systematized his theory of speech acts (Searle 1969; 1975)—the urge for a fundamental clarification (Searle 1993a; 1993b; 1998), which led him to formulate a social *ontology*. Staying *in partibus infidelium*, that is, in the very deconstructionist Paris he was opposing, he must have thumped the table and said, "Garçon, un Demi, Munich, à pression, s'il vous plait," thereby underlining that, with his act, he was not producing a beer nor a table: he was placing an order to an already existing waiter, and the only thing he produced was a contract between him and the *garçon*. The latter (provided he did not get offended for being addressed like in a Jean Gabin film) had to bring him a beer, just like Searle had to pay. The act, therefore, as I have shown in chapter 4, produced an object, which in turn was made possible by other invisible objects—norms, prices, regulations and so on.

Now, how to stop the postmodernist *dèrapage*? Searle probably noted, I imagine, that the most solid and visible thing in this whole contract were the money he left on the table (he curiously did not mention the *receipt* that the waiter had printed as soon as Searle, by paying, had extinguished his debt, but I will come back to this). Hence Searle's theory: social objects represent higher-order objects produced through performatives, which nonetheless—contrary to what postmodern thinkers believe—possess a physical basis, like the metal or paper with which we pay. Thus he had circumscribed the sphere of the performative (which only counts for social objects) and anchored the world of social objects to the world of physical objects, *pace* postmodernists who thought that a toothache is socially constructed. Not so: the precise opposite is true, namely that *even social objects need physical supports*. Here, though, things got a bit out of hand for Searle.

In fact, on one hand, when he claims that the real model for social objects is money, which needs metal or paper as a support for its higher-order functions, Searle is very realist. Yet there is a huge number of social objects (complex entities like states, universities, or firms) that have no physical counterpart endowed with evident borders. There are others (debt, for instance) that seem to lack by definition *any* kind of physical counterpart. Therefore it is as if Searle took by the letter Reinach's metaphor that social objects are as solid as trees and houses, acting like the neo-Kantians who, smelling spiritualism in the transcendental I, looked for categories in brain gyri.

On the other hand, though, precisely because of his speech act theory, Searle maintains a high degree of conventionalism in his approach—something that, as I will show, leads him to claim, for instance, that "anything can count as money" (try to *pay* in mountains or mice and you will notice it is not so). In other words, after trying to anchor strictly (and not largely, as I will try to do by recurring to *inscriptions*) the social object to the physical object, he confers an unprecedented power to social construction—without considering, for instance, that it seems highly implausible that there should be a state including celestial bodies from outside the solar system, because evident material constraints would make it ungovernable. (It suffices to think, in a more realistic example, of Charles V's difficulties with an empire on which the sun never set).

In short, this is the point: the legitimate *desideratum* of Searle's ontology has to be formulated differently to keep a lot of the good part of it but also to correct its most obvious and onerous flaws. I will start from the beginning.

Weak realism: How it works. The starting problem is that of figuring out what keeps the social and the physical objects together, namely what keeps together—say, the price and the beer, the money and the paper it is made of. Searle's idea is roughly the following:

X counts as Y in C
where
X = physical object
Y = social object
C = context
"counts as" = collective intentionality

What is needed to obtain from a mere piece of colored paper (a physical object) money (a social object) is a function that applies the following rule: X (e.g., a piece of paper) counts as Y (e.g., money) in a context C (e.g., a given state in a given time). Such a function is attributed by means of constitutive rules that, unlike the more familiar regulative rules (for instance, the rule of right-hand traffic), are not designed to regulate a preceding situation that is independent from the rules themselves, but rather they bring the situation itself into being (as is obvious in the case of games: the rules of chess, for instance, are not meant to put order in a preexisting situation in which there are chess boards, pawns, and other pieces, but rather they give a meaning to all such things).

So far, all is clear. Undoubtedly, this explanation looks quite reasonable. The rules that are involved in the attribution of a function create social objects (pawns or philosophy professors) out of physical objects (tiny pieces of wood, human beings). Searle points out that the attributed functions are not conventional, even if they originate from rules. In fact, it would be a mistake to think that there may be some equivalence between "following a rule" and "following a convention," because, as Wittgenstein (1953) has noted, this would mean that there is no difference between following a rule and the mere belief that one is following a rule; between playing chess and the mere belief that one is playing chess; or (if we consider an instance of regulative rule) between looking at a clock and just imagining a clock to know the exact time. In other words, if I lose a chess piece I may well replace it with, say, a beer bottle cap, for the piece is conventional.[2] However, its function is not: the cap will have to behave exactly like, say, the bishop, and therefore move only diagonally. At least if I want to play chess and not merely pretend that I am playing chess.

Advantages and problems. The first advantage of such an account is that of ruling out the view that makes social objects absolutely conventional, a view that dates back at least to Rousseau's idea of the social contract (Rousseau even suggested the conventionality of the language used in stipulating the contract). So, without going too far, I made a first point against postmodern thinkers.

Secondly, social objects have been connected directly not only to the rules that create them but also to the physical objects that constitute their *inferiora*. Now, assuming that collective intentionality plays the same role in Searle's theory as the act in Twardowski-Meinong's scheme whereas the physical object plays the same role as the object, Searle's social ontology would have the following structure:

Physical object
↓
Collective intentionality
↓
Social object

Then, it is worth noticing—and this is important in view of what I shall say next—that in Searle's account the distinction act-inscription-object boils down to the simple dichotomy act-object. The theory of collective intentionality, in fact, privileges the act, whereas in the idea that social objects supervene on physical objects what is privileged is the object. Unlike the theory I have previously rejected, here the terms at issue are two instead of three:

Act

~~Inscription~~

(Physical) Object

Does this work? No, it does not. Firstly because it is hard to avoid the impression of a certain circularity: on one hand, language is a social object; on the other, it is the condition for social objects. In addition to this general problem, there are two major issues afflicting Searle's theory: first, a problem that concerns the act and, second, a problem that regards the object.

PROBLEMS WITH THE ACT

Football mysteries. I will take the example of football to test Searle's theory. The basic idea is that we have physical objects, for instance a grass field, a leather sphere, and men (or women) in shorts running and kicking the ball to one another. Out of all this, though, social objects are produced: that is, a pitch, a ball, players, and a match. How? Thanks to a magic wand: "collective intentionality."[3] Searle (1995, 41) writes, "[There is a] continuous line that goes from molecules and mountains to screwdrivers, levers, and beautiful sunsets, and then to legislatures, money, and nation-states. The central span on the bridge from physics to society is collective intentionality, and the decisive movement on that bridge in the creation of social reality is the collective intentional imposition of function on entities that cannot perform these functions without that imposition." The idea, at least in principle, seems simple and efficacious.

What works. What comes into play in a football match are precisely physical objects—playing football is different from thinking about playing football, watching a match is different from dreaming about one—subject to natural laws: think of the ball's trajectory or the players' performance. Yet, other laws (score, win or lose, penalty, offside, and so on) impose themselves upon the physical ones. These other laws are of a very different kind: the ball that, with a certain trajectory, scores a goal on Sunday can be the same that, with the same trajectory, hits the net on Monday but without scoring because no match takes place that day. In short, physics is not enough. Take the following experiment: Try to imagine a sequence of coordinates relative to an object in various instants T_1, $T_2 \ldots T_n$, subsequent to the instant T_0 in which a force was applied to it. The force must be sufficient to describe the trajectory, but many factors can alter it, and this is why the outcome is not always the one wished for.

What is this description about?[4] It is about a penalty shot. Does it describe it adequately? It does not. It is unlikely that supporters from both teams would be willing to witness the scene with calm scientific composure. The reaction of rage (or joy, depending on the team) is due to the belief that a football match is not only a succession of physically determined causes and effects. And it does not seem very intelligent to claim that football matches do not exist given that, in reality, they are nothing more than a series of actions and reactions that can be explained with the help of the laws of physics. It would be like saying that the best way to enjoy a match would be to watch it through an atomic microscope. What is missing? Here is the second point: Some do it better than others, and some are just completely hopeless, but basically it works like this: You have to push hard enough, and this can be not that easy because at times you can be tired or nervous or choking under pressure. And it is not that easy to sense the spectators' eyes looking at you, filled with expectations. Then, when you have to do it two or three times a week, it can be really stressful.

It is again a description of a penalty shot, where the object aimed at (the net) is omitted. Things cannot be explained only through physical causes: aims are needed as well. So, as Leibniz noticed, a description of the conquest of a stronghold like the following would be rather bizarre: "It was because the particles of powder in the cannon having been touched by a spark of fire expanded with a rapidity capable of pushing a hard solid body against the walls of the place, while the little particles which composed the brass of the cannon were so well interlaced that they did not separate under this impact" (1908, § 19; trans. modified). Instead, we should say that "the foresight of the conqueror brought him to choose the time and the proper means and how his ability surmounted all obstacles" (ibid.). Good for him.

It is incredible how many things become incomprehensible when and if one ignores their destination: imagine the odd effect a toaster, a vacuum cleaner, or a computer would have if you did not know what they were for (it is already hard enough when you do know their purpose). This is so true that, in our naïve psychology, we are led to conceive of physical reality itself as intentional. Like in the memorable scene from *Acquainted with Grief*, which describes lightning hitting the countryside hills in Brianza and causing ineffable problems, only to discharge itself (its goal) in a bath:

There, with a remarkable shot, and after the annihilation of a grand piano, he plunged into the dry tub of the maidservant. This time he flattened forever into the mysterious nullity of the earth's potential. . . . The mason of Villa Enrichetta, with the common sense of all villagers, advanced a hypothesis of his own, for that matter highly plausible: that the final withdrawal of the yellow beast, so he called it, was due to his finding the latrine's pipes clogged, whereupon he couldn't make use of the passage necessary to such a lightning. (Gadda 1969, 25)[5]

There is yet another circumstance one must consider, having to do with *collective* intentionality. Playing football is like speaking a language: you have to share many things, and only within that sharing can one recognize oneself as an individual. It is only within a language that billions of people spoke before me (and millions more speak around me) that I can meaningfully say something like "I, Maurizio Ferraris, was born in Turin." In the same way, it is only within a system of rules shared by all (fans, referee, players) that scoring a goal can make sense (something that will make my team happy and displease the other). This, of course, does not entail that individualities disappear: they are nothing but drops of water that exist only if there is a sea. Take this example:

> If he figures out that I am aiming for the right, he will go right. I should let him believe that my objective is to aim for the left. But he might understand that my real objective is for the right, and then the best thing would be to make him think that I will aim for the right and then shoot to the right. Even better, I will make him believe that I am aiming for right but I mean to make him think that I will shoot to the left while I really intend to shoot to the right and, in the end, shoot to the left.

Suppose these are the thoughts of a striker before a penalty kick. Apparently, two monads are facing each other: the striker and the goalkeeper. Two mysterious and inaccessible subjects. It is not really like that: the striker wants to score, the goalkeeper hopes to make a save. On their part, the two teams can say the same thing that Charles V said: "My cousin Francis and I are in perfect accord—he wants Milan, and so do I." Yet, not everyone is playing the same game.

Here is the point: we do not have to do with subjects confronting each other outside of any sharing. We might imagine that one would trip, another one would push, and yet another one would score a goal with a hand and thus win the World Cup (proving that the hand truly is the absolute tool). Yet, we cannot imagine that, in order to win, a goalkeeper would pierce the ball with a knife. You cannot do that, and he would not win if he did. This is how, in Searle's view, social reality works. Prior to the conflict there is always a common world of aims and rules:[6] the same common world due to which money is for paying, independently from our considerations of it (proof of God's benevolence or the devil's manure).

What does not work. So far, so good. I have philosophically unveiled the mystery of social reality. The reasoning works, the hypothesis is persuasive. In fact, it seems that children pass from an allocentric phase, in which they are not yet individuals, to an egocentric phase, where they start from their own I. That society precedes individuals was theorized long ago, and it is indeed hard to understand how a society could be made starting from monads.[7] So far, it is therefore all clear. Also, a physical localization for collective intentionality was discovered: that the field of pertinence of social objects coincides with that of intentional objects is very plausible; what then makes these contents objective (or, rather, intersubjective) could be neuro-physiological characters like the "mirror neurons," which preside over our awareness both of ourselves and the others.[8]

But things get more complicated when we probe further and ask: What exactly is collective intentionality? Is it able to bridge the gap between the physical and the social? Is it able to explain *all* of social reality? *Where* does this intentionality reside?

As to the first question, what is the nature of collective intentionality, the fact that the neurons responsible for it have been found still does not tell us what it is. It is not hard to see in Searle's hypothesis a sort of re-proposal of Dilthey's objective spirit. Humans' will, thoughts, intentions, desires, and hopes are solidified in institutions: families, societies, states, railway stations, post offices, outings to the country, and university departments. This gives us a good idea, but not a very clear one: if we replace "collective intentionality" or "objective spirit" with "supersoul" the problem will immediately become obvious.

As to the second point, the possibility of bridging the social on the physical is quite difficult to accomplish. Molecules do not have an aim; they do not manage to harmonize the physical and the psychic. *We*, in an already given context, attribute an end to the world and its parts. Likewise, it seems an exaggeration to think of a universal teleological order (the only thing that, in Searle's hypothesis, would allow the passage from X to Y) in which the *same* intentionality would work for Gadda's lightning and the football match.[9] In short, the introduction of an aim is explicatively useful, but one surely cannot claim that collective intentionality constitutes the origin of social objects—because it lacks a determining character.

In fact, one could object that collective intentionality is similar to the aesthetic common sense Kant (1951, § 32) talks about in regard to the judgment of taste. When I find a thing or a person beautiful, I imagine humankind would share my judgment. This proves the fact (which is intuitively very solid) that a sharing exists. Of course. Yet, Kant's idea is that the sharing is hypothesized but not binding: I am not surprised if something I like is disliked by another, while I would be very surprised if my fifty euro bill counted as nothing for someone else. In Searle's opinion, though, the two facts should be equivalent.

As to the second point, namely the generalizability of this theory, can we be sure that it works in all cases rather than just for, say, soccer, American football, and basketball, but not for other less amusing games such as driving in traffic or paying taxes? A passionate basketball player, Searle's colleague Michael E. Bratman (1992) justifies a weak version of collective, "shared" intentionality along these lines:[10]

> I intend that we want to shoot a basket and pass you the ball. You, like me, intend that we want to shoot a basket. Our intentions are stable. For the action of shooting a basket to be a cooperative shared activity it is not necessary that our respective action plans coincide: it is sufficient for them to overlap, at least partially. Obviously, if I pass you the ball, it is because I intend this and think that you, like me, intend that we want to shoot a basket. The overlapping of action plans guarantees the interdependence of intentions: our intentions are interrelated. I do not simply intend to realize my action plan, I also intend to support you in the realization of your own.

This is the core of Bratman's reasoning: my intention is not added to yours. The bond between the subject's intentions is not simply cognitive: it is not enough that I intend that and also think that you also intend that. My intention depends on yours and vice versa: if the other players stopped playing, I would stop as well, because my intention would cease to be.

What Bratman does not say, though (and this also holds true for basketball), is what a rule is, how it works, what counts as a court, a penalty, and so on. All this without considering that, if this was the mechanism, then a shared intentionality would not exist before the age of four, that is, before the development of a theory of the mind. Moreover, if (as I suggested earlier) you think of a situation like "driving in traffic"—or, even better, "paying taxes," "fighting for the homeland," "buying a theater ticket"—then Bratman's definition seems factitious. Even in the simplest cases, involving a limited number of people, satisfying all the conditions listed above would be difficult, requiring a long and expensive negotiation. It would be even worse if we were to read the behavior of firms in terms of intentionality. We would have a description of an irresponsible, egoistic, highly competitive psychopath with delusions of grandeur,[11] as we learn from reading a company's self-presentation as if it depicted an individual (it is clear that, in a firm, the understatement required by the fact that self-praise is no recommendation does not apply).

And the problems don't stop there. Collective intentionality (rather, intentionality in general) does not explain even the paradigm case of social object that Searle himself privileges, namely money. There are two problems here.

First, Searle claims that "anything can count as money"; since monetization is in large measure due to convention, this claim seems reasonable, but only up to a point. In addition to pieces of metal and paper, bags of salt and shells are (or have been used as) currency, but never tables or cows, because they cannot be easily managed and handed over. Then one might as well go for the barter, where one could use old and worthless coins as buttons for Tyrolese clothes. Likewise we cannot use as coin soap bubbles, carbonized paper, grains of sand, atoms, or fresh meat. The sequences of ones and zeroes in a computer have certainly taken the place of cash in a very large number of transactions, but their physical representation is an object three by two inches in size, is thin enough to fit in a wallet, is resistant enough not to break, and is made of plastic that does not melt or dissolve in water. The ontological constraints turn out to be closely related to the ecological constraints, given that at the North Pole even a pound of fresh meat might count as money, but there would remain restrictions on physical size: imagine a banknote that was a mile long. Therefore, intentionality is far from omnipotent.

It is also worth noting that Searle does not state that "anything can count as senator" (which should be allowed by his theory), and this for the banal reason that a senator ought to be a person—or at least look like one. Caligula's horse Incitatus was not really a senator, although Caligula had all the necessary power to confer him that status. Whereas in Ridley Scott's *Blade Runner* there are androids who become senators, which seems to suggest that even in science fiction you need a humanoid appearance to make a career.[12]

Second, and more seriously, the intentionality of money is far from certain.[13] As Carl Menger (1840–1921) observed, money came about in a way that was itself unintentional though as a result of intentional actions.[14] For sure, history provides examples of goods that have been declared to be tender by legislative act, but in most cases the law has simply recognized as money goods that had already taken on this role. It is economic convenience that calls on individuals, who are aware of their own advantage and irrespective of the public interest, to exchange their own goods with others that can be counted on in a wider market. They will prefer those goods that embody the features that make them fit to be means of exchange.[15]

In cauda venenum: where is collective intentionality? The point is not secondary, but it turns out to be crucial since, at least as regards the social world, not only is there no entity without identity (see Quine 1941, § 6; 1958, 23), there is also no identity without residence, even if it is a temporary abode. Now, there is a banal answer to the question of where individual intentionality, considered both as representation and as volition, is to be found: *in our heads*—roughly speaking, behind the eyes, under the hair and between the ears. But it would be much harder to answer the question where collective intentionality is: is it scattered about in the air? Little by little, if we try to find an answer, we will notice that this obscure and ungraspable intentionality lies in *texts*. I will show in the chapter 8 how central this aspect is—which Searle neglected due to his antitextualist syndrome.

PROBLEMS WITH THE OBJECT

From the physical to the social, and back. I shall leave the first problem (that of the act) unsettled and focus on the second question, the one that concerns the theory of social objects as higher-order objects.

Such a theory has two problems. First, it is unclear (as long as collective intentionality is not clarified) how exactly one can create a social object out of a physical object. Second, even accepting collective intentionality, it is far from clear, given a particular social object, how one can straightforwardly individuate a corresponding physical object. Searle's theory is in what can be labeled as a "Gestalt" predicament: it aims at explaining how we get a higher-order object from a lower-order object, but it fails to account for the opposite direction, from the higher-order object to the lower-order one.

From the physical to the social. To show the difficulties that affect the path from the physical to the social I will examine three examples that have been put forward by Searle himself (it is worth noting that one of them has been subsequently abandoned by him).

1. *The wall.* To explain the passage from the physical to the social, Searle offers the example of the transformation of a wall into a border. The idea is that first there is a physical object, a wall that separates the inside from the outside and defends the community. Then, little by little, the wall disintegrates, leaving nothing but a row of stones, which are useless as an obstacle but which have transmuted into a social object, a border: it is the same as the yellow line in a post office or an airport that indicates where to wait one's turn.[16] Now, we can understand how, in disintegrating, a wall can, in some circumstances become a border. But it is not at all clear how—on the basis of this simple analogy, a fortuitous situation that may have actually occurred, but how often we do not know—we got to the yellow line or the centerline on the highway. The question is further complicated by the following consideration: If a physical object really could constitute the origin of a social object, then *every* physical object would turn into a social object and every wall would constitute a border. But this clearly is not the case, as anyone who wants to knock a wall down in his or her house knows, so long as this operation does not contravene some norms that are not necessarily related to the wall's physical stability.

2. *Marking the territory.* Still on the question of the passage from the physical to the social, I would like to note a point that will become important as I proceed. Before adducing the case of the wall, Searle cited animals that mark their territory, but then he decided to abandon the example because it seemed inadequate.[17] Why inadequate? Not in an absolute sense, given that it is a good example, but it does not suit Searle's theory. In effect, there is no moment in which the trace constitutes a *physical* limit. The

trace is a smell and an olfactory limit does not make for impenetrability, for all that it fulfills its performative role. *Right from the start* it is something that does not begin as a physical obstacle to then become a social obstacle, but it arises as a trace, which in its essence is mildly physical and strongly social.[18] The case of marking territory could have been a good example of how *fiat* borders[19]—those that are established by a decision—turn out to be quite indifferent to how they are embodied, so that, from this point of view, there is no difference between an olfactory trace and the Great Wall of China. And if Searle had followed up, rather than privileging money and the wall, he would have saved himself a lot of trouble, in particular that (which I will dwell on later) of how to explain with his theory those social objects, such as debt, that do not have any physical counterpart. For, according to weak realism, there is a world of difference between a wall and a debt: the former is the presence of something; the latter is the absence of something. By contrast, the trace that marks a territory establishes a means by which, being present as an olfactory given, it can refer to an absence, which is the animal that has marked the territory. In this sense, it constitutes a superordinate structure as much to the wall as to the debt.[20]

3. *Money.* All this points to an even more general consideration. The example of money, which Searle adduces as the normal case of a social object, constitutes an exception. Because it is relatively easy to transform a button into a coin to deceive a blind man, and then once again use it as a button. But in the overwhelming majority of cases, the operation looks much more complex, if not impossible. And this is a very serious limitation that compromises the paradigm status of the example adduced. Indeed, it is easy to claim that simply by inscribing a piece of metal we get a social object, and that, once heavy use has effaced the inscription, we have a physical object again. But this, as I said, is not at all the norm, but rather an exception.[21]

From the social to the physical. On to the second aspect of the problem, regarding the reversibility from the social to the physical. It is fairly intuitive to say that a banknote is also a piece of paper, or that a president is also a person. Just so, when Searle is alone in a hotel bedroom, there is only one physical object, but many social objects: there is a husband, an employee of the State of California, an American citizen, a person with a driver's license, and so on. In this case, the return from Y (social) to X (physical) is smooth. Things are quite different if we consider other (and not so unusual) circumstances, which give rise to difficulties that were acknowledged long before Searle's theory of social objects and which have to do with both objects and events. I will review three paradigmatic cases.

Heidegger's state. It is the example of a social object that is usually very big. In his *Introduction to Metaphysics*, Heidegger (2000, 37) writes: "A state—it *is*. What does its Being consist in? In the fact that the state police arrest a suspect, or that in a ministry of the Reich so and so many typewriters clatter away and record the dictation of state secretaries and ministers? Or 'is' the state in the discussion between the Fuhrer and the English foreign minister? The state is. But where is Being situated? Is it located anywhere at all?" It is a hard task that of individuating which physical objects constitute the being of the state: probably the borders, maybe the army and the public administration or the political apparatus. But are, say, the Tuscan cigars owned by the Italian senators still part of the state? If the answer is no, why not? One could claim that it is an ill-formulated question. Someone else might object that is a simple case of linguistic vagueness: the meaning of the term *state*, just like that of *mountain*, was never determinately fixed, so that wondering where the being of a state is, is much like asking where the being of the Matterhorn is.[22] But from the standpoint of a descriptive metaphysics, I would state that there are teachings of state doctrine, whose meaning should be defined enough to hold a course on it, write books about it, and so on. In short, if the question was simply ill-formulated or the term was merely vague, then we would have to wonder on what bases we can state that the Italian Embassy in Bucharest belongs to Italy and not Romania. Therefore we cannot simply avoid it, since it captures the core of our social ontology, namely, the circumstance that such a relevant entity for our life was never regarded as such.

Ryle's university. The second problem is what Ryle (1949) has defined as "the myth of the ghost in the machine," in his discussion of Cartesian dualism (How does the *res cogitans* emerge from the *res extensa*? Is it a kind of miracle?). Here Ryle makes an analogy with the relation between a social object such as the university and the physical objects with which it can be identified. It would be rather surprising, Ryle points out, if one asked, "Where is the university?" after having visited the library, the departments, the teaching rooms and so on: the social object "university" results from a composition of objects, whose formal structure and formal constraints have to be carefully analyzed. This is to say that we should not look for some strange essence that is supposed to lie behind libraries and rectorates. Of course, this is just a negative indication. However, to hold that there really are ghosts in (or behind) the objects would amount to saying that computers can really think and that we should acknowledge civil rights to machines that have passed the Turing test. The hypothesis (brought forward in chapters 4 and 8) that the being of the university, as well as that of the state, lies in inscriptions seems instead to offer a positive indication.

Merleau-Ponty's battle. In one of his late courses at the Collège de France, commenting on Heidegger's passage quoted earlier, Merleau-Ponty (1958) added a (not so Teutonic) reference to Stendhal's *Charterhouse of Parma*: "Fabrizio: where is the Battle of Waterloo? It is in everything you see and beyond." In fact, in the social world, there are also social *events* such as battles, weddings, soccer games, and birthday parties.[23] The problem is that the boundaries of events are even more elusive than the boundaries of objects (see Borgini and Varzi 2005)—suffice it to say that in seventeenth-century armies the ensigns' task was to declare a battle over; and when ensigns were no longer used things did not get better.[24] Therefore, once again: what is exactly the object or set of objects that lies under the battle event?

Reductions. Are there alternative solutions? We could always try, for instance, to *reduce* social objects that are too complex to smaller ones. I shall expose this solution only as an experiment, since—as readers will easily notice—it can hardly be regarded as viable.

1. *Hitler's bunker.* In 1453, the Western Roman Empire was confined to Constantinople's urban perimeter. And this is not the only example. For instance, there was a moment, ten years after the *Introduction to Metaphysics* was first published, in which the being of the German state was totally confined to a single place, namely the Reich Chancellery bunker.

2. *Little Big Horn.* Since the previous example was that of a battle, the Battle of Berlin, maybe Merleau-Ponty's question can be answered. Moreover, at least in the case of the battle of Little Big Horn, we do know where it took place and when it ended: when the chief of the Indian coalition killed Custer.

3. *Napoleon in Saint Helena.* The argument looks even stronger if we consider the fact that Napoleon in Saint Helena, differently from Hitler in the bunker, did not represent the French state but was only a historical figure in disgrace and an ill fifty-year-old man. Therefore, there truly

was more of the German state in the bunker than the French state in Saint Helena.

Though a seemingly attractive strategy, any reduction is bound to fail, because, banally, a vast number of social objects lack an evident physical counterpart (like shares in the stock market). So how can this be fixed?

SMITH'S CORRECTION

As Barry Smith (2003a, 25) pointed out, we very often have to do with Y entities that are independent of any X, "entities which (unlike President Clinton and Canterbury Cathedral and the money in my pocket) do not coincide ontologically with any part of physical reality." In Smith's view, these are "representations." "The blips in the bank's computers merely *represent* money, just as the deeds to your property merely *record* or *register* the existence of your property right" (2003b, 145).

In making room for the dimension of representations, Smith reshapes Searle's theory, implying a somehow significant change in the distinction act-inscription-object. Smith's scheme would then be roughly the following:

Act

~~**Inscription**~~

(Ideal) Object: Representation

De Soto's capital. In this sense, Smith stresses representation in De Soto's passage (2000, 49; emphasis added):

> Capital is born by *representing* in writing—in a title, a security, a contract, and other such *records*—the most economically and socially useful qualities. The moment you focus your attention on the title of a house, for example, and not on the house itself, you have automatically stepped from the material world into the conceptual universe where capital lives.[25]

The underlying idea is that if social objects ultimately are intentional (i.e., a common good that is in our head rather than in the world, and not in the form of mere psychological acts), then their appropriate sphere is the sphere of shared representations.

Blindfold chess. To get a better grasp on the notion of "representation," Smith describes them as "quasi-abstract entities," offering the example of blindfold chess. The idea is that chess can be played without any physical support. It can be played on the Internet, where the board is not present in the way that the physical chessboard is: it has two localizations, corresponding to the two computers. What is more, two masters can play in their minds without even having a board represented on the screen. In such cases, it is easy to see that the "mental" chess would not correspond to any actual psychological representation on the part of the players, but it would rather be an ideal object.

Smith applies this model to money: after a certain point and making use of evolved technology, we begin to do without the physical counterparts, which are replaced by traces in a computer. Here too we have a social object to which no physical object corresponds, but only a representation. This representation is objective for it is different from the mental acts, say, of chess players, shareholders, or of all the people who normally deal with money.

One hundred thalers. Yet, is it really true that the blips in a computer are not physical at all? Are they really *res cogitans*—totally separate from *res extensa*? It is enough to visit a technological cemetery, be it a Chinese recycling plant or just a corridor in my university department cluttered with computers no longer in use, to see how much plastic and silicon are necessary to support magnetic traces. Unless we say that a computer possesses a

Strong realism
Social objects are as solid as physical objects.

Strong textualism
Physical objects are socially constructed.

Weak realism
Social objects are constructed upon physical objects.

Weak textualism
Social objects are constructed by idiomatic inscriptions (small physical objects).

soul distinct from its body, we have to allow that the blips are material: not a representation, as Smith claims, but an inscription, as I do.

In short, it is hard, if not impossible, to say that, in the case of money that has been transformed into computer traces, there are only representations and nothing physical to support them, even if the body is not large. But suppose that it is so, that representations need nothing physical. In that case, there is no way to answer the questions: What is the difference between one hundred real thalers and one hundred ideal thalers? And how do we distinguish the representation of one hundred thalers from one hundred thalers merely imagined or dreamt? Here (see diagram) is the result.

8

WEAK TEXTUALISM

"The triumph of hope over experience" is what Samuel Johnson famously said about second marriages. One truly needs a lot of hope because—unless the act had been canceled (and the only institution in the world that can do that is the Roman Rota)—there can never be a Catholic marriage after the first one: this is how strong *inscriptions* are, as the constraints of social ontology.

DERRIDA'S MARRIAGE

On January 31, I bought a shirt on sale. I did not have any cash ("money" in the traditional sense) and, what is worse, my ATM card was totally useless (it was the last day of the month and I had no credit left on it), so to the cashier's question "Credit card or ATM?" I had to answer, "Credit card, please." The cashier put the card (which doubles as an ATM card) in a little machine, and started with a single gesture a process on a gigantic network; some time later a printed piece of paper came out of the machine.

This is a rather ordinary situation, but it involves a quite peculiar archaism: I had to sign that piece of paper. This is quite bizarre; think about it for a moment. Had I used the ATM card, I would have had to make use of an idiomatic inscription as well, although of a more technological kind—referring to the original signature through which I signed the bank disposition when I requested an ATM card.

I could have done it even in absence of any technology. Suppose that I got married on January 31. In that situation, my wife, the witnesses, and I would have had to sign a register, in conformity with the ritual. Moral: for a social object to exist—whether it is the purchase of a discounted shirt or a marriage—there has to be an *inscription*, which in addition has to be *idiomatic*. This can be the answer to Searle's dilemma, but only with a radical change of perspective, through a modest Copernican revolution putting at the center of the stage the third—until now neglected—element in Twardowski's scheme, namely *content* (which I suggested in chapter 4 should be renamed "idiomatic inscription").

Idiomatic inscriptions. As I have shown, the trouble with weak realism lies in the fact that either we link social objects to physical ones—leading to vast, vague, or negative social objects—or we regard social objects as mere "representations," but then postmodernism would be just around the corner, given that we would not be able to make any principled distinction between one hundred real thalers and one hundred ideal thalers. Of course, a solution is needed, and Searle (1995, 35) has provided us with a suggestion: "Often, the brute facts will not be manifested as physical objects but as sounds coming out of peoples' mouths or as marks on paper—or even thoughts in their heads."

Why is this passage so important? Sounds, signs, and thoughts are not big physical objects like states or persons: they are composed of a relatively small number of molecules. However, they still have some physical thickness: a sound involves vibrations, a thought implies a certain electrical activity in the brain, and something similar can be said of the signs on a piece of paper.[1] It is then an object with very few molecules, and the truly important aspect of money is the small amount of molecules that compose the signature of the issuing authority that sanctions its validity. These count much more than the large number of molecules making up its form and matter, given that a very big banknote can be worth less than a small one. That small but crucial number of molecules, then, is not too different from the blips on a bank computer. Therefore Searle's problem related to the existing difference between a banknote and the blip on a bank computer disappears. They are, in the end, objects of the same kind, sharing the same distinctive features, which are valid also for what Searle calls "status indicators" such as, for instance, passports and driver's licenses.[2] Which is exactly what I wished to demonstrate:

1. A social object is *inscribed*. It has a small amount of molecules (much less than the massive physical objects lying at the basis of Searle's

theory) but nonetheless such molecules are *something*, and not a simple representation. That small amount of molecules can account for Smith's elusive notion of "quasi-abstract entity": it would be an entity that is recorded somewhere in space.

2. A social object is also *idiomatic*, that is to say it is recorded in specific ways. Even in a gold coin, a great part of the matter constitutes an excipient, while the active principle is indeed the idiomatic inscription.[3]

These two features allow us to read in a different way what De Soto says in the often quoted passage: "Capital is born by representing *in writing*—in a title, a security, a contract, and other such *records*—the most economically and socially useful qualities." Capital's crucial aspect then is identified with *writing* and *documents*, not just with mere "representations." And De Soto, who mentions Derrida in his book referring explicitly to *Grammatology*,[4] shifts decisively toward a theory of writing: for a good to be distributed, means are needed to make the immobile (like a land or a housing property) mobile (almost like a phone): and this is why writing, being mobile, lasting, and defined is so important.[5] De Soto read in this light, bearing in mind not so much the *genesis of the capital* but rather the clarification of the *necessary condition for social objects*, yields an overturning of Searle's formula:

Not
X counts as Y in C
But
C constitutes X as Y

Where C = inscriptions, which seems good proof of the fact that, *in the sphere of social objects*, there is nothing outside the text. This formula, though, might still appear as rather strong, because it features a genetic claim (C constitutes), which is why I prefer the weaker formula I proposed in chapter 4, namely:

Object = Inscribed Act

This should be understood as the necessary but not sufficient condition.[6] For a social object to exist, there must be an inscribed act of some kind; but this does not mean that any inscribed act is a social object (and a legitimate social object), given that there must still be a society, whose genesis cannot be exclusively explained through inscription; and in this society there are *intentions*, rather vague entities (especially in the form of *collective intentionality*) but not purely and simply replaceable by inscriptions.

With these considerations in mind, Derrida's textualism—which I am trying to re-elaborate—founds the specific nature of social objects not on the act and neither on the object (whether ideal or real), but rather on its idiomatic record or mode of presentation. In my scheme, it looks like this:

~~Act~~
Inscription
~~Object~~

With this premise, I intend to do four things in the following paragraphs:

1. Explain what the *trace* is, as it is the ontological substrate of the whole theory.
2. Define the kind of trace that is relevant to a human ontology (and probably also an animal one), namely *recording*.
3. Specify the nature of the trace pertinent to a social ontology, namely *inscription*.
4. Justify why it has to be *idiomatic*, that is, causally dependent on an individual intervention.

In other words, I shall work on the following progression from the physical to the social:

Trace (world)
↓
Recording (mind)
↓
Inscription (society)
↓
Idiom (single individual)

Or, more visually speaking:

Trace (table)
↓

Recording (*tabula*)
↓

Inscription (document)
↓

Idiom (signature)

As you can see, my aim is to simply *differentiate* what Derrida unified. I will draw from this a less suggestive theory, perhaps, but one that I hope will be able to account for the nature of social reality.

TRACE

By *trace* I mean something that, with a limited number of molecules, functions as a physical support for a recording. Only in the case of social objects does the trace possess a constitutive value. In the world of physical objects traces only exist for minds capable of recognizing them, therefore there are no traces *as such*. In the world of ideal objects,[7] traces intervene only in the socialization of a being that, in itself, does not depend on inscriptions. Things are different for the constitution of a social object: without traces there are no minds (theory of the *tabula*), but only for minds are there traces.

From atoms to parliaments. In my hypothesis, it is the trace, and not collective intentionality, that provides the bridge uniting atoms and parliaments.[8] In fact, it is concrete in its physical consistency (word, computer file, animal trace to mark the territory, mnestic inscription, or writing on paper) and abstract in its reference function.

Here it might be useful to quote a philosophical example. In a passage from his *Aesthetics: Lectures on Fine Art*, Hegel (1998, 354–57) talks about the Egyptian religion. Egyptians had come to an imperfect notion of immortality, they had not truly understood it: in fact, they looked for it in the embalming of the dead. In this imperfect notion of the spirit, though, there is some sort of truth—Hegel writes—because death happens twice: once as death of the natural, the second time as death of what is *only* natural—and therefore as the birth of the spirit. A knot in your handkerchief is both a knot and a memo; a memo on your mobile phone is both a physical thing and a reminder of something else; ash is both a natural being and the trace of fire. So, back to Hegel and his Egyptians, the mummy as such is not spirit, but it is not simply nature either, because a mummy (unlike a corpse) is a social object—as anyone who goes visit Lenin's mummy will notice since, at times, they even change his clothes.

And now to this simple question: In the case of an animal marking its territory, is it writing a law or answering some natural need? There are some difficulties in establishing whether this kind of mark belongs to nature (after all, it is a physical thing as well as the satisfaction of the animal's natural needs) or to culture (at the same time, in fact, it signals a border, which is social given that nothing in it constitutes a physical obstacle). Yet that mark is the necessary condition for a process that will end in the act of signing a credit card receipt. Moral: *we have truly found the bridge between the physical and the psychic, and this bridge is not intentionality but the trace.*

Weakening. One more point. With respect to Searle's collective intentionality or to Derrida's thesis that "there is nothing outside the text," my use of the trace is a weakening. I start from a fact (there is a society) and then note that this society would not exist without traces. In short, *the trace presupposes a constituted society, but a constituted society essentially needs traces.* I believe this solution has two advantages:

1. With respect to collective intentionality, it is clearer. If you want to understand what a trace is in the social world, just open your wallet or drawer, go to a library, look in the streets, and you will find all the traces you need. If you want to understand what a trace is in the natural world, there is a vast choice: snail drool, scars, erosion, wood grains, and so on. Now, back to social traces, a society truly needs traces and I challenge anyone to prove me wrong. If you take them away—all the records, inscriptions, *tabulae*, and styles—then you will no longer have a society.

2. With these limitations, my theory also weakens Derrida's thesis. It is not that "there is nothing outside the text," rather "there is nothing *social* outside the text" and inscription constitutes the necessary but not sufficient condition for the construction of social reality. Traces do not create reality as such, but without traces society cannot exist.

RECORDING

As for recording, I have little to add to what I said in Part I of the book. A trace, in one's mind or for one's mind, becomes a record; this record can, at times, assume a social value—such as when the police turn into evidence a piece of DNA attached to a cigarette (smoking is bad for you!).

Therefore, there are traces only for minds. Nonetheless, if the hypothesis of the mind as *tabula rasa* holds, there are no minds without traces that, at a certain level of complexity, can be even specified as intentions and interpretations.[9] Imagine that—like in Christopher Nolan's film *Memento* (2000)—one has a very limited memory: in such a case, could we speak of individual intentionality? And now suppose that only telepathy existed: would we communicate any better? We would probably not communicate at all because, again, what we call "intentions" are sediments of traces.[10] This is all the more evident for intentions of a social nature: it is hard to consider as "originary" (i.e., independent from inscriptions) the intention of becoming a researcher, a colonel, or a Sir. Now, consider a very common and very human behavior such as envy: a rival of mine gets a reward, so now I want it too. Is this originary intentionality? I doubt it.

Moreover, Searle is convinced that only human beings possess an authentic intentionality and that all the other living organisms and animals kinds are derivatives. This opinion is problematic, given that it leads us to the question about animal intelligence: if you say that animals are automata (that they do not have an originary intentionality) how can you exclude that you are not an automaton yourself?[11] It is an argument on which much has been written, but I wish to limit myself to an observation. Why call upon a both originary (only human) and collective intentionality when the simple recording of a trace—that is, memory—allows us to understand what we are talking about? My thesis, of an Aristotelian matrix, is therefore the following: *the nature of the social bond is expressed by imitation much more and much better than by collective intentionality* (fashion and advertising figured this out very well). The individual condition for imitation is indeed what I defined as *recording* (a man with no memory will never be a good actor). All this is presented as a uniform development—as long as there is a mind, traces become recordings and, as long as there is a society, the latter become inscriptions. At this point, a traffic police officer stops us, asking for our driver's license and registration, and all is clear.

INSCRIPTION

What is an inscription? By *inscription* I mean a recording endowed with a *social* value. As I said, I do not intend to explain the origin of society: I take it for granted. It is within a society that words, something written, or a handshake become relevant. There is nothing in the social world that can do without inscriptions. Take the following examples:

> All Italian firms (5.9 million) must be *registered* with the Register of Companies, which constitutes the primary source of certification for their constitutive data, just like a civil registry is for the citizens' data.
>
> The *cadastre* is the comprehensive *archive* of all the real estate of a country.
>
> The *subscription* to the website is free and offers access to many online services.
>
> Need a domain *registration?* Looking for inexpensive hosting? *Register* with us!
>
> Read, approved and *signed.*

Starting from this consideration and getting to the core of the matter, I will now try to show how this theory—resting upon inscription as the social variant of recording—allows us to account for *all* social entities, including those that were problematic in Searle's theory. In my examples, I will try to clarify my theory by focusing on the following five points:

1. Social objects do not necessarily require speech acts.
2. The identity of a social object depends on the few molecules of its inscription.
3. The determining inscription is not necessarily a legal document.
4. The counterpart of inscription can also be a negative entity.
5. Once inscribed, a social object exists with such power that, to make it disappear, a supernatural intervention is needed.

Marriages, war declarations, wills, and fines. First point: *Pace* Austin, social objects do not necessarily require speech acts. With regard to this, Austin is aware of the fact that one cannot claim that "getting married is saying a few words," but rather that "getting married is, in some cases, simply saying a few words," since in certain cultures it is enough to live together in order to be considered as married. This entails that the speech act is not the *eidos* but only a manifestation, and that *the necessary condition of a performative is that there is a recording*: that is, a form of inscription conforming to a ritual. The role of recording is confirmed by the fact that, in the Italian civil rite, after the "I do" of both contracting parties, the civil state officer asks, "Have the witnesses heard?";[12] all this is followed by the formal writing of the official records. The same happens at exams, which are not valid unless the speech act has a corresponding record and, to stick with the university metaphor, the social object "full professor" is constructed through written records: public competitions, curriculum vitae, documents, and so on. Even leaving logocentrism aside, it seems that privileging marriage influenced Austin's analysis.

On one hand, there are acts (like war declarations) that *de facto* rarely happen in presence. It seems implausible that the King of France would go to the Queen of England's palace saying, "I declare war on you"—it is not excluded that she might reply, "And I declare you under arrest," and that would be it. It is better to write it down, and inscriptions will be able to do without words, merely requiring (for instance, through a preventive attack) an acknowledgment. In other cases, it is not even necessary to address the enemy directly: it might suffice to address Parliament, and the act will count as a declaration because it will be assumed that (through press, radio, and television) the message will reach its addressee, even though he did not witness the formulation of the act.[13]

In other cases, even more interesting in that they were considered by Austin—who nonetheless did not draw the obvious conclusion from them—the act, *de jure* and not only *de facto*, can only exist in writing. Consider one of the examples of the performative made by Austin: "I give and bequeath my watch to my brother." Now, since this is a will, the act will come into effect and produce an object only when the owner will not be able to utter *a single word*. Little by little, therefore, speech acts are turning into a small island in an ocean of written acts—moreover, the speech formula itself depends on writing (when I proclaim someone a doctor in Philosophy I read from a paper, so as not to get it wrong).

On the other hand, it would be rather bizarre to claim that you necessarily need a speech act to be fined for parking where prohibited: how long would one have to wait for an officer? And how many officers would be needed? In some instances, like in the case of fines for excessive speeding, the traffic enforcement camera is doing the job of a human officer—it cannot speak and has no originary intentionality. Even with human officers, a look of reproach or approval can strengthen or compromise prestige—a social object *per se* in Searle's classification. Again, the crucial element is recording, not the speech formulation.

Poland, Fiat, Telecom, and Vodafone. Second point: *Pace* Searle, the identity of a social object depends on the few molecules of its inscription and not on the (many, few, or nonexisting) molecules of the physical object that it might refer to. To verify this, I start from an object with many molecules indeed: Poland.

If you look at an up-to-date map of Poland, you will see Warsaw's current position in the east of Poland; most of the postwar territorial acquisitions were made at Germany's expense. If you look at a map that shows Poland in 1941, under German occupation, Warsaw is located in the west, near the border. Now take a map that represents Poland in the 1920s, when it was territorially very large because its two neighbors, Germany and the Soviet Union, had had some problems in the past (a lost war and a revolution respectively). Warsaw is at the center of a vast territory pushed slightly toward the west. Or look at Poland in Napoleon's times. At that time, Warsaw was located near the eastern border. However, it is worth noting that in 1772 Warsaw was located near the northern border. At this point in your research, it should come as no surprise that in a 1300 map Warsaw does not even exist within then Poland. Moral: the identity of Poland does not derive from the molecules that make up its territory, but rather from the treaties, written registrations, and agreements, all of which share the interesting feature of being signed at the bottom.

Now take the example of a social object whose physical support, for all its size, does not consist in as many molecules as a state, such as a heavy equipment firm like Fiat. In the 1930s, Fiat's physical being consisted of the plant at the Lingotto in Turin, in its workers, employees, and directors, in the person of Giovanni Agnelli the elder, and in the cars. But is that how it is now? Obviously not. The Lingotto might become a museum, a hotel, or a convention center that no longer belongs to Fiat, the workers have (almost) been done away with, the property relations have become more complex and ramified, and yet Fiat continues to exist, and its problems are not matters of identity. One may also note that the cars that have always been and still are around, constitute the being of Fiat only until they are sold; after that they become part of the purchaser's property. The magic by which a car is no longer part of Fiat but becomes mine is a *contract*, which is a form of registration that features two signatures, that of the buyer and that of the seller.[14] And contracts of this sort, along with the accounting books, packets of shares, communications and letterhead notepaper, faxes, wage packets and so on (i.e., *inscriptions*), underlie Fiat's identity. We might say that it has a "characteristic activity"[15] but, just like Poland, it does not depend on its physical molecules: in the end, the signatures that define Fiat will turn out to be only a few less than those that define Poland.

Now consider a service company, such as the Italian telephone provider Telecom. Fifty years ago, it was known as Sip (and before that, Siptel). What physical molecules define its identity? Here, too, we have a certain number of operators, office buildings and also, bizarrely, the handsets (which were owned by the firm) and the landlines. Now that anyone can buy the telephone he or she wants, the Telecom set is no longer the only phone in the home, and today they are in a minority in homes from which the landline phone is, in any case, disappearing. Moreover Telecom has gradually lost its monopoly on landlines. Should we conclude that it has become a different thing? In one sense yes: it is no longer the company with the Italian monopoly that it once was. But, just as its identity through the passage from Siptel to Sip to Telecom did not depend on phones and wires, so now—as ever—its identity consists in signatures and documents, which is to say in inscribed acts. In short, the phones and the wires can disappear or change hands without this necessarily bringing about the disappearance of Telecom. It is enough that the inscriptions do not disappear: there would be big trouble if they did.

So then, where is the being of Vodafone? Phrasing the question this way has the advantage of taking lots of molecules out of the picture. In fact, Vodafone has never owned telephones or lines, given that it specializes in mobile phones. So where is the being of Vodafone? What are the molecules it consists of? A few years ago, one may have been tempted to answer that Vodafone's being consisted in the image of its official endorser, model Megan Gale. But of course this cannot be so. Megan Gale *represented* Vodafone, she never *was* Vodafone. And she was never a Vodafone *property* (one can rent a car, but not a person, it would be slavery).

So *where is* the being of Vodafone? The answer is easier than expected: in the SIM card, quite apart from its support; in acts deposited in court, quite apart from their support; and in shares, quite apart from their support. All these are so many kinds of inscription and signature: the code deposited on the SIM card is in essence a signature, which establishes a conceptual unity between a bit in a bank's computer, a genetic code, and a trace of ink on paper.

Fiorentina, Israel, and Madagascar. Third point: A determinative inscription need not be a legal document.

Take the social object that is the Florence soccer team Fiorentina.[16] AC Fiorentina was founded on August 26, 1926, and folded in July 2002, thus officially ceasing to exist. A new association, Florentia Viola, was founded on August 3, 2002, following the failure of AC Fiorentina in 1926 to sign up to the B Division of the Italian League, and Florentia Viola took the place of the old club in the hearts (and memories) of its fans. The new club used the old strip and the old stadium, but it was a new social object, with new players in a different league (C2). More than a year later, president Della Valle acquired the old brand Fiorentina at a bankruptcy auction, but the name of the club was still different from the previous one (the new team was called ACF Fiorentina SpA). Having nothing in common with the registration of Fiorentina, Florentia is, to all intents and purposes, a new social object, a new team with new players in a new championship. But the fans and the public at large continued to view it as the old Fiorentina and attributed to it the identity and the victories that Fiorentina had won in the past, even though that society is legally dead. On August 20, 2003, an ontologically paradoxical event took place: with the expansion of the B Division from 20 to 24 teams, three of the teams that had been relegated to the C Division the year before were saved and, given the failure of Cosenza to sign up, Fiorentina was promoted for sporting merit. This event was decreed by the Tribunale Amministrativo Regionale (TAR, Regional Administrative Tribunal) and the Federazione Italiana Giuoco Calcio (FIGC, Italian Football Federation), which are official juridical and federal organs. But it is a mystery what sporting merit they could find in a club that had been founded barely a year before. Florentia was probably the only professional team not to have won even a junior title! What had happened? Quite simply, the titles won by the old Fiorentina were attributed to Florentia, forgetting that they were distinct objects from the juridical point of view inasmuch as they referred to different registrations.

How are we to deal with this? We seem to have a situation converse to that of the Ship of Theseus, the metaphysical puzzle that, in Hobbes's version,[17] presents us with two ships, one of which has had all its parts replaced one by one and the other that has been built using just the parts that were replaced: which of the two is the true Ship of Theseus? In the case of Fiorentina, we have to do with entities that keep some of the physical components (in particular, one of the players) but that, in the space of a few years, give rise to two distinct social objects: how can we justify the continuity? Not on a physical base, because only one player survived; nor yet on a legal base, given that the two firms are distinct. The continuity is rather a matter of tradition: it was Florence's team, it had its own fans and it was perceived as the continuation of the old team. Moral: the *being of the social object Fiorentina is in the records*, which, however, are not only those of the notary public but rather in the memories of the fans, newspapers, and television.

Moving on to the case of Israel: Is its identity given by the fact that, nearly two thousand years after the destruction of the Temple of Jerusalem, a state was set up that occupied in part the same physical land or by the fact that it is the land that the Bible talks about? It is hard to decide, because the two issues are closely intertwined. Nevertheless if one of Theodore Herzl's projects had been realized by the reconstruction of Israel in Argentina, the state of Israel would have been right there, with its continuity guaranteed by the written tradition of a Messianic religion and not by the molecules of a wholly different territory.

In some cases, the inscriptions can be not only extralegal but misleading and can nevertheless impose themselves relative to appeals to physical objects. Madagascar was another place suggested at the beginning of the 1940s as a destination for the State of Israel. The result would have been the same as that of Herzl's Argentine project. But there would have been the added complication that what we today call Madagascar, the large island in the Indian Ocean, designated a territory on the African continent and came to be used for the island only as a result of repeated errors.[18] Now, no one today is in doubt that Madagascar is that island, and it would be eccentric to try to return to the old denomination by way of an appeal to the identity of physical objects, *whose writ no longer runs*.

Parmalat. Fourth point: The counterpart of an inscription can also be a negative entity, as in the case of a debt, which is not in the debtor's nor the creditor's pocket. So where is the social object? Once more, it is an inscription that helps us out.

In the January 4, 2004, edition of the Italian newspaper *La Repubblica* we read:

> According to the original plans, they should have been hidden, like a corpse, in a hole dug in the night in the middle of the Po Plain, right behind the headquarters of Parmalat. But instead they ended up in the wrong hands, those of the Milan magistrates, and led to several arrests. I am referring to three sheets of paper on which, a few hours before the scandal exploded, the Parmalat accountants had summarized the balance sheet of Bonlat—that is, the disposal-company of the group, which was designated to receive all the debts (along with a good deal of the secrets) of Tanzi and his partners. Three sheets of paper whose contents *La Repubblica* now reveals.

Now, to dig a hole in order to bury three sheets of paper was a very original idea indeed. Would burning them, swallowing them, tearing them up into tiny little bits, or even flushing them down the toilet, as is shown in movies, not have been more practical alternatives to making the three sheets disappear? And yet that is not what they did. The head honchos at Parmalat wanted to go the whole hog: another hole in the ground behind the firm, which calls for time on a moonless night and can, in the end, be discovered. With the result that the three sheets were found first by the magistrates and then by *La Repubblica*. Why? Because they were still *inscriptions*.[19]

Roman Rota. Fifth and last point: Once it is inscribed, a social act constructs so robust an object that it calls for a supernatural intervention to make it disappear. Take the annulment of a marriage.[20] Canon 1142 of the Code of Canon Law establishes that the Pope, for the good of souls, may dissolve a marriage and specifies that "'may be dissolved' means 'by grace' and with a dispensation, inasmuch as it is an administrative provision and not a sentence." Which is tantamount to saying that there was nothing anywhere ever: where there is a sentence, as happens in the case of a divorce, we have to recognize the existence of an object. To the best of my knowledge, this is the only case that contradicts the formula object = inscribed act.

IDIOMS

The role of idioms. To come to the final ingredient of the hierarchy ascending from atoms to parliaments: the idiom. As demonstrated, I replaced objects (physical or ideal, Searle's X and Smith's Y) with inscriptions. This allowed me to overcome the difficulties facing the two thinkers' theories. There is still a problem, though: behind the social object there should be some kind of intention. I think we might avoid this rather mysterious entity by clarifying that the inscription needs to be *idiomatic*. By *idiom* I mean the specific mode of presentation of an inscription that links it to a single individual. Its most evident model is the signature (on a document, a check, a banknote) but it can also be a peculiar way of expression like a person's tone of voice. Unlike intention, it is manifest and can be verified. In this last paragraph I wish to argue for the relevance of the idiom by underlining three points:

1. The most recurring mode of expression of the idiom is the signature, an almost omnipresent element—both directly and indirectly—in social reality.
2. Its aim is the identification of the object through a chain linking it to a signer.
3. Precisely inasmuch as it concerns identification, the idiom plays a decisive role in the validation of social objects, in which there is no realization without identification.

Signatures. I will attempt a phenomenology of this patent and yet mysterious object. I receive by e-mail the following request: *nous vous serions obliges de bien vouloir nous faire parvenir ce prérapport dument signé le plus rapidement possible.* This might cause me some problems, because I am rather slow with the computer: how can I send a signature? And why do they want it? Is a message not enough? Do they really care so much for my scribble? And, more generally speaking, why all those statesmen signing a treatise, and why all those solemn declarations made in the first person, with their own voice and their peculiar accent?[21] Why, at a wedding, does one not say "of course" instead of "I do," and why does one have to do it in a normal tone and not in falsetto? Perhaps to ascertain the intention? Of course; but this ascertaining takes place precisely through an idiomatic inscription.

Hence the paradigmatic role of the signature. When we sign something, we give rise to something that is *absolutely unique*: the signature should be just that, put in that moment on that day; *in principle repeatable*: if I were to be forever changing my signature, I could not sign anything, which is why the bank asks us to deposit a signature; *wholly private*: no one can sign my signature in my place; *essentially public*: if I were to create a signature that I use only for myself, while I used another in public, only the latter would really be a signature.[22] Now, note that although it plays a decisive role in social reality, *the signature is not an object, but a content.* However, in its essence the signature is always distinct from the name, as can be easily shown. In fact, I can write:

Maurizio Ferraris

Maurizio Ferraris

Maurizio Ferraris

Maurizio Ferraris

These are not four different names, but it is the same name (the same object) in four different styles. I can even write:

Maurizio Ferraris

It is still just a name (now written in a font that mimics handwriting), but we still do not have a signature. And if I wanted to regard it as signature, then it would be a fake one. Here is why *le style c'est l'homme* seems to grasp social reality much better than *nomina sunt homina*. The single individual lies entirely in his signature.

Individualization. What ties an individual to the style and the style to the signature? First and foremost, his or her difference from the object. It is worth noting that, with the same object, contents can vary. Think of Flaubert's *Madame Bovary* and the same story (the same object) recounted by another writer; this is what happens for instance in classical tragedy or in historical novels that have the same subject, say the invasion of Normandy. Likewise two paintings of the same subject, for instance Anthony and Cleopatra or the Flight into Egypt, can turn out to be completely different. But this does not happen to ideal objects: Pythagoras's theorem remains the same irrespective of the writing surface, of the chalk or pen used to draw the figures, of the colors, of how precisely it is executed or the size of the representation.[23]

One might say that this is nothing but aestheticism, that is, a marginal experience. I doubt it: otherwise it would be unclear why we are so powerfully guided, in social life, by forms and styles. In short: Why do people want designer clothes? Let us try to imagine a society that really knows where aesthetics begins and ends. Would it be a society that regulates itself only by the act and the object, leaving style for, as once was the phrase, Sunday idling? Not at all, as can be shown easily.

A certain gentleman goes to a *vernissage* and appreciates the artist's style (i.e., the content). He is free to do so because he is in an art gallery and not in a law court or an office: no one can criticize him for his deplorable *penchant* for the style, since he is precisely in the place set aside for the exhibition of stylistic features. Everything is in order, then, because this is Sunday idling. However, something happens that is rather embarrassing for the theory of the marginality of content. If he likes a painting and his bank account allows him to, the gentleman can pull out his check book and write first a number (which is surely an object) and then the name of the artist or, more likely, the gallery owner (and here too we have an object); at this point, he will add at bottom right something like his own name, but not in any old fashion: what he will trace is precisely his signature. In that moment, he will become the owner of the painting, which is another idiom, itself validated by its author by a signature at the bottom right.

If there is any disagreement, a court, which is anything but indifferent to signatures, will decide. Suppose that the gentleman in question has all that money because he is the manager of a firm. More signatures there, not to mention the strange survival of the medieval blazon that is the logo.

It is quite different from the *names* Fiat, IBM, or Pirelli. It seems that behind the logo's precise form of presentation there lurks an intention on the firm's part, which is not necessarily present in the mere mention. In principle, and apart from the exceptional case of JHVH, the *name* of Fiat,

Charlemagne, or Freud can be repeated by anyone, but not a *logo*, a *monogram*, or a *signature*. Sticking to the logos, for Fiat, IBM, or Pirelli to become more than a mention of the firm, what is needed is another idiomatic presentation, which is to say a signature. And it is not by chance that the Italian for *signature* is *firma*, presumably to evoke the sense in which a right to sign undergirds those actions that constitute the identity of the business.

Now imagine instead that the rich collector made his money with a patent[24] or, less likely, with a book. Stylistic elements here as well. First of all, note that a person who bought the book can very well destroy it in front of the author's eyes,[25] but she cannot appropriate the *literal expression* of the author's ideas, independently from the language in which they are written. This means, contrary to Searle's theory, that the physical basis is irrelevant to the constitution of the identity of the social object. Also, contrary to Smith's thesis, the ideal representation does not suffice to construct a real social object.

Leaving aside the obvious case of trademarks (which are essentially logos referring to signatures),[26] I will focus on the apparently more problematic case of patents, which regard the ownership of an idea. Suppose the art collector made his pile because he invented and patented the Tetra Pak. He could not protect the idea, any more than he could privatize the parallelogram, but he could get rich precisely through the idiomatic application of a geometrical solid, making the most of the peculiarities of size, of the material used, and of the way the thing is opened. That peculiarity, thanks to the patent, is tied to his name and, thereby, to his signature. (The fact that certain fruit juices have baroque and bizarre openings probably depends on this circumstance: the producers wanted to bypass our collector's patent).

Validation. Here is the grand finale. The moral is very simple: for social objects to exist, there must necessarily be inscriptions validated by signatures. Perhaps, though, there is a problem *in extremis*: if Smith, with his theory of representations, could not distinguish *de jure* one hundred ideal thalers from one hundred real ones, I, with the theory of idiomatic inscriptions, cannot distinguish *de facto* one hundred ideal thalers from one hundred real ones, nor one hundred real thalers from one hundred fake ones (for instance, real IBM shares from counterfeit ones). The first circum-

Strong realism	**Strong textualism**
Social objects are as solid as physical objects.	Physical objects are socially constructed.
Weak realism	**Weak textualism**
Social objects are constructed upon physical objects.	Social objects are constructed by idiomatic inscriptions (small physical objects).

stance might seem to refer to Searle's view (you cannot prescind from the physical object), the latter would reveal the insufficiency of the appeal to the signature. At this point even the last theory on social objects would be lost (see diagram).

Now, I do not think this is so: not all of the theories should be crossed out. First of all, it is a problem *de facto* and not *de jure*, therefore (at least from a philosophical point of view) it is less important; secondly, the theory of idiomatic inscriptions seems to be a solution both for ideal/real and for true/fake.

One hundred real thalers entail a number of traces. Because, not being really *ideal* (even Kant was wrong on this: they are *imaginary*, the representation of a social object that has its beginning and end in time) they require an inscription, and they require it *necessarily*. It is necessary that someone imagines those one hundred thalers and, if he does, there must be some trace of it: a couple of neurons must have been involved. Now, what distinguishes one hundred real thalers from one hundred imaginary ones? The fact that in real thalers inscriptions are much more clear, constant, and defined. Try to imagine a twenty-dollar bill, then look at a real one, and you will see what I mean. Therefore, inscription is not only a formal element: it offers a criterion to distinguish ideal from real. In external objects— checks, contracts, banknotes—the distinction is very clear, constituting the difference between an imagined object and one existing in the external world.

The real can be *empty*, like a Parmalat share or a bad check. In this case, philosophically, there is not much to be done. Nonetheless, since I claimed that inscription is a necessary but not sufficient condition, I do not see here an objection to my theory: it is necessary that there are inscriptions, but this does not mean that they are sufficient—as creative finance well knows.

Finally, the real can be counterfeit. Here the idiomaticness of the inscription becomes crucial. On this point (and in this very sense) it is relevant to quote Saul Kripke's theory (1972, 102), a theory of the name that seems to presuppose the theory of the signature. In order to be what it is, an object can change many and even all of its properties, apart from one: its *origin*. *This is exactly what the signature tells us*, especially in its differing from the name: I can write as many names as I wish, but I can sign only with my own, in a specific way, and that scribble indicates continuity with the origin (it was me, I was there, signing).

Here is a counterproof of this, with which I wish to end this treatise on writing, mobile phones, and social reality and through which I thank three masters. Take the following postcard, addressed to Gadamer and signed by Derrida, Vattimo, and myself (which I then forgot to send out). The postcard shows four names and three signatures; Gadamer's name in the address, of course, does not count as a signature, and would have stayed the same even if it was written with Vattimo's or Derrida's handwriting.

Why then is Gadamer—unlike Derrida, Vattimo, and Ferraris—a name and not a signature? For a very simple reason: its origin is not Gadamer, but Ferraris, who wrote the address. Counterfeiters write names that are

Social Objects: Realism and Textualism

not their own on banknotes, sign in the place of someone else (namely the only one who is legitimately authorized to do so), and this is why their banknotes are fake: that is it. I realize that I have only offered philosophical arguments, but it was all I had to offer. If you really need to distinguish a real banknote from a fake one, buy one of those the tobacconists use: it is all you need.

EPILOGUE

It's a long time since I wrote to you, Frau Milena, and even today I'm writing only as the result of an incident. Actually, I don't have to apologize for my not writing, you know after all how I hate letters. All the misfortune of my life—I don't wish to complain, but to make a generally instructive remark derives, one could say, from letters or from the possibility of writing letters. People have hardly ever deceived me, but letters always—and as a matter of fact not only those of other people, but my own. In my case this is a special misfortune of which I won't say more, but at the same time also a general one. The easy possibility of letter-writing must—seen merely theoretically—have brought into the world a terrible disintegration of souls. It is, in fact, an intercourse with ghosts, and not only with the ghost of the recipient but also with one's own ghost which develops between the lines of the letter one is writing and even more so in a series of letters where one letter corroborates the other and can refer to it as a witness. How on earth did anyone get the idea that people can communicate with one another by letter! Of a distant person one can think, and of a person who is near one can catch hold—all else goes beyond human strength. Writing letters, however, means to denude oneself before the ghosts, something for which they greedily wait. Written kisses don't reach their destination, rather they are drunk on the way by the ghosts. It is on this ample nourishment that they multiply so enormously. Humanity senses this and fights against it and in order to eliminate as far as possible the ghostly element between people and to create a natural communication, the peace of souls, it has invented the railway, the motor car, the aeroplane. But it's no longer any good, these are evidently inventions being made at the moment of crashing. The opposing side is so much calmer and stronger; after the postal service it has invented the telegraph, the telephone, the radiograph. The ghosts won't starve, but we will perish [Kafka 1999].

Mobile phones existed already during Kafka's time. Surely they existed before home phones: they were letters and, before that, inscriptions, maybe wax or clay tablets. The first limit of my work then is that I did not grasp the spirit of the age; I did not capture that cheeky ghost. I only described something that has always been there and that now has merely become more powerful thanks to the mobile phone.

Still, I can console myself with this: through the reference to inscription and signature, I hope to have made social ontology clearer, since I underlined (it is writing after all, what else could I do?) a basic characteristic that many had failed to notice. That said, there is still a lot of work to do. I can only threaten the reader with the final words of Sartre's (2003, 647) *Being and Nothingness*: "We shall devote to them a future work."

NOTES

FOREWORD

1. This text was originally published in the weekly column La Bustina di Minerva, "L'Espresso," December 15, 2005.

INTRODUCTION: WHERE ARE YOU?

1. And in the meantime the requests have increased, such as the direction of a program of National research on the ontology of intellectual properties and its transformations in the computer age (2002–4); the definition, in courses, seminars, and articles, of the notion of "social objects"; the collaboration on this topic with Barry Smith at the IFOMIS in Leipzig and Saarbrücken, with the support of the Alexander von Humboldt-Stiftung (June–August 2004); the participation, in May 2004, in the "Telecom Italia Journey," in Cosenza, where for the first time I thought of the issue of "where are you?" (as a theoretical problem, of course: on the practical level I was well-accustomed to it).

2. Even though, in Japan and Korea, novels are actually sent via text in an episodic form. See http://www.repubblica.it/2005/b/rubriche/scenedigitali/japan/japan .html. But this is another story, which I will talk about later, and that maybe has the advantage of iconographic writing.

3. A perfect documentation on the state of things can be found in Di Lucia (2003).

4. Shakespeare, Hamlet, 1.5.166.

5. I am not exaggerating nor making things up, or rather, reality—as always—surpasses imagination. In the Islamic law (for example, in short-term marriages in Iran) it is technically possible to divorce via a text message.

1. SPEAKING

1. See Nyìri (2005a). I will often refer to these texts, which now constitute a bible of the mobile phone, or at least more than a Pentateuch, since eight volumes have been published so far (2002, 2003a, 2003b, 2003c, 2005a, 2005b, 2006, 2007). I refer the reader back to them for a bibliography on the mobile phone, an enormous field that I will not even try to sketch out here.

2. The mother might therefore stalk Gino and her daughter by using a system of topographical research: the mobile phone processes the satellites' signal and sends it to a server, which processes the customer's position it received and sends the cartography of the area. The customer's terminal, still communicating with the server, inserts a destination. The server processes the route, the distance, and the arrival time, sending the itinerary and driving information to the customer's terminal, who sees it on the screen. On the mobile phone's screen appears a three-dimensional and detailed street map that, turn after turn, not only shows the route to follow (the directions can also be delivered by a voice) but also indicates the presence of gas stations, restaurants, hospitals, train stations, airports and so on) including information that might determine the destination itself (for instance, by sending the weather forecast). This is what normally happens, if all goes well; un-like a friend of mine who, going from Portofino to Genoa, was invited to turn left, into the sea.

3. It also works the other way round. There are areas in Trieste where Vodafone has no network; the mobile phone will connect to the Slovenian network, and there is little you can do about this: either you manually set your phone so it con-nects to Vodafone only, or it is a matter of time before you receive a text telling you that you can call Italy from abroad by dialing 0039 before the number. Those who go to Trieste for the first time might be induced to reconsider their geopolitical no-tions. The locals simply avoid calling from the risky zones. I thank Alessandra Ja-comuzzi for this and other mobile phone adventures.

4. The commercial does not lie, it merely ascertains a fact. It has been proven (Bert 2005) that there are people who leave the hairdresser, take a picture of them-selves, and send it to their spouse or friend asking "how do I look?"

5. Giuseppe Turani, "La Repubblica," December 15, 2003: "It is a Wi-Fi phone. There is no need for wires anymore. And not even to have a bulky object on your desk. The new phone is this. You charge it with a wire, just like mobile phones. The advantages are many. To begin with, it is truly not bulky. Furthermore, it is mobile (within the office area, that could also be a whole building). Therefore, if one goes to a colleague, it is enough to have it in one's pocket to be able to answer from any place. And also to call, of course. The Wi-Fi phone is, in a word, a sort of office phone. The old phone dies and this one arrives, very simple and very handy."

6. Consider the sad story of "Fido"—a typical dog name—by Telecom, which appeared toward the end of the 1990s. It was a cordless phone connected to the landline, but with reception in the whole city. It had a short and unhappy life, taken over by the mobile phone like the Polish chivalry brigades by German tanks in 1939. Giving up, Fido turned to a mere cordless phone destined for the house only. From the causes of this failure emerges the power of the mobile phone, which I will analyze in the following chapters. With Fido you could not write; Fido was not private (so that if you left with Fido the others in the house were left without a phone, and you received their calls without being able to pass them over; Fido was subjected to the fragile but subsistent criteria of *politesse* of the home phone: no calls after 10 PM, no calls at meal times, nor during the siesta. All this has disappeared with the mobile phone. Now we say: "I'll call. If he's asleep the phone will be off" (not always, though! What if it was on?). From Fido's sacrifice, nonetheless, another parasitism of the home phone with respect to the mobile phone has emerged: that is, home phones allowing to send text messages. Here, once again, the home phone falls behind the mobile phone and one of its *apparently* anomalous but winning features.

7. The original Italian is: Quando, segnal de' popoli, / Ti collocò sul monte, / E ne' tuoi labbri il fonte / Della parola aprì. / . . . Tal risonò moltiplice / La voce dello Spiro: / L'Arabo, il Parto, il Siro / In suo sermon l'udì.—Trans. by Kenelm Foster

8. From Kafka (1919): "The emperor—it is said—sent to you, the one apart, the wretched subject, the tiny shadow that fled far, far from the imperial sun, precisely to you he sent a message from his deathbed."

9. By law, a customer who switches mobile phone companies or buys a new phone has the right to keep his old number, and the new company has to guarantee it at no extra cost. Not to mention the market of personalized phone gadgets: peculiar ringtone, perhaps differentiated according to who is calling, color, ornaments. In Japan *all* mobile phones are endowed with a little hook on which you can attach the so-called straps: small pendants of various kinds—some are branded and cost from 4,000 yen (40 euros) up. In short, everyone wants to have his or her *own, unique* phone, all and forever *theirs*.

10. And with the warrant for *privacy* Stefano Rodotà has rightly placed the new matter on the agenda. I thank Pier Giuseppe Monateri for this suggestion.

11. As my student Davide Grasso points out: "In the phenomenology of the mobile phone (and of moral action) you illustrated to us, not much importance was given to the missed call, understood as a single ring of the phone, but I think it is noteworthy for two reasons that are represented by two different situations. A) Meeting up: If I receive a missed call in reply to a text in which I had written 'See you tonight at the usual pub?,' the missed call is both an assent and a promise, constituting thereby a social object with no use of speech and not even the alphabet, but merely through a trace, a record in the memory (of the phone). B) Courting: A

missed call to the courted person stands for a whole lot of words said or written, meaning them all (and often better), because who receives it can fantasize freely about their significance; I think this is interesting because it has to do with trace and, if I understood correctly what it means, with *différance*. Moreover, receiving such a minimal trace on the phone can generate real hopes and fancies, perhaps leading to a date, i.e., a social object." This does not work only for Turinese pubs; the semantics and pragmatics of missed calls, evidently dictated by economic reasons, is precisely the same in sub-Saharan Africa. See Donner (2005).

12. In the Israeli society, the diffusion of the mobile phone is often tied to security issues. See Cohen and Lemish (2005).

13. "We think in names" Hegel stated (1830, § 462), and today we could add "we call names, no longer numbers."

14. See Luca Fazzo, "La Repubblica," November 17, 2004, on the intercepting system produced by Telecom and installed in Campobasso's prosecutor's office.

15. We should therefore stigmatize the sadism of certain mobile companies that do not show the number also for ordinary use: at least, it looks like sadism, but at the same time the legitimate aspiration to secrecy is understandable.

16. See the essays collected in Nyìri (2003a), a monographic volume on the topic.

17. Or "Auditel," even, given the increasing recourse to text messages in television votes.

18. Kant (1766, 2:363), stigmatizing Swedenborg's folly, describes the world of the mobile phone: "The positions of the spirits, relative to each other, have nothing in common with the space of the corporeal world. Hence in what concerns their spirit-positions, the soul of someone in India may often be the closest neighbour of someone in Europe, *and in contrast to this, those who according to the body live in the same house, could be very far apart according to these relations*" (emphasis added).

19. I thank my friend Antonello Giugliano for suggesting the title of this paragraph.

20. It is not excluded that they already did it at their time, because in a way every confession is, literally, a connection. Take Rousseau's *Confessions*: they are an open letter, a very long e-mail addressed to mankind in which (with the slightly blackmailing style typical of mails offering you loans with dubious benefits) Jean-Jacques begs the whole world to read it and not to annihilate the unique and useful portrait he offers of himself. The same goes for Augustine, who realized the incongruence of confessing to God, who knows everything, and said to himself: of course, God knows everything, but I wish to confess not only to Him and in my heart, but also in a written form (i.e., by e-mail) and in front of many witnesses (i.e., in connection with mankind). This is how you make truth, according to Augustine: "This would I do in my heart before Thee in confession: and in my writing,

before many witnesses" (*Confessions*, 10.1.1). A blog, which is a kind of public diary online, meets all of the Bishop's requirements.

21. See Derrida (1980b) for a truly beautiful treatise on post.

22. Developed and discussed in Ferraris and Varzi (2003).

23. In accordance with the intuition underlying the project of a "descriptive metaphysics," with the aim of grasping the constant features of human thought. See Strawson (1959).

24. This concept was crucial to Aristotle's philosophy, brought back to the fore by the psychology of perception (Gibson 1979), and applied to social ontology by Barry Smith (1998).

25. Ferraris (2001; 2002, 97–107). This perspective refers to the notion of "invariance under transformation" discussed by Nozick (2001), as well as the conservative character of common sense, rehabilitated by Strawson (1959).

26. See Lévi (1994). What emerged, rather than collective intelligence, is mass stupidity—which is not exclusively postmodern.

27. The Italian original, from Leopardi's poem *La Ginestra*, is "Dipinte su queste rive / Son dell'umana gente / magnifiche sorti e progressive.—Trans.

28. The song is "La Topolino Amaranto."—Trans.

29. Hitchcock offers a vast number of examples, being a master in imagining improper uses for the phone such as using the wire to tie someone up.

30. Descartes (1641), First meditation: "the visions that come in sleep are like paintings: they must have been made as copies of real things." See Ferraris (2004a; 2004d).

31. Science historian Ian Hacking (1999, 1) proposed a list of objects that, according to postmodern thinkers, are socially constructed: the notion of "authorship," that of "brotherhood," the child viewer of television, danger, emotions, facts, gender, homosexual culture, illness, knowledge, literacy, the medicalized immigrant, nature, oral history, postmodernism, quarks, reality, serial homicides, technological systems, urban schooling, vital statistics, women refugees, youth homelessness, Zulu nationalism, mind, panic, the eighties. During a workshop on underage motherhood, a Catholic agent declared: "And, obviously, I am a social construction *myself*; we all are."

32. For recent presentations of ontology see Andina and Barbero (2003), Bottani and Bianchi (2003), Casati (2003), Ferraris (2003c), Kim and Sosa (1999), Loux (1998), Mulligan (2000), Nef (1998, 2004), Poli and Simons (1996), Runggaldier and Kanzian (1998), Smith (1995b), and Varzi (2001, 2005).

33. One should not be surprised by the intrinsic difficulty of other questions, like those concerning the essence of kisses, flips, U-turns, murders, hairstyles, holes, shades, smiles. See Casati and Varzi (1994), Casati (2000), and Varzi (2001).

34. Koepsell (2000) examines phenomena like software, the Internet, e-mails (but not the mobile phone, which at the time was not regarded as a part of cyberspace)

with the aim of making them compatible with common sense ontology. See also Koepsell (2003).

35. Technically, they are *affordances*, that is, performances offered by the object independently from the intentions it was built with (a low table can occasionally work as a chair and undoubtedly a cat sees no difference between a chair and a table). The notion of *affordance* was theorized by Gibson (1979) but is already present in Gestalt theory, where Kurt Lewin spoke about *Aufforderungscharakter*.

36. When I wrote this book originally, tablets had only just been invented. For this translation, I updated my examples as necessary to include the latest technology.

37. In fact, this still holds true. Tablets do not supply those functions.

38. Meinong is not alone in this task, because he works at a time that, in retrospect, seems characterized by a great deal of ontological enthusiasm. A formal theory of objects had been elaborated, contemporaneously, both by Husserl and by another of Brentano's pupils, Kazimierz Twardowski (1866–1938), whom I will talk about later. Contrary to what Meinong believed, metaphysics in its historical development had been far from indifferent to this matter, which appears also in simple experience—the experience that, in order to deny the existence of a square circle, imposes us to picture it as an object, otherwise we would be denying the existence of something vague, maybe even anything.

39. Next to *Objekte* and *Objektive*, Meinong also lists the *"Dignitative"* (*Gegenstände* apprehended by [possible] feelings) and the *"Desiderative"* (*Gegenstände* apprehended by [possible] desires), although only in his mature theory of objects; see, for instance, Meinong (1923). For the purpose of my argument, these can be ignored here.

40. It is a reasonable task, but not that easy to enact. Many years later, in a popular book of his, Russell (1930) wrote, almost *en passant*: "No new thing under the sun? What about skyscrapers, aeroplanes, and the broadcast speeches of politicians? What did Solomon know about such things?" and in the only note of the book "*Ecclesiastes* was not, of course, really written by Solomon, but it is convenient to allude to the author by this name." Further down he wrote: "Napoleon envied Caesar, Caesar envied Alexander, and Alexander, I daresay, envied Hercules, who never existed" (Russell 2012, 16, 58). In other words, it is hard to do without the reference to inexistent objects, because there is plenty of them in our lives. With his polemic, though, Russell sanctioned Meinong's fame beyond Graz as well as an empire that was soon going to be nonexisting. He started a process that in the frame of a century brought Meinong back to the fore of the debate on ontology and metaphysics. For more on this, see Orilia (2002) and Barbero (2003; 2005).

41. If fact, Meinong treats the objective both like a proposition (that can be true or false: "the rose is red") and like a state of things (subsisting or nonsubsisting: the fact that the rose is red or not). Nonetheless, given that truth is a characteristic that

Meinong regards as "subjective" and directly dependent on the subsistence of the objective (a true objective is subsisting and judged, i.e., grasped by a subject), the objective might seem rather like a state of things or, in other words, a *Wahrmacher*: that which makes a proposition true. And just like objects are divided into existent, subsistent, and nonexistent, so objectives are divided into subsistent and nonsubsistent. A subsistent objective is "the sum of the interior angles of a triangle is 180°"; a nonsubsistent objective is "$2+2=5$." Luckily these distinctions, once again, are not relevant for my discussion.

42. One might wonder in what way something dependent on a person's belief can become a bearer of characteristics that are independent from that person. The answer is simple and lies in the universally accepted principle according to which the ignorance of a law does not entail impunity. In other words, it is assumed that someone living in a certain society knows its rules and observes them, even without sharing them.

43. Cyberspace also possesses a very concrete physical location and is dependent on the physical support containing it (see Koepsell 2000). I will come back to this in chapter 7, in my discussion on Smith's correction.

44. The notion of "intentionality" means precisely that, when we think, we always think of something: "Every mental phenomenon is characterized by what the Scholastics of the Middle Ages called the intentional (or mental) inexistence of an object, and what we might call, though not wholly unambiguously, reference to a content, direction toward an object (which is not to be understood here as meaning a thing), or immanent objectivity. Every mental phenomenon includes something as object within itself, although they do not all do so in the same way. In presentation something is presented, in judgment something is affirmed or denied, in love loved, in hate hated, in desire desired and so on. This intentional non-existence is characteristic exclusively of mental phenomena. No physical phenomenon exhibits anything like it. We could, therefore, define mental phenomena by saying that they are those phenomena that contain an object intentionally within themselves" (Brentano 1995, 88–89).

45. I will develop this point in chapter 4.

46. One possible objection could be the following: why does this classification not contemplate psychic objects, like the dream I had last night? The reason is almost banal. These objects are too volatile, they are not properly part of the physical world nor of the ideal world where theorems are, and they can be shared only somewhere in my mind. Therefore, they constitute a mere appendix of the subject and do not possess, in principle, that ability to be shared that lies at the basis of the definition of an object—which is such only insofar as it is also such for someone else (and this is undoubtedly the case with social objects). Another objection could be: what is the difference between an artifact (which I classified as a physical object) and a social object? After all, in regards to time, a chair and a contract are

alike: they were not there, and then they started existing at a given point. Nevertheless, once the chair is made, it can exist even if no one remembers it. The contract, instead, disappears in the absence of inscription.

2. WRITING

1. Some companies have activated a service for which, after each call, you get a text message telling you how much credit you have left. I imagine the advantage is the transparency of your balance, knowing every second how much you have and how much a phone call is. The outcome, though, demonstrates the validity of the saying according to which the road to hell is paved with good intentions. Imagine making twenty phone calls in an hour—under certain circumstances, it can happen. You then get twenty text messages and spend quite some time deleting them, so as not to fill up the SIM card's memory. All this while you are in a hurry, so much so that you are making twenty calls in an hour. Even without using extreme examples, it is still fatiguing. Of course, with an extra call you can deactivate the service, but a synthesized gentle voice will let you know that the request will be fulfilled in the next forty-eight hours.

2. This is rightly said with regard to mobile phones; see Nyìri (2002).

3. The first signs of writing, it is said, appeared around 50,000 years ago with the *homo sapiens*: we might as well claim that the first writings, or at least the first recordings, not necessarily encoded, appeared with man.

4. A barbarity that Vico ungenerously attributes to Cola di Rienzo (poor guy), who was made barbaric because of political necessities.

5. Ong underlined the differences between orality and writing, enacting the paradox, as old as the *Phaedrus*, for which the word (understood as origin) is thought of and described retrospectively starting from writing. With the just as paradoxical outcome of praising writing in an even excessive way: "A literate person, asked to think of the word 'nevertheless,' will normally (and I strongly suspect always) have some image, at least vague, of the spelled-out word" (Ong 2002). What a bizarre experiment: asking someone to *think* and then use the fact that she is thinking of an image (what else could you think of?) as the proof of the pervasiveness of writing!

6. See, for instance, McLuhan (1964). McLuhan outlines a sort of Hegelian dialectic culminating in the final chapters, dedicated to cinema, radio, television, and weapons (understood, though, as psychological weapons, like television messages and icons, and not like intelligent missiles in the search of a mobile phone).

7. *Confessions*, 6.3.3: "[Ambrose] read, his eyes travelled across the page and his heart sought into the sense, but voice and tongue were silent."

8. See in particular Derrida (1967b, 47–56). For a presentation of the problem, see Ferraris (2003a, 67ff).

9. Also, in Italian, the digraph *ch* (sounding K) is now being written and shortened as *k*, funnily reproducing the formula of the Placito di Capua, the first attestation of Italian vulgar: "sao ke kelle terre" (I know that those lands).

10. This pathography can also be found in many alphabets, in certain primers for children and some formulas that preceded by far the computer revolution, where we find a mixture of alphabet and ideograms ("I ♥ NY," "I ♥ my dog" and so forth).

11. Arousing some strange forms of indignation. For instance, Rousseau complained about people starting to pronounce *vingt* exactly as it is written.

12. In fact, in front of an ideogram one either knows how to read it or does not even know what it means (unless the ideogram maintains some kind of similarity to what it denotes, which happens very rarely).

13. Italian saying, meaning "do not overdo it when you speak, keep it simple."—Trans.

14. Originally published at http://www.bibop.it/area_stampa/scritturaprovv.htm (site discontinued).

15. Excerpted from "The Library of Babel," http://jubal.westnet.com/hyperdis cordia/library_of_babel.html.

16. *Bouvard et Pécuchet* is an unfinished satirical work by Gustave Flaubert, published posthumously in 1881. *Zeno's Conscience* is a 1923 novel by the Italian writer Italo Svevo.—Trans.

17. An argument that was popular in Athens around the age of the Peloponnesian Wars—namely when writing, invented centuries before, started to be taught in elementary schools in Attica—went like this: a person who knows the *grammata* knows everything, because everything is written or writable. The argument is obviously flawed, because if everything can be written and read one still needs the time to read and write; also, everything can be written, including "Aristotle was born in Llandudno," but it remains to be seen whether it is true (this is often the feeling that accompanies us when we surf the Web). The library, then, is enriched with many books, but it also gives voice to Bacon's complaint that on many disordered shelves are gathered disorderly repeated books, adding mistakes, slips, and typos to a material that could be very well contained in one book only.

18. It is said (or rather, once again, it is *written*) that it is a new kind of communication, like the synthetic and allusive language of text messages and so on. Now, take a form of communication more literarily organized, like a book or a newspaper. Given that they do not pass through the mediation of a composer, but only through an automatic spell-checker, they are full of typos that would have been inconceivable before (and a book is not at all better than a newspaper in terms of mistakes, unlike it used to be). One could say: newspapers used to be full of typos, which no longer happens thanks to the spell-checker. Obviously, it is no so. Once, recognizing as English the text I was writing, (because of a couple of English

words I had used) the spell-checker had turned "i programmi" into "I programme." Luckily the two lines where the misdeed happened were underlined in red, but this is often not the case. The word *programme* is not necessarily underlined: it can act unexpectedly. This is the reason for the new typos. I have recently read *caput mondi* (the program had recognized the Latin *caput* but had corrected that *mundi* as not quite Italian). Mereology, a very respectable discipline born out of formal ontology, regularly turns into merceology. Generally, we witness the law of what philologists call *lectio facilior*, namely the tendency to normalize unusual expressions, considering them as mistakes. Yet, this is not always the case, given that to "reify," unless you have told your computer, becomes "deify" (although reification is as frequent as deification). The highest price is paid by proper names: the philosopher of science Giorello becomes *girello* (merry-go-round), the philosopher of language Leonardi becomes the poet Leopardi—usually, at least, Umberto Eco is safe. Once again, though, these are effects of writing, not of the spoken word.

19. "Life . . . is a tale told by an idiot, full of sound and fury, signifying nothing." Shakespeare, *Macbeth*, act 5.

20. Despite the increasing presence of web designers, websites are often extraordinarily ugly. Sometimes they seem like a derivation of the book that does not consider the differences between reading a book and visiting a website (it is one of the things that mostly go unnoticed). Too often websites are heavy, baroque, polychrome, and polymorphous, and therefore hard to use. The British classicist Eric Havelock, in his book *The Muse Learns to Write* (1986), tackles the transition from orality to literacy when the Homeric poems started to be transcribed. A useful supplement, for a transformation of the same extent, could be *The Muse Learns to Surf*.

21. It is Searle's (1992) thesis, which indeed seems problematic to me (as I will argue in chapters 7 and 8), not so much because of the idea of computer intentionality, but because it attributes a primary and fundamental intentionality to humans.

22. It is not by chance that sales prospects for processor producers who invested a lot on computing power were left disappointed. The majority of people do not need devices of impressive computing power and typically use only a small part of the functionality offered by computer applications.

23. Within the limits I outlined in chapter 1.

24. "Internet calls are back in fashion," *La Repubblica*, October 9, 2003.

25. "An American society offers an incredibly cheap contract. A device to call via Internet. Vonage offers a device through which one can connect the phone to the net, and make phone calls at zero cost." *Corriere della Sera*, July 11, 2003. Obviously, today the service is also available in Italy.

26. It therefore seems problematic to see in text messages an "improper" use of the mobile phone, as suggested by Del Corno and Mansi (2002). Such a use would

be, say, that of a screwdriver used as a dagger (they speak, in fact, of "improper weapons"), whereas in this case it is a very proper function that we merely did not know about. So much so that commercials make no distinctions between writing and calling. A recent one, moreover, advertises the possibility of "surfing and texting unlimitedly."

27. Until recently, it was rare to see people taking pictures, especially in a city that doesn't see many tourists. Now everyone is taking pictures: in streets, in restaurants, anywhere; someone always seems to be immortalizing (i.e., recording) a moment, or looking at a picture that was just sent to them.

28. In this case the user is not too clever, but this is another story.

29. This point will be developed in chapter 3.

30. "Man is the most intelligent of animals because he has hands" (Diels-Kranz 1974, 59 A 102).

31. "The soul is like a hand: the hand is the tool of all tools, the soul is the form of all forms" (*De Anima*, 432a, 1–3). In *De Partibus Animalium* (687a, 10–35), Aristotle objects to Anaxagoras as follows: "Now it is the opinion of Anaxagoras that the possession of these hands is the cause of man being of all animals the most intelligent. But it is more rational to suppose that his endowment with hands is the consequence rather than the cause of his superior intelligence. . . . The invariable plan of nature in distributing the organs is to give each to such animal as can make use of it."

32. In the *Phenomenology of Spirit*, there is a paragraph on physiognomics: "It is the hand most of all by which a man manifests and actualizes himself. It is the living artificer of his fortune. We may say of the hand that it is what a man *does*, for in it, as the active organ of his self-fulfillment, he is present as the animating soul; and since he is primarily his own fate, his hand will thus express this in-itself." In short, it is through our hands that we have control over our destiny. But the hand, Hegel (1998, 189) tells us, like writing (and analogously to the voice), is also an expression of individuality, an exteriorization of the internal: "Thus the simple lines of the hand, the timbre and compass of the voice as the individual characteristic of speech—this too again as expressed in writing, where the hand gives it a more durable existence than the voice does, especially in the particular style of handwriting—all this is an expression of the inner." The literal and explicit reference to Aristotle's definition of the hand as "universal tool" can be found in the *Encyclopaedia* (Hegel 1830, § 411).

33. From Mozart's *Don Giovanni*, 1.9: "là ci darem la mano / là mi dirai di sì."

34. See Clark (2003, 9). It might be interesting to look at a phenomenology of the various words for *mobile phone* in other languages. In Italy it is called *telefonino* (small phone) as well as *cellulare* (cell, with *phone* being implied), which refers not to its external size but to its internal functioning. *Cell phone* is the American term, whereas *mobile phone* is the British one (although this has changed in

recent years, with Americans increasingly using the British variant). In fact, in Italy one can also call it *mobile*, but only to distinguish it from the *fisso* ("fixed" home phone). The fundamental essence of the device is also described in French, where it is called *portable*. The moral of this lexographic reconstruction is that with the mobile phone *all* the phone is in your hand, not only that cornet (which had the technical prophetic name of "micro-telephone," that is *telefonino*).

35. Is it possible to find an image of the mind alternative to the *tabula rasa*? In fact, one could at least update it: the SIM card, or the recorder, for instance. Or maybe the flow of pure experience (which exists, though, only if there is some possibility of recording). Or a sponge (again, something that absorbs and records, like Flaubert's Bouvard: absorbing paper). One can object that the mind is active: of course, but it acts on manipulating previously written material. One could object that memories are selected or even made up: indeed we are talking about a *tabula rasa*, that is, a wax board, not a gravestone. The best model, here, would be the possibility of recording and deleting provided by the computer.

36. In a way, it is already like that: think of the so-called blogosphere, the interconnected whole of web blogs, which has its own rules as well as its blog stars (real online celebrities, often writing under a pseudonym and being completely unknown in "real" life, that is in the world of news).

37. In Japanese, *keitai*, another name for the mobile phone, originally means (again) portable, and it is an adjective used for various portable objects. Significantly, *keitai kasa* are the small umbrellas that fit into a handbag. Yet, *ketai,* on its own, is only used to designate the mobile phone, as if it were the portable item *par excellence.*

3. RECORDING

1. Lietta Tornabuoni, "La Stampa," March 19, 2005, review of the film *Hostage*, USA 2004.

2. Almost all of the immigrants' uprisings in "temporary stay centers" have made use of mobile phones. Also, among the reasons of suffering denounced by the residents there are the restrictions on the use of the phone, which to them becomes the only possibility of contact with the external world; not so much with friends or relatives, but mainly with lawyers—in a situation of complete lack of legal assistance.

3. For instance, it is known and attested that the prevailing function of videophones is the *commemoration* of aspects of everyday life (Kato 2005, 215). This has unexpected outcomes and side effects: the images of the tortures in Abu Ghraib were taken with a videophone and sent by the soldiers to friends and relatives to let them know about their bravery.

4. I will come back to this (see chapters 4 and 8), but there are circumstances where the distinction between the two levels is more evident, like in thrillers. A policeman says to the person he stopped: "you are under arrest" (this is first of all an act) and *then* tells him what his rights are (which is a communication).

5. The Italian academic grading system ranges from 0 to 30, and 18 is the minimum grade to pass.—Trans.

6. A possible objection is: when an official orders something to a subaltern he makes a performative, even if there is no need for a record. It is not so: the subaltern will, indeed, record the order in his mind and will show he has understood: *yessir, oui mon general, Jawohl.*

7. Derrida's comment (1968a) on Plato's condemnation of writing is famous.

8. *De Anima*, 430 a1. I focused on the images of the *tabula* in Plato, Aristotle, Locke, and Leibniz among others in Ferraris (1997).

9. See the presentation and the comment in Derrida (1967a, 235ff).

10. Hegel 1830, § 459, annotation. See Derrida's comment (1970, 139–52).

11. This had, in fact, attracted Leibniz's attention. Leibniz was fascinated by the idea of a symbolic logic and a communication of ideas not passing through an imprecise medium like language.

12. Furthermore, Hegel underestimates the agglutinative nature of ideographic writing: there is no need to invent a new character, it suffices to combine two characters for the complex form to assume a different meaning that is not reducible to the two *inferiora*.

13. See also Derrida (1967a, 235ff).

14. The true objective of writing is the creation of symbols that would stand in for words (Gelb 1952, 97), therefore the only writing that does not miss its target is the phonetic one (212); see also the description of the evolutional stages from painting to writing.

15. Apparently, McLuhan's passion for orality had an affective origin: his very pious mom read to him from the Bible when he was a child.

16. I extensively developed this hypothesis in Ferraris (1997), which overall represents the attempt at making the Kantian transcendental and the Aristotelian theory of the mind as a *tabula* converge. I refer the reader to this text for more on the erudite and curious background of this apology of writing.

17. In fact, the mobile phone seems to favor precisely this function of capitalization, see Donner (2003).

18. Mobile phone–based services are not uncommon these days. In Austria you can buy opera or train tickets using a mobile phone (see http://paybox.at/). In the United States, you can get tickets for movies and other events using services such as Fandango. Some banks let you know, via text messages, the amount, date, and place of the payment every time you use your credit card. Even before you sign a receipt you get a text stating that a payment in the

amount of x euros was just requested at the restaurant where you just asked for the bill.

19. This is paradoxical for a fanatic enemy of science such as Rousseau (1993, 15): "In fact, whether we turn to the annals of the world, or eke out with philosophical investigations the uncertain chronicles of history, we shall not find for human knowledge an origin answering to the idea we are pleased to entertain of it at present. Astronomy was born from superstition; eloquence from ambition, hate, flattery, and falsehood; geometry from avarice, physics from vain curiosity; all, even moral philosophy, from human pride."

20. As is known, the long-feared apocalypse at the end of the last millennium did not take place: computers kept working notwithstanding the scarce foresight of the first programmers, who did not expect a millenary Reich.

21. Proust compares his memory to a casket and thus justifies the writing of the *Recherche*.

22. See Freud (1895, 204–7), where he speaks of ϕ impermeable neurons and ψ permeable ones.

23. This is why James (1907, 102) tries to reformulate the theory of *adaequatio* in a rather baroque way: "To 'agree' in the widest sense with a reality, *can only mean to be guided either straight up to it or into its surroundings, or to be put onto such working touch with it as to handle either it or something connected with it better than if we disagreed*" (emphasis added). And this, honestly speaking, is not very convincing.

24. We may see it in Quine (1951), an author so different from Heidegger, but influenced by the pragmatist tradition. Truth is not *adaequatio intellectus et rei*, but the insertion of the *datum*, the *given*—as such a flickering entity—in a context, that is, in the schema of physics as in the best conceptual scheme. This is not that different from Gadamer (1960), who claims roughly the same thing, apart from the fact that he takes the tradition instead of physics, and language instead of conceptual scheme.

25. The most important twentieth-century formulations of the theory of truth as *adaequatio* are those by Russell, Wittgenstein, and Moore, in which *adaequatio* is understood as correspondence to facts. More recently, philosophers like, on one hand, Kevin Mulligan, Barry Smith, and Peter Simons and on the other, David Armstrong have defended (if not a theory of truth as correspondence) the correspondentistic intuition for which there exist entities that make true things true: these entities are the *Truth-Makers* (Meinong's *Wahrmacher*). See Mulligan, Simons, Smith (1984). For a general overview of the ongoing debate and for a moderately skeptical position on the existence of *Truth-Makers*, see Caputo (2004). Also, to arouse the curiosity of erudite readers: "The factor of truth" is the title of Derrida's comment (1975) on Lacan's seminar on Poe's *The Purloined Letter*, where Derrida starts from the thesis that truth *is* correspondence (to be understood also

as the post, just as *facteur* in French means "postman") of the proposition to the thing. Yet, Derrida observes that correspondence does not always reach its destination—which (neither for Derrida nor for us) does not constitute an objection to the assumption that something like *adaequatio* represents an indispensable ingredient in order to speak of truth.

26. This is the thesis of the nontruth, subsequently used by Schiller, and hinted at by James too.

27. Plato (*Taethetus*, 161c).

28. See Nagel (1997, 69): "I believe the simplest rules of logic are unrevisable. . . . The aim of universal validity is compatible with the willingness always to consider alternatives and counterarguments—*but they must be considered as candidates for objectively valid alternatives and arguments.*" And: "We discover objective reason by discovering that we run up against certain limits when we inquire whether our beliefs, values, and so forth are subjective, culturally relative, or otherwise essentially perspectival. Certain forms of thoughts inevitably occur *straight* in the consideration of such hypotheses—revealing themselves to be objective in content. And if we envision the possibility of coming to regard them after all as subjective, it must mean that we imagine making them the focus of other thoughts whose validity is truly universal. . . . [T]he appeal to reason is implicitly authorized by the challenge itself . . . any considerations against the objective validity of a type of reasoning are inevitably attempts to offer reason against it, and these must be rationally assessed" (23–24).

29. See Husserl (1966, 98). For a development of those arguments, see De Palma (2004), from which I take the previous quotes from Husserl and Nagel, and whose considerations have been decisive for my reasoning.

30. See Frege (1977, 25): "In thinking we do not produce thoughts, we grasp them. For what I have called thoughts stand in the closest connection with truth. What I acknowledge as true, I judge to be true quite apart from my acknowledging its truth or even thinking about it. That someone thinks it has nothing to do with the truth of a thought."

31. The analogies with Gentile's *Theory of Mind as a Pure Act* (1916) are obvious.

4. CONSTRUCTING

1. A similar misunderstanding can be found in Stout (1910–11), who underlined that if truth depends on judgment (of a subject), then we have to do with idealism, and potentially subjectivism. Russell (1912) replied that, although judgments happen in the mind, their truth or falsity does not depend on the subject, but on a correspondence with the thing, in which the mind plays no role at all. I thank Guido Bonino for this indication.

2. Davies (2005). The distinction between *type* and *token* was proposed by the American philosopher Charles Sanders Peirce (1839–1914); see Peirce (1902, Book II, ch. 6, IV, § 537).

3. For a more detailed analysis from the historiographical point of view, see Ferraris (2003d).

4. For an excellent presentation of the performative, see Bianchi (2003, 55ff).

5. Ugo Foscolo, *Dei sepolcri*, vv. 91–93. Literal translation: "from the day when weddings, courts and altars/gave human beasts piety/for themselves and others."—Trans.

6. Here is a short list, just to give an idea: offices, titles, distinctions, institutions; borders, political and administrative entities (cities, regions, counties, states, quasi-states, empires), and other objects created in a *fiat* like land possessions; collective entities like political parties, religious orders, bands, mafia, football teams, battalions, processions; legal objects and other ones depending on legal decisions; status objects and collective ones like works of art and other kinds of artifacts that, apart from being physical objects, also possess characteristics that depend on the social sphere. A legion, as I have shown, even if it is an almost invisible one, but not a foreign legion: rather, a very domestic jungle, defining the obscure and tenacious thread of our existence.

7. Both the "practice theory" in Foucault (1969) and the "theory of communicative action" in Habermas (1981) rest on this rather problematic assumption.

8. On Reid, see Schulthess (1983) and Schumann-Smith (1990).

9. On Reid's realism, see Spinicci (2000).

10. See Austin (1962a) and Burckhardt (1990).

11. Wittgenstein (1953, 6): "Think of the tools in a tool-box: there is a hammer, pliers, a saw, a screw-driver, a ruler, a glue-pot, glue, nails and screw.—The functions of words are as diverse as the functions of these objects."

12. Swift (2011, 227): "Since words are only names for things, it would be more convenient for all men to carry about them such things as were necessary to express a particular business they are to discourse on. And this invention would certainly have taken place, to the great ease as well as health of the subject, if the women, in conjunction with the vulgar and illiterate, had not threatened to raise a rebellion unless they might be allowed the liberty to speak with their tongues, after the manner of their forefathers; such constant irreconcilable enemies to science are the common people. However, many of the most learned and wise adhere to the new scheme of expressing themselves by things; which has only this inconvenience attending it, that if a man's business be very great, and of various kinds, he must be obliged, in proportion, to carry a greater bundle of things upon his back, unless he can afford one or two strong servants to attend him."

13. Famous line from *The Bethroted* by Alessandro Manzoni.—Trans.

14. See Searle (1969; 1975).

15. Literal translation of line 42 of the poem *La Rassegna di Novara* by Costantino Nigra ("usi a obbedir tacendo").—Trans.

16. Also, Austin (1979) was essentially interested in the constitution of a conceptual geography as the linguistic analysis of common sense (whose tools consist of the dictionary, the law, and psychology), and did not care about the formalization of categories. The twofold circumstance of the reference to ordinary language and of the rhapsodic character of the analysis exposed this perspective to the obvious objection that ordinary language is full of confusion and incongruences, and that it does not constitute an indisputable authority (to which Austin replied that it was a starting point, not an end, although he explained neither what the end should be nor how it could be reached).

17. I will develop these arguments extensively in chapter 8.

18. See Reinach (1913), Schumann-Smith (1987), and Mulligan (1987).

19. The fact that acts are producers of objects, after all, merely gives shape to a common intuition: the promise outlasts the act of promising, it is distinguishable from it. Marriage lasts after the wedding and, to be canceled, it requires another act: divorce.

20. In Italian, the term *carta* means both paper and card, so the reoccurrence of the word is even more evident.—Trans.

21. Obviously I do not have to think of it continuously, it is enough for me to know it. I know that two days ago I promised someone something, but right now I am not thinking about it. Yet I know, a promise is a "dispositional" attitude and the possibility of remembering that I promised, if I am in the condition of doing so.

5. STRONG REALISM

1. In his short but dense presentation of the problem, Varzi (2005, 85–89) observes that the sphere of social ontology—notwithstanding Reinach's (1913), Znamierowski's (1924–30), and Dewey's (1925) proposals—constitutes a crucial but largely unexplored terrain, and acknowledges Searle's (1995) and Smith's (2003a and 2003b) merit for reviving a long forgotten debate. In my treatise, I start from the presupposition that problems of social ontology were tackled in the twentieth century also by the continental tradition (typically, by Heidegger, Foucault, and Derrida) and it is on this basis that I propose the realism/textualism and strong/weak typologies that will guide me in the testing of my theory.

2. Sacco (1993; 1989; 1990). See also Sacco (1989, 5:39–40; 1990; 1993, 689–702). The notion of a "cryptotype" corroborates the claim that law *preexists* linguistic expression: "The law does not need the word. The law pre-exists the articulated word. Even today, the law recognizes the dichotomies that are freighted with meaning, which are due to the continued actuality of instruments with which it

operated even before man had the word and did not yet use the word to create juridical facts" (Sacco 1990, 14).

3. For this reason, Reinach's theory should not be confused with natural law theories that, for instance, derive the notion of *state* from that of *contract*, without realizing that the notion of contract *presupposes* that of state. The mere fact of distinguishing juridical objects from physical, psychic, and ideal objects excludes the legitimization of natural law. There is nothing like a "natural law," because in the thing that we call "nature" there is no "right." Law is not to be found in nature any more than the *Mona Lisa* is to be found in colors.

4. Roman Ingarden (1893–1970), Reinach's student, extended this perspective to the analysis of literary works and art artifacts in general; see Ingarden (1931). For an approach that was recently updated, see Thomasson (1999).

5. See Ferrari (2003, 193–95). For the specifically juridical approach, see Kalinowski (1967).

6. This approach finds its greatest expression in Nicolai Hartmann (1882–1950); see Hartmann (1949), starting from a criticism of Husserl, accused of reducing reality to consciousness.

7. In this sense, Stanislaw Leniewski (1916), professor of philosophy and mathematics in Warsaw and one of Husserl's students, proposes a formalization of ontology "from below," that is, à la Aristotle, starting from the presupposition that the rules discovered through an analysis of this kind are no less necessary than those found by Kant when he was inferring categories from the system of pure judgments of the intellect.

8. The outcome of this hyperbole would be the statement by La Mettrie (1748–65): "To be a machine, to feel, to think, to know how to distinguish good from bad, as well as blue from yellow, in a word, to be born with an intelligence and a sure moral instinct, and to be but an animal, are therefore characters which are no more contradictory, than to be an ape or a parrot and to be able to give oneself pleasure."

9. See Gargani (1997), Bretone (1998), Lancieri (2003). For the centrality of the object in classical ontology, see Kobau (2004).

10. *Nomina sunt consequentia rerum.* Justinian, *Institutiones,* bk 2, 7, 3.—Trans.

11. A few examples: not to put your elbows on the table so as not to bother your neighbor; to eat only with the right hand in the Muslim world because the left one is considered impure; to use only nonsharp knives to avoid any physical threat.

12. See Lipmann (1923), Hayes (1979), Bozzi (1989; 1990), and Casati and Smith (1994).

13. See Smith (1997). At the origin of the approach underlying this perspective is the experience of Gestalt psychology between the end of the nineteenth and the beginning of the twentieth centuries; Gestalt psychology focused on the transcendence of complex structures with respect to their elementary components; see Ehrenfels (1890), Wertheimer (1923); and, for a theoretical elaboration, Smith (1988).

14. Hence the constant difficulties, from natural law theories onward, of a physicalist approach to legal problems; see Jasanoff (1995) and Moore (2002).

15. See Smith (1995). These are "familiar objects" (Ayer 1940, 2), a pompous definition, if one compares it, for instance, to things in Austin: "modest-sized specimen of dry goods" (Austin 1964, 8). This indication can be useful also to capture some characteristics of social objects, whose temporal existence is often commeasured to the bodily extension and the temporal length of an individual's life.

16. See Gibson (1979, 46). For ecology in psychology, see Barker (1968), Barker et al. (1978), and Schoggen (1989).

17. The relativism born out of the comparison between customs has been a traditional argument against moral institutions: The Greeks honored their dead, the Persians burnt them. Nevertheless, the way in which this reasoning imposed itself in antiquity and then in the eighteenth century with Montesquieu maintained a material root (the difference in customs is based on the difference in climates; see Montesquieu [1748]). In other words, relativism never merely rested upon the idea of pure convention. The passage to postmodern relativism is founded on a fallacy: the consideration that different customs and legislations have different formal manifestations; it concludes that there is also a substantial diversity, while it is easy to see that the same normative content is expressed in various ways. In France, what is not forbidden is allowed. In Germany, what is not allowed is forbidden. It seems like a huge difference, but the vast majority of permitted and forbidden things coincide in the legislation of the two countries.

18. This time in accordance with the project of "descriptive metaphysics" by Strawson (1959). On the debate between "revisionist" (or, better, "prescriptive") metaphysics and "descriptive" metaphysics see Haack (1979) and Varzi (2001; 2005).

19. I owe these two examples to Paolo Di Luca, whom I thank.

20. This duty is a *Sollen*, that is, a categorical imperative, not a material necessity.

6. STRONG TEXTUALISM

1. This position is the same as the one held by the very strong thought that chose to call itself "weak thought"; see Vattimo and Rovatti (1983).

2. Something similar, but with greater consequences, moving from psychic experiences to historical events, happened in 1991 during the first Gulf War. The evening of the first attack, philosopher Gianni Vattimo was on television, explaining that the war was not going to happen, as it was a postmodern conflict made with media and not weapons. Vattimo had just concluded his argument when, on the screen behind him, things went crazy: the attack had just started. Could this be the empirical confutation of a theory? For postmodern thinkers, it could not—just

like a radical skeptic will never be persuaded that he is burning (he could very well be *thinking* to be on fire). So much so that a few years later, after much reflection, French sociologist Jean Baudrillard (1995) published a book in which he *ascertained* and not *foresaw*, that the Gulf War *had never happened* and it was all media fiction, so the images on our screens and behind Vattimo's back were fake.

3. In fact, a great part of Heidegger's inquiry regards the determination of individual dispositions, be they existential conditions (boredom, angst) or attitudes toward objects (things and tools), and the sphere of social ontology is generally defined as "inauthentic." That is to say that authenticity lies in the subject, and objects are rather related to the realm of inauthenticity. So, at this point, the subject conquers being that "is given" (or denied) to man just like Zerlina gives herself to Don Juan (There we'll be hand in hand, dear, / There you will say, "yes," remember what I said about the hand in Heidegger). This is confirmed by the metaphor that man is the shepherd, the guardian, and the sentinel of being. So, in Da Ponte's words: "Oh, che caro galantuomo! / Vuol star dentro colla bella, / Ed io a far la sentinella!" ("Oh, what a gentleman! / He wants to stay inside with the beauty / And I, guarding like a sentinel!"). Thus sings Leporello (*Don Giovanni*, act 1, scene 1), and thus Heidegger (1929, 27): "the fact that existential being lies in nothing, founded on hidden angst, makes of man the sentinel (*Platzhalter*) of nothing."

4. See Rorty (1979) for his general theory, and Rorty (1991, 237–64) for his specifically political view.

5. Also, one should not think that our lives are a continuum of decisions in which ontology and epistemology, being and knowing take part. Critical issues emerge on a vast number of minor or minimal points that require no debate. The two extremes of those willing to discuss everything and those who would avoid debating even in bioethics, because the eternal being has already decided, are hyperbolic cases. The approach that deconstructs the false assumptions behind terms like *terrorism*, *democracy*, or *rule of law* seems entirely sensible and sharable, whereas someone willing to deconstruct *roast chicken* or *Mount Blanc* is wasting her time.

6. Derrida (1967a, 227–28): "There is nothing outside of the text [there is no outside-text; il n'y a pas de hors-texte]. . . . In what one calls the real life . . . there has never been anything but writing; there have never been anything but supplements, substitutive significations which could only come forth in a chain of differential references."

7. Searle (1995, 159): "Derrida, as far as I can tell, does not have an argument. He simply declares that there is nothing outside of texts. . . . And, in any case, in a subsequent polemical response to some objections of mine, he apparently takes it all back: he says that all he meant by the apparently spectacular declaration that there is nothing outside of texts is the banality everything exists in some context or other!"

7. WEAK REALISM

1. As Finnish philosopher Raimo Tuomela (1995, 202) did. As I will show, the first formulation of the notion of "collective intentionality" is his. For recent developments in social ontology see Gilbert (1989), Cohn (1997), Smith (199), and Koepsell and Moss (2003).

2. Of course, this function is a convention within the larger convention of chess.

3. As I mentioned earlier, the term was coined, before Searle, by Raimo Tuomela. For an overview and a discussion of the debate, see Carli (2004).

4. This description was suggested to me by Lorenzo Baravalle, whom I thank.

5. The very same scene can be found in Daniel Dennett (1989, 22): "An electrician once explained to me how he worked out how to protect my underground water pump from lightning damage: lightning, he said, always wants to find the best way to ground, but sometimes it gets tricked into taking second-best paths. You can protect the pump by making another, better path more obvious to the lightning."

6. You do not believe me? Then tell me what on earth is going on here (and I am not talking about a Martian game, but about a simple American football game, namely Searle's favorite case): After the first fifteen minutes the match seemed to be clearly in the Chargers' hands, who were leasing 24-0. Rolf Benirschke had scored a thirty-two-yard *field goal*, Wes Chandler had returned a *punt* directly in *touchdown* for fifty-six yards, Chuck Muncie's run for a yard and Dan Fouts's eight-yard *end zone* passage to James Brooks had built an apparently unreachable advantage for San Diego. Then, the Dolphins' reserve *quarterback*, Don Strock, was called to replace David Woodley and unexpectedly scored seventeen points. (The emphasis is on technical/conventional terms.)

7. See Durkheim: "*The totality of beliefs and sentiments common to the average citizens of the same society* forms a determinate system which has its own life; one may call it the *collective or common conscience*. No doubt, it has not a specific organ as a substratum; it is, by definition, diffuse in every reach of society. Nevertheless, it has specific characteristics which make it a *distinct reality*. . . . It is thus *an entirely different thing from particular consciences*, although it can be realised only through them. it is the physical type of society, a type which has its properties, its conditions of existence, its mode of development, just as individual types, although in a different way. . . . *Juridical, governmental, scientific, industrial*, in short, all special functions are of a psychic nature since they consist in systems of representations and actions. They, however, *are surely outside the common conscience*" ([1893] 1933, 80–81; emphasis added).

8. See Gallese (2003), Fogassi et al. (2005), and Nakahara and Miyashita (2005).

9. See Kant's confutation of Leibniz's teleology: "Snow in cold countries protects the crops from the frost; it makes human intercourse easier (by means of

sleighs). The Laplander finds in his country animals by whose aid this intercourse is brought about, that is, reindeer, who find sufficient sustenance in a dry moss which they have to scratch out for themselves from under the snow, and who are easily tamed and readily permit themselves to be deprived of that freedom in which they could have remained if they chose. For other people in the same frozen regions marine animals afford rich stores; in addition to the food and clothing which are thus supplied, and the wood which is floated in by the sea to their dwellings, these marine animals provide material for fuel by which their huts are warmed. Here is a wonderful concurrence of many references of nature to one purpose; and all this applies to the cases of the Greenlander, the Lapp, the Samoyede, the inhabitant of Yakutsk, etc. But then *we do not see why, generally, men must live there at all.* Therefore to say that vapour falls out of the atmosphere in the form of snow, that the sea has its currents which float down wood that has grown in warmer lands, and that there are in it great sea monsters filled with oil, because the idea of advantage for certain poor creatures is fundamental for the cause which collects all these natural products, would be a very venturesome and arbitrary judgement" (1790, § 63, trans. J. H. Bernard; emphasis added). Only if there effectively was a providential order of the physical world, then intentionality could grant the passage from atoms to honorific titles, from the physical to the social. But it would be like claiming (to refer to Voltaire's ironic remark) that lice were created to induce us to cleanliness.

10. I thank Cristina Becchio, to whom I owe the exposition of Bratman's argument.

11. *The Economist*, May 6, 2004, on the film *The Corporation*: "Like all psychopaths, the firm is singularly self-interested: . . . And, like all psychopaths, the firm is irresponsible. . . . It is grandiose, always insisting that it is the best, or number one. It has no empathy, refuses to accept responsibility for its actions and feels no remorse." I owe this indication to Roberto Casati.

12. This argument was developed by Giulia Alberti, Davide Biasoni, and Gemma Lupi in 2004–5 in the master's program in Philosophy in Turin.

13. I owe this indication to Maria Grazia Turri.

14. C. Menger: "The origin of money can be fully explained only if we know how to see in the social institution its unreflective product, the involuntary result of the specifically individual activity of the members of a collectivity" (1985, 155).

15. In this context, it may be helpful to note a pretty clear proof of the unintentional nature of money on the basis of my Italian readers' experiences. About a decade ago, many national currencies were replaced by the euro, and clearly this process was fully and strongly intentional, given that it was preceded by popular referenda, parliamentary votes, and institutional acts of various sorts. Now, what is the psychological result of this noteworthy intentional ingredient? The fact is that those who had been brought up with their national currency initially viewed

the euro as an abstract currency, which they tended to convert in the old currency, with unfortunate economic consequences. It will be different for children who have been brought up with the euro: for them, who have not seen it as the result of intentional deliberation, it will be a fully concrete currency.

16. The yellow line *must not* be crossed, unlike those walls that *cannot* be crossed. Which is another problem that Searle does not focus on sufficiently.

17. "In an earlier version of this argument, I used the ethnologists' example of groups of animals marking limits to their territory. In such a case, as in the example of the primitive tribe, the barrier is not a sheer physical obstacle like a wall or a moat but is, in some sense, symbolic. But I am not certain that the ethnologists are justified in attributing so much collective intentionality to the animals, so I have substituted the tribal example to make the same point" (Searle 1995, 40n). Therefore, according to Searle, it is not excluded that animals mark their territory by mere chance, or only to satisfy physiological needs—so it could be out of a physiological need that the chimpanzee returns the stick to its rightful owner. Searle concludes, "when we discuss the role of language in the next chapter we will see that the distinction between the linguistic and the prelinguistic is important. Fine, but to what extent? It is, in fact, implausible that the chimpanzee would say to itself 'I must return the stick to its rightful owner', but this does not at all lead to considering his action as a simple reflected act—leaving aside the possible objection that, if we have no proof of animals' intentionality, then we should wonder if men are at all intentional either or whether it just *seems* to us that there is such a thing as intentionality" (ibid.).

18. I do not know when I started thinking that, had I cut off my teddy bear's label, something terrible would have happened to me. Probably, the mere fact of not cutting it from the start created something that, through iteration, led to a taboo. Note the fundamental difference with respect to the wall example. It is not that the object physically resists and, afterward, generates a prohibition. A taboo similar to the teddy bear's could have been produced by a yellow line: it is enough that, say, someone decides that crossing a random yellow line would cause his death.

19. For instance, city borders. A city can contain a *bona fide* border (like a river) without ceasing to be *one* city, even if it is made up of three different cities like Budapest—which was born in the second half of the nineteenth century from the unification of Buda, Pest, and Obuda, regardless of the great border imposed by the Danube (which in fact for a long time divided Buda and Obuda from Pest).

20. I wish to underline, as regards the act-inscription-object tripartition, that the trace perfectly plays the role of content, in that it is the animal's *signature*. I will return to this in the next chapter, discussing weak textualism.

21. At the base of Searle's alchemy there is a linguistic and conceptual problem. Searle talks indifferently of "money," but he seems to confuse two things, given that he seems to be thinking of currency when he speaks of money as the physical

X. But money and currency are not the same. Shillings are money, but not currency. Currency is concrete, money is an abstract buying power that, if need be, I can replace with a pistol to get the people in the bank to give me some cash. In such a case, it would be bizarre to say that X (the pistol) counts as Y (money) in the context C (the bank); and it would be stranger still to say that the pistol counts as *currency*. We can thus see that in the case of *money*, X counts as Y does not hold; in the case of *currency*, X counts as Y holds only because we assume that X is already currency and Y is money.

22. For instance, what is the exact atom where the Matterhorn ends and the Po Valley starts? This linguistic and ontological problem of vagueness, already tackled by Rousseau (1923), has been recently reconsidered by van Inwagen (1983, 1988), Tye (1990), Williamson (1994, 1998), Horgan (1995), Keefe (2000), Varzi (2001b), and Hill (2001).

23. On the conceptual problems with events, see Casati and Varzi (1996).

24. For instance, when exactly did the battle of Waterloo begin? On June 18, 1815, when Napoleon was preparing his assault on Brussels, or on June 17, when Grouchy tried to communicate with Blücher while Ney was looking for Wellington? Or on June 16, when Grouchy actually defeated the Prussians, but made the mistake of not chasing them? Or when Napoleon invaded southern Belgium? Or when he returned from Elba (in this last case the battle would have had its beginning in Borodino, so that Pierre Bezuchov and Fabrizio del Dongo would have witnessed the same battle without understanding much of it)?

25. It is in Smith's interpretation that representation is highlighted. As I have shown, in fact, Smith recognizes the role of recording, but regards it as purely preparatory to representation, and therefore as marginal or accidental.

8. WEAK TEXTUALISM

1. To claim (with Searle) that the sounds emitted from people's mouth are not physical is to deny ultimately that acoustics constitutes a branch of physics. By contrast, to suppose (with Smith) that the representations in people's minds do not need a physical X causally related to the social Y means professing a dualism between the *res extensa* and the *res cogitans* that not even Descartes would have supported, given that the Cartesian view posits a pineal gland uniting matter and soul. In my hypothesis, the gland becomes the *tabula* and the molecules (ink, paper, silicon, neurons, enzymes) necessary for an inscription. This little amount of matter needed for the construction of a social object is, before and after Descartes, the "subtle body" or the "spiritual flesh" (see Griffero 1999; 2001; 2004). The reference is not casual: in §§ 1–5 of his *Logical Investigations*, Husserl insists on the function of *Dokumentierung* offered by language, seeing in it a form of "spiritual flesh."

2. Searle (1995, 119–20), in a way, takes writing and even signatures into account: "In complex societies common status indicators are passports and driver's licenses. They indicate the status of the bearer as someone who is legally entitled to travel to and from foreign countries or is legally qualified to drive. The most common device for status indication is the written signature. Signing a document may create a new institutional fact, but the continued existence of the written signature indicates, other things being equal, the continued existence of the fact. The signature on the document persists in a way that the live performative does not and thus is able to play its role as a status indicator." But his anti-Derridean ardor (or, more positively, his loyalty to the tradition of speech acts) did not allow him to realize the implications of such a circumstance.

3. The Arab caliph used to pay his tribute to Byzantine emperor Justinian II in *nomismata*, the Byzantine coins. In 692 the emperor started to coin nomismata with a portrait of Christ on them; the caliph paid the due amount of gold with coins without the portrait of Christ and this was a sufficient reason for Justinian to declare war on the caliph (Treadgold 2001, 135). By this I do not mean to say that matter is irrelevant. A fifty euro banknote has a certain form, color, filigree, and matter; if it were different (triangular, made of cork), the inscription "50 Euro" would not suffice to make it legal. In the same way, we cannot obtain fifty euro, from a "37 Euro" or a "13 Euro" note given that such notes do not exist (whereas the number 50 can be in fact obtained and stays the same whether you add up 13 and 37, 49 and 1, 25 and 25, no matter the support of my calculations). As for idiomatic form, one may observe that checks coming from different banks have different colors and shapes. But what makes a check idiomatic, and therefore valid, is the signature of the owner of the bank account. Again, a signature is made of few molecules, arranged in a specific way (a signature is not simply a name), and it is meant to guarantee the presence of the owner of the check when it was written.

4. De Soto (2010, 237): "The French philosopher Jacques Derrida recalls in *De la Grammatologie* how Jean Jacques Rousseau argued that writing was an important cause of human inequality."

5. As for De Soto, I am leaving aside his problematic interpretative hypothesis of the capital, which overshadows the role of work with the role of distribution (which is like sending Marx away and calling Adam Smith back). I also neglect the fact that the economic therapy proposed by De Soto for the Third World requires much longer than is desirable.

6. Perhaps, my formula object = inscribed act could be defined in a more similar way to Searle's (following Laura Borlengo's suggestion): X counts as Y in T where X = idiomatic inscription, Y = social object, and T = text. Note that by stating X = idiomatic inscription I am outlining a class of objects that are a subset of Searle's X (X = physical object), but I avoid all the difficulties that Searle encountered.

7. See my considerations in chapter 6, in the section "The Moral of the Story."

8. For a more detailed version of my theory of the trace (ichnology) I refer the reader to my *Documentality. Why It Is necessary to Leave Traces* (2012).

9. See Wittgenstein (1980, § 185): "When I see the milkman coming, I fetch my jug and go to meet him. Do I experience an intending? Not that I know of. (Any more than I try to walk, in order to walk.) But if I stopped and asked, 'Where are you going with that jug?' I should express my intention."

10. As Derrida (1967b, 57–61) noted, in his first "Logical Investigation" Husserl distinguishes between indication and animated expression, the first being signs only if there are expressions; but expressions are still a subset of signs.

11. In this sense, I wish to recall a thought experiment elaborated by Robert Nozick and reworked by Daniel Dennett (1987, 398–99). Imagine very intelligent aliens that need not explain social activity through intentional attitude but simply resort to a microphysical analysis. Dennett's idea is that, as clever as the aliens may be, their attitude would be only externally conform to social reality, but they would truly be doing something else. Aliens would therefore not possess an originary intentionality but, in the best-case scenario, a derived intentionality (which is tantamount to saying that we give them instructions that they represent as intentions, or that we read their reading in an intentional sense when it is far from it). It could be so. Yet, I still wonder how we know that we possess an originary intentionality.

12. This is like asking, "Have they recorded?" Otherwise words would be wasted and utterly pointless—which is also the way in which Plato, in his *Theaetetus* (191c–d), qualifies the insufficiencies of a *tabula rasa* without the right consistency (too soft, so that it cannot hold the recording, or too hard, so that it cannot be inscribed). For an excellent analysis of testimony, see Vassallo (2003, 24–32).

13. Take, for instance, the following speech by Franklin D. Roosevelt at the Congress of the United States: "On the morning of December 11, the Government of Germany, pursuing its course of world conquest, declared war against the United States. The long-known and the long-expected has thus taken place. The forces endeavoring to enslave the entire world now are moving toward this hemisphere. Never before has there been a greater challenge to life, liberty, and civilization. Delay invites greater danger. Rapid and united effort by all of the peoples of the world who are determined to remain free will ensure a world victory of the forces of justice and of righteousness over the forces of savagery and of barbarism. Italy also has declared war against the United States. I therefore request the Congress to recognize a state of war between the United States and Germany, and between the United States and Italy." It is a performative, and yet it respects none of Austin's conditions. Literally, one could think that it is not a war declaration, since it could be argued that Roosevelt is simply informing Congress (they declared war against us), deploring the attackers, praising the attacked and the advantages of a possible reaction; and that he is asking for a war declaration. In reality, it is not so:

by addressing Congress for the authorization of a war declaration he is, in fact, declaring war. Not on the present Congress, but on Hitler (who is absent).

14. Again, one might object that the signature presupposes an agreement, and therefore an intention. I agree, but it must be admitted that, as I mentioned earlier, intentions are hard to verify and that a straitjacket contract is valid for what is written on it, and submits to all the clauses written in tiny character on the back. If it depended on the intentions of the poor guy who signed it, it would cease to exist or have never existed.

15. Which significantly shrunk in time: the Fabbrica Italiana Automobili Torino was just like the Sacred Roman Empire that, according to Voltaire, was no longer sacred, nor Roman, nor an empire.

16. This case was presented by Davide Fassio, master's student.

17. See Hobbes (1655, II, ch. 11, § 7). For recent discussions see Chisholm (1976, 89–113), Simons (1987, 199–204), Wiggins (2001, 76–106), and Varzi (2003). See also Carrara and Giaretta (2004).

18. See Evans (1985). It is an argument against Kripke's theory, which—in the more codified area of monetization—I will refer to later.

19. This also works with Enron. Among the comments on the company's bankruptcy, a financial newspaper had a top ten list of the things you could do with an Enron share, the first one being "use it for sanitary disposal and other bathroom activities."

20. I refer to the analysis by Maria Teresa Busca, master's student.

21. Imagine Mussolini proclaiming Italy's entry into the war, on June 10, 1940, with a Turinese accent, or Badoglio announcing the armistice on September 8, 1943, in Roman dialect: would they have been credible? These are matters of detail, but it is worth to keep them in mind.

22. These characters are present in performances that can, under specific circumstances, replace signatures, such as handshakes. When two statesmen come to an agreement, even verbally, they probably shake hands; then they repeat the gesture in front of TV reporters, and these public replicas are all authentic (it is *them* shaking hands)—even though the first public handshake was repeating the private one (which is not necessary, the public one is the one that matters) and the subsequent ones were only to the benefit of television.

23. With a little adventurous extension, it can simply indicate a modus operandi. It is often said that "the thief left his signature"—which is obviously neither a signed card (unless the thief is Arsène Lupin) nor fingerprints—that is, a certain style that reoccurs, even in different circumstances (robbery, housebreaking, and so on)

24. I developed a more detailed analysis of this point in Ferraris (2003b), although starting from different theoretical presuppositions.

25. Kant (1785, n86): "The author and the owner of the copy may both say of it with equal right: it is my book! but in a different sense. The first takes the book as a

writing or a speech; the second as the mute instrument merely of the delivering of the speech to him or to the public, i.e. as a copy. This right of the author's, however, is no right in the thing, namely, the copy (for the owner may burn it before the author's face), but an innate right in his own person, namely, to hinder another from reading it to the public without his consent, which consent can by no means be presumed, because he has already given it exclusively to another." In the case of photography, author's rights have curious consequences: if I wish to reproduce an image of myself, I have to ask for the photographer's permission.

26. The sentence "That branch of the lake of Como" is Manzoni's; but Manzoni is certainly not the author of the story of two lovers who are hounded by a country gentleman (in fact, it may well be a Walter Scott story). What matters is the idiom, his peculiar style, which is protected in all the languages into which a book can be translated, independently from the chosen medium: book (printed in whatever fonts and shapes), radio, CD, and, of course, also cinema and television (where what is conveyed is hopefully not just the story, but also the characters' temper, the form of the dialogue and so on: a TV version of the *Bethroted* in which Lucia were a gigantic woman, Renzo a dwarf, and Padre Cristoforo a drunk with green hair, would be just a parody).

REFERENCES

Augustine. n.d. *Confessions*. Translated by Edward Bouverie Pusey. http://www
.sacred-texts.com/chr/augconf/augo1.htm.

Ajani, Gianmaria. 2003. "A proposito del trapianto di nozioni vaghe." In *Io com-
paro, tu compare, egli compara: che cosa, come, perché?*, edited by Bertorello
Valentina, 3–19. Milano: Giuffrè.

Andina, Tiziana, and Carola Barbero, eds. 2003. "Storie dell'ontologia." *Rivista di
estetica* n.s. 22.

Aristotle. 1984. *The Complete Works of Aristotle*. Vols. 1 and 2. Edited by J. Barnes.
Princeton, NJ: Princeton University Press.

Armstrong, David Malet. 1997. *A World of States of Affairs*. Cambridge: Cambridge
University Press.

Augé, Marc. 1992. *Non-Lieux*. Paris: Seuil.

Austin, John L. 1962a. *How to Do Things with Words*. Oxford: Oxford University
Press.

———. 1962b. *Sense and Sensibilia*. Edited by Geoffrey J. Warnock. Oxford: Oxford
University Press.

———. 1979. "A Plea for Excuses." In Austin, John L. *Philosophical Papers*, 175–204.
Oxford: Oxford University Press.

Ayer, Alfred. J. 1940. *The Foundations of Empirical Knowledge*. London:
McMillan.

Barbero, Carola. 2003. "Chi è Madame Bovary?" *Rivista di estetica* n.s. 24: 18–23.

———. 2005. *Madame Bovary: Something Like a Melody*. Milano: Albo Versorio.

Barker, Roger G. 1968. *Ecological Psychology. Concepts and Methods for Studying
the Environment of Human Behavior*. Stanford, CA: Stanford University
Press.

Barker, Roger G. et al. 1978. *Habitats, Environments, and Human Behaviour. Studies in Ecological Psychology and Eco-Behavioural Science from the Midwest Psychological Field Station, 1947–1972*. San Francisco: Jossey-Bass Publishers.

Baron, Naomi S. 1998a. "Letters by Phone and Speech by Other Means: The Linguistics of E-mail." *Language and Communication* 18: 133–70.

———. 1998b. "E-mail as Contact Language: The Evolution of a Modality." *International Conference on Speech, Writing and Context: Literacy and Linguistic Perspectives*. Nottingham: Nottingham University, 16–19 July.

Baudrillard, Jean. 1995. *Le crime parfait*. Paris: Galilée.

Bert, M. 2005. "Adaptive Ethnography: Methodology for the Study of Mobile Learning in Youth Culture." In Nyíri 2005a.

Bianchi, Claudia. 2003. *Pragmatica del linguaggio*. Roma-Bari: Laterza.

Borges, Jorge L. 1941. The Library of Babel. Translated by James I. Irby. http://jubal .westnet.com/hyperdiscordia/library_of_babel.html.

Borghini, Andrea, and Achille C. Varzi. 2005. "Event Location and Vagueness." *Philosophical Studies* 128, no. 2: 313–36.

Bottani, Andrea, and Claudia Bianchi, eds. 2003. *Significato e ontologia*. Milano: Franco Angeli.

Bozzi, Paolo. 1989. *Fenomenologia sperimentale*. Bologna: Il Mulino.

———. *Fisica ingenua*. Milano: Garzanti.

Bratman, Michael E. 1992. "Shared cooperative activity." *The Philosophical Review* 101: 327–41.

Brentano, Franz. 1907. *Untersuchungen zur Sinnespsychologie*. Leipzig: Duncker & Humbolt.

———. 1995. *Psychology from an Empirical Standpoint*. London: Routledge.

Bretone, Mario. 1998. *I fondamenti del diritto romano. Le cose e la natura*. Roma-Bari: Laterza.

Brook, Andrew. 2005. "My BlackBerry and Me: Forever One or Just Friends." In Nyíri 2005a, 305–12.

Burkhardt, Armin, ed. 1990. *Speech Acts, Meanings and Intentions*. Berlin and New York: de Gruyter.

Caputo, Stefano. 2004. *Fattori di Verità*. PhD diss., Università del Piemonte Orientale.

Carli, Eddy. 2004. "Intenzioni e intenzionalità collettiva." *Isonomia. Rivista dell'Istituto di Filosofia, Università degli Studi di Urbino "Carlo Bo,"* 1–17. http:// www.uniurb.it/Filosofia/isonomia/2003carli.htm.

Carrara, Massimiliano, and Pierdaniele Giaretta, eds. 2004. "Ontologie analitiche." *Rivista di estetica* n.s. 26.

Casati, Roberto. 2000. *La scoperta dell'ombra*. Milano: Mondadori.

Casati, Roberto, and Barry Smith. 1994. "Naive Physics: An Essay in Ontology." *Philosophical Psychology* 7: 225–44.

Casati, Roberto, and Achille C. Varzi. 1994. *Holes and Other Superficialities*. Cambridge, MA: MIT Press.

———, eds. 1996. *Events*. Dartmouth: Aldershot.

Casati, Roberto, Maurizio Ferraris, and Achille C. Varzi. 2003. "Il paradigma dell'oggetto." *Il Sole 24 Ore*, March 9.

Chisholm, Roderick. 1976. *Person and Object. A Metaphysical Study*. London: Allen & Unwin.

Clark, Andy. 2003. *Natural Born Cyborgs*. Oxford: Oxford University Press.

Clark, Andy, and David Chalmers. 1998. "The Extended Mind." *Analysis* 58: 10–23.

Cohen, Akiba A., and Dafna Lemish. 2005. "When the Bombs Go Off the Mobiles Ring. The Aftermath of Terrorist Attacks." In Nyíri 2005b, 117–28.

Collin, Finn. 1997. *Social Reality*. London: Routledge.

Cooper, John M., ed. 1997. *Plato: Complete Works*. Indianapolis, IN: Hackett.

Costa, Vincenzo. 1996. *La generazione della forma. La fenomenologia e il problema della genesi in Husserl e in Derrida*. Milano: Jaca Book.

Croce, Benedetto. [1902] 1958. *Estetica come scienza dell'espressione e linguistica generale*. Roma-Bari: Laterza.

Davidson, Donald. 1973. "Radical Interpretation." *Dialectica* 27: 313–28.

Davies, Richard. 2005. "Tipi e gettoni: i limiti del nominalismo e gli oggetti della proprietà intellettuale." In *L'ontologia della proprietà intellettuale: aspetti e problemi*, edited by Andrea Bottani and Richard Davies, 70–102. Milano: Franco Angeli.

Debray, Régis. 1993. *L'Etat séducteur: les révolutions médiologiques du pouvoir*. Paris: Gallimard.

Del Corno, Franco, and Gianluigi Mansi. 2002. *SMS. Straordinaria fortuna di un uso improprio del telefonino*. Milano: Raffaello Cortina Editore.

Dennett, Daniel. C. 1989. *The Intentional Stance*. Montgomery: Bradford Books.

De Palma, Vittorio. 2004. "Il *cogito* e l'evidenza. La critica di Husserl a Descartes." *La Cultura. Rivista di filosofia, letteratura e storia* XLII: 447–68.

Derrida, Jacques. 1962. *L'origine de la géométrie*. Paris: Puf.

———. 1967b. *La voix et le phénomène*. Paris: Puf.

———. 1968a. "La pharmacie de Platon." In Derrida 1972.

———. 1968b. "Ousia et Grammé. Note sur une note de Sein und Zeit." In Derrida 1972.

———. 1970. "Le puits et la pyramide. Introduction à la sémiologie de Hegel." In Derrida 1972.

———. 1971. "Signature, événement, contexte." In Derrida 1972.

———. 1972. *Marges de la philosophie*, Paris: ed. de Minuit.

———. 1975. "Le facteur de la vérité." In Derrida 1980.

———. 1980a. "Envois." In Derrida 1980b, 11–273.

———. 1980b. *La carte postale. De Socrate à Freud et au-delà*. Paris: Flammarion.

———. 1985. *La main de Heidegger*. In Derrida 1987, 415–51.

———. 1987. *Psyché*. Paris: Galilée.

———. 1988. *Limited Inc*. Evanston, IL: Northwestern University Press.

———. 1998. *Of Grammatology.* Baltimore, MD: Johns Hopkins University Press.

Descartes, René. 1641. *Meditationes de prima philosophia.* http://www.wright.edu /~charles.taylor/descartes/medl.html.

De Soto, Hernando. 2001. "The Mystery of Capital." *Finance & Development* 38, no. 1.

Dewey, John. 1925. *Experience and Nature.* Chicago: Open Court.

Dilthey, Wilhelm. 1905. "Studien zur Grundlegung der Geisteswissenschaften." In *Gesammelte Schriften.* Vol. 7, 3–75. Teubner: Leipzig-Berlin.

———. 1907. "Das Wesen der Philosophie." In *Gesammelte Schriften.* Vol. 5, 339–416. Teubner: Leipzig-Berlin.

———. 1910. "Der Aufbau der geschichtlichen Welt in den Geisteswissenschaften." In *Gesammelte Schriften.* Vol. 7, 79–188. Teubner: Leipzig-Berlin.

Di Lucia, Paolo, ed. 2003. *Ontologia Sociale. Potere deontico e regole costitutive.* Macerata: Quodlibet.

Donner, Jonathan C. 2003. "What Mobile Phones Mean to Rwandan Entrepreneurs." In Nyíri 2003c, 393–410.

———. "What Can Be Said with a Missed Call? Beeping via Mobile Phones in Sub-Saharian Africa." In Nyíri 2005a, 267–76.

Döring, Nicola et al. 2005. "Contents, Forms and Functions of Interpersonal Pictorial Messages in Online and Mobile Communication." In Nyíri 2005a, 169–75.

Dummett, Michael. 1993. *Origins of Analytical Philosophy.* London: Durckworth.

Durkheim, Émile. [1893] 1933. *The Division of Labour in Society.* Translated by George Simpson. Glencoe, IL: Free Press.

Ehrenfels, Christian Von. 1890. "Über 'Gestaltqualitäten.'" In *Vierteljahrsschrift für wissenschaftliche Philosophie* 14: 242–92.

Evans, Gareth. 1985. "The Causal Theory of Names." In *The Philosophy of Language,* edited by Aloysius P. Martinich, 271–83. Oxford: Oxford University Press.

Ferrari, Massimo. 2003. *Categorie e apriori.* Bologna: Il Mulino.

Ferraris, Maurizio. 1988. *Storia dell'ermeneutica.* Milano: Bompiani.

———. 1995a. *Mimica. Lutto e autobiografia da Agostino a Heidegger.* Milano: Bompiani.

———. 1995b. "Kant e l'esemplarità dell'esempio." In *Filosofia 94,* edited by Vattimo, Gianni, 147–72. Roma-Bari: Laterza.

———. 1997. *Estetica razionale.* Milano: Raffaello Cortina Editore.

———. 1998. *L'ermeneutica.* Roma-Bari: Laterza.

———. 1999. "Perì mail." *aut aut* 289–290: 115–19.

———. 2001. *Il mondo esterno.* Milano: Bompiani.

———. 2002. "Inemendabilità, ontologia, realtà sociale." *Rivista di estetica* n.s. 19: 160–99.

———. 2003a. *Introduzione a Derrida.* Roma-Bari: Laterza.

————. 2003b. "Problemi di ontologia applicata: la proprietà delle idee." In Bottani, Andrea and Claudia Bianchi 2003, 104–15.

————. 2003c. *Ontologia*. Napoli: Guida.

————. 2003d. "Oggetti sociali." *Sistemi intelligenti* XV, no. 3: 441–66.

————. 2004a. "Necessità material." *Isonomia. Rivista dell'Istituto di Filosofia, Università degli Studi di Urbino "Carlo Bo,"* 1–30. http://www.uniurb.it/Filosofia /isonomia/Ferraris.htm.

————. 2004b. *Goodbye Kant! Cosa resta oggi della Critica della ragion pura.* Milano: Bompiani.

————. 2004c. "L'opera d'arte come fidanzata automatica." *Rivista di estetica*, n.s. 26: 153–70.

————. 2004d. "Matrix e la mozione degli affetti." In *Dentro la matrice. Filosofia, scienza e spiritualità in Matrix*, edited by Massimiliano Cappuccio, 55–72. Milano: Albo Versorio.

————. 2012. *Documentality: Why It Is Necessary to Leave Traces.* New York: Fordham University Press.

Ferraris, Maurizio, and Achille C. Varzi. 2003. "Che cosa c'è e che cos'è. Un dialogo." In *Nous. Postille su pensieri*, 81–101. Lecce: Milella.

Floridi, Luciano. 2003. "On the Intrinsic Value of Information Objects and the Infosphere." *Ethics and Information Technology* 4: 287–304.

Fodor, Jerry. 1983. *The Modularity of Mind.* Cambridge, MA: MIT Press.

Fogassi, Leonardo et al. 2005. "Parietal Lobe: From Action Organization to Intention Understanding." *Science* 308: 662–67.

Foucault, Michel. 1961. *Histoire de la folie à l'âge classique.* Paris: Plon.

————. 1966. *Les Mots et les choses.* Paris: Gallimard.

————. 1969. *L'Archéologie du savoir.* Paris: Gallimard.

Frege, Gottlob. 1879. *Begriffschrift. Eine der arithmetischen nachgebildete Formelsprache des reines Denkens.* Halle: Nebert.

————. 1884. *Die Grundlagen der Arithmetik. Eine logisch-mathematische Untersuchung über den Begriff der Zahl.* Breslaw: Köbner.

————. 1892. "Über Sinn und Bedeutung." *Zeitschrift für Philosphie und philosphische Kritik* 100: 25–50.

————. 1918–19. "Der Gedanke. Eine Logische Untersuchung." *Beiträge zur Philosophie des deutschen Idealismus* I: 58–77.

————. 1977. *Logical Investigations.* New Haven, CT: Yale University Press.

Freud, Sigmund. 1895. "Entwurf einer Psychologie." In Freud, Sigmund. 1950. *Aus den Anfängen der Psychoanalyse.* London: Imago Publishing Co.

Freud, Sigmund. 1924. "Notiz über den 'Wunderblock.'" *Internationale Zeitschrift der Psychoanalyse* 11: 1–5.

Gadamer, Hans-Georg. 1960. *Wahrheit und Methode.* Tübingen: Mohr.

Gadda, Carlo E. 1969. *Acquainted with Grief. A Novel*. New York: George Braziller Inc.

Gallese, Vittorio. 2003. "La molteplice natura delle relazioni interpersonali: la ricerca di un comune meccanismo neurofisiologico." *Networks* 1: 24–47.

Gargani, Alberto. 1997. *Dal corpus delicti al Tatbestand*. Milano: Giuffrè.

Gehlen, Arnold. 1957. *Die Seele im technischen Zeitalter: sozialpsychologische Probleme in der industriellen Gesellschaft*. Hamburg: Rowohlt.

Gelb, Ignace. J. 1952. *A Study of Writing, the Foundations of Grammatology*. London: Routledge & K. Paul.

Gibson, James. J. 1979. *The Ecological Approach to Visual Perception*. Boston, MA: Houghton Mifflin.

Gilbert, Margaret. 1989. *On Social Facts*. New York: Routledge.

———. 1993. "Group Membership and Political Obligation." *The Monist* 76: 119–31.

Goodman, Nelson. 1951. *The Structure of Appearance*. Cambridge, MA: Harvard University Press.

Graf, Roland. 2005. "Traces, Places and Self-Evidence. Aspects of 'Space' on Cellular Phones." In Nyíri 2005a, 97–102.

Griffero, Tonino. 1999. "I sensi di Adamo. Appunti estetico-teosofici sulla corporeità spiritual." *Rivista di estetica* n. s. 12: 119–225.

———. 2001. "Corpi spirituali." In *L'altra estetica*, edited by Maurizio Ferraris and Pietro Kobau, 147–205. Torino: Einaudi.

———. 2004. "Uguale eppure diverso. Il 'corpo spirituale': problemi ontologici e identitari." *Rivista di estetica* n.s. 27: 49–115.

Haack, Susack. 1979. "Descriptive and Revisionary Metaphysics." *Philosophical Studies* 35: 361–71.

Habermas, Jürgen. 1981. *Theorie des kommunikativen Handelns*. Frankfurt/M.: Suhrkamp.

Hacking, Ian. 1999. *The Social Construction of What?* Cambridge, MA: Harvard University Press.

———. 2002. *Historical Ontology*. Cambridge, MA: Harvard University Press.

Hartmann, Nicolai. 1949. "Alte und neue Ontologie." In *Kleiner Schriften, Band III: Vom Neukantianismus zur Ontologie*, 333–37. Berlin: De Gruyter, 1958.

Havelock, Eric A. 1986. *The Muse Learns to Write: Reflections on Orality and Literacy from Antiquity to the Present*. New Haven, CT: Yale University Press.

Hayes, Pat. J. 1979. "The Naive Physics Manifesto." In *Expert Systems in the Micro-Electronic Age*, edited by Donald Michie, 242–70. Edinburgh: Edinburgh University Press.

Hegel, Georg W. F. 1998. *Phenomenology of Spirit*. New Dehli: Motilal Banarsidass Publisher.

———. 1971 [1830]. *Hegel's Philosophy of Mind: Being Part Three of the "Encyclopaedia of the Philosophical Sciences."* Oxford: Clarendon Press.

———. 1998. *Hegel's Aesthetics: Lectures on Fine Art*. Vol. 1. Oxford: Oxford University Press.

Heidegger, Martin. 1919. "Brief an Elisabeth Husserl." *Aut aut* 222–23: 6–14.

———. 1927. *Sein und Zeit*. Gesamtausgabe. Vol. 2. Edited by Friedrich-Wilhelm von Herrmann. Frankfurt/M.: Klostermann.

———. 1929–30. *Grundbegriffe der Metaphysik*. Gesamtausgabe. Vols. 29–30. Edited by Friedrich-Wilhelm von Herrmann. Frankfurt/M.: Klostermann.

———. 1935. *Einführung in die Metaphysik*. Gesamtausgabe. Vol. 40. Edited by Petra Jaeger. Frankfurt/M.: Klostermann.

———. 1935–36. *Basic Writings from "Being and Time" (1927) to "The Task of Thinking" (1964)*. London: Taylor & Francis, 1977.

———. 2000. *Introduction to Metaphysics*. Translated by Gregory Fried and Richard Polt. New Haven, CT, and London: Yale University Press.

———. 2004. *What Is Called Thinking?* London: Perennial, HarperCollins.

Hill, Christopher, ed. 2001. "Vagueness." *Philosophical Topics* 21: 1–244.

Hobbes, Thomas. 1655. *De Corpore*. http://www.archive.org/stream/thomhobbes malmeo3molegoog#page/n120/mode/2up.

Hoften, Claes von, and Elizabeth Spelke. 1985. "Object Perception and Object-directed Reaching in Infancy." *Journal of Experimental Psychology: General* 114: 198–211.

Horgan, Terry, ed. 1995. "Vagueness." *Southern Journal of Philosophy*, suppl. 33: 1–261.

Husserl, Edmund. 1900–1. *Logische Untersuchungen*. In Husserliana XVIII. Den Haag: Nijhoff, 1975.

———. 1918–26. "Analysen zur passiven Synthesis. Aus Vorlesungs- und Forschungsmanuskripten." In Husserliana XI. Den Haag: Nijhoff, 1966.

———. 1929. *Formale und transzendentale Logik*. In Husserliana XVII. Den Haag: Nijhoff, 1974.

Ingarden, Roman. 1931. *Das Literarische Kunstwerk*. Halle: Max Niemeyer.

James, William. 1907. *Pragmatism: A New Name for Some Old Ways of Thinking*. New York and London: Longmans, Green & Co.

———. [1909] 1970. *The Meaning of Truth: A Sequel to "Pragmatism."* New York and London: Longmans, Green & Co. and Ann Arbor: University of Michigan Press.

———. [1904] 1976. "Does 'Consciousness' Exist?" In William James, *Essays in Radical Empiricism*, 3–19. Cambridge, MA: Harvard University Press.

Jasanoff, Sheila. 1995. *Science at the Bar: Law, Science, and Technology in America*. Cambridge, MA: Harvard University Press.

Johansson, Ingvar. 1989. *Ontological Investigations. An Inquiry into the Categories of Nature, Man and Society*. London: Routledge.

Kafka, Franz. 1919. *A Message from the Emperor*. Translated by Marc Harman. http://www.nybooks.com/blogs/nyrblog/2011/jul/01/message-emperor-new-translation/.

————. 1999. *Letters to Milena*. London: Random House.

Kalinowski, Georges. 1967. *Le Problème de la vérité en morale et en droit*. Lyon: Emmanuel Vitte.

Kant, Immanuel. [1766] 1900. *Dream of a Spirit-Seer*. London: Swan Sonnenschein & Co. and New York: Macmillan Co.

————. 1785. *Essay three of the injustice of counterfeiting books*. http://staffweb.hkbu .edu.hk/ppp/fne/essay3.html.

————. [1790] 1951. *Critique of Judgment*. Translated by Bernard, John H. New York: Hafner Publishing Company.

Kato, Fumitoshi. 2005. "Seeing the 'Seeing' of Others: Conducting a Field Study with Mobile Phones/Mobile Cameras." In Nýri 2005a, 215–22.

Katz, James. 2005. "Magic in the Air: Spiritual and Transcendental Aspects of Mobiles." In Nýri 2005a, 283–88.

Keefe, Rosanna. 2000. *Theories of Vagueness*. Cambridge: Cambridge University Press.

Kim, Jaegwon, and Ernest Sosa, eds. 1999. *Metaphysics: An Anthology*. Oxford: Blackwell.

Kobau, Pietro. 2004. *Essere qualcosa. Ontologia e psicologia in Wolff*. Torino: Trauben.

Koepsell, David. R. 2000. *The Ontology of Cyberspace*. La Salle: Open Court.

————. 2003. "Libri e altre macchine: artificio ed espressione." In Casati 2003, 429–39.

Koepsell, David. R., and Laurence Moss, eds. 2003. "John Searle's Ideas About Social Reality." *American Journal of Economics and Sociology* 62: 285–309.

Kripke, Saul. 1972. "Naming and Necessity." In *Semantics of Natural Language*, edited by Donald Davidson and Gilbert Harman, 253–355, addenda 763–69. Reidel: Dordrecht.

La Mettrie, Julien Offray de. 1912. *Man a Machine*. Chicago: Open Court Publishing.

Lancieri, Alessandro 2003. *Il concetto di res nel Diritto Romano e nelle Disputationes Metaphysicae di F. Suárez*. Tesi di laurea in filosofia teoretica, Università di Torino.

Leibniz, Gottfried W. 1684. *Meditationes de cognitione, veritate et ideis*.

————. 1695. *Système nouveau de la nature et de la communication des substances aussi bien que de l'union qu'il y a entre l'âme et le corps*.

————. [1686] 1908. *Discourse on Metaphysics, Correspondence with Arnauld and Monadology*. Chicago: Open Court Publishing Company.

Leśniewski, Stanisław. 1916. *Podstawy ogólnej teoryi mnogosci*. Moskow: Prace Polskiego Kola Naukowego w Moskwie.

Lévi-Strauss, Claude. 1955. *Tristes Tropiques*. Paris: Plon.

Lévy, Pierre. 1994. *L'Intelligence collective. Pour une anthropologie du cyberspace*. Paris: La Découverte.

Lewin, Kurt. 1926. "Vorsatz, Wille und Bedürfnis." *Psychologische Forschung* 7: 330–85.

Licoppe, Christian, and Yoriko Inada. 2005. "Seeing one another onscreen and the construction of social order in a mobile-based augmented public space. The uses of a geo-localized mobile game in Japan." In Nyíri 2005a, 71–79.

Lipmann, Otto. 1923. "Das Wesen der naiven Physik. Grundsätze einer Prüfung der Fähigkeit zu intelligentem physischen Handeln." In Otto Lipmann and Hellmuth Bogen. *Naive Physik. Theoretische und experimentelle Untersuchungen über die Fähigkeit zu intelligentem Handeln*. Leipzig: Barth.

Loux, Michael J. 1998. *Metaphysics. A Contemporary Introduction*. London: Routledge.

Lyotard, Jean-Francois. 1979. *La condition postmoderne*. Paris: Ed. de Minuit.

Manzoni, Alessandro. 1834. *The Betrothed*. London: R. Bentley.

Madison, Gary B. 1993. *Working through Derrida*. Evanston, IL: Northwestern University Press.

Marconi, Diego. 2005. "Contro la mente estesa." *Sistemi Intelligenti* 3: 389–98.

Marx, Karl. [1842] 1975a. "The Divorce Bill." In *Rheinische Zeitung* 353. In *Marx and Engels Collected Works*. London: Lawrence & Wishart.

———. [1842] 1975b. "Proceedings of the Sixth Rhine Province Assembly. Third Article. Debates on the Law on Thefts of Wood." In *Rheinische Zeitung* 298–300. In *Marx and Engels Collected Works*. London: Lawrence & Wishart.

McLuhan, Marshall. 1964. *Understanding Media: The Extensions of Man*. New York: New American Library.

Meinong, Alexius von. [1899] 1971a. "Über Gegenstände höherer Ordnung und deren Verhältnis zur inneren Wahrnehmung." *Gesamtausgabe*. Vol. 2. Graz: Akademische Druck- und Verlangsanstalt.

———. [1904] 1971b. "Über Gegenstandstheorie." *Gesamtausgabe*. Vol. 2. Graz: Akademische Druck- und Verlangsanstalt.

———. [1923] 1971c. "Zur Grundlegung der allgemeinen Werttheorie". *Gesamtausgabe*. Vol. 3. Graz: Akademische Druck- und Verlangsanstalt.

Menger, Carl. 1985. *Investigations into the Methods of the Social Sciences*. Translated by Lawrence H. White, and Louis Schneider. New York: New York University Press.

Merleau-Ponty, Maurice. 1958–61. *Notes des cours. 1959–1961*. Edited by Stéphanie Ménasé. Paris: Gallimard 1996.

Metzger, Wolfgang. 1941. *Psychologie–Die Entwicklung ihrer Grundannahmen seit der Einführung des Experiments*. Darmstadt: Steinkopff.

Montesquieu, Ch.-L. Secondat de. 1748. *L'esprit des lois*. http://www.gutenberg.org/files/27573/27573-h/27573-h.htm.

Montuschi, Eleonora. 2003. *The Objects of Social Science*. London and New York: Continuum.

Morena, Luca. 2002. "I confini delle cose." *Rivista di estetica* 20, no. 2: 3–22.

Moore, M. S. 2002. "Legal Reality: A Naturalist Approach to Legal Ontology." *Law and Philosophy* 21: 619–705.

Mulligan, Kevin, ed. 1987. *Speech Act and Sachverhalt. Reinach and the Foundations of Realist Phenomenology.* The Hague: Nijhoff.

———. 1998. "From Appropriate Emotions to Values." *The Monist* 841: 161–88.

———. 2000. "Métaphysique et ontologie." In *Précis de philosophie analytique*, edited by Pascal Engel, 5–33. Paris: Puf.

———. 2002. "Getting Geist–Certainty, Rules and Us." *Cinquantenaire Ludwig Wittgenstein, Proceedings of the 2001 Tunis Wittgenstein Conference*, 35–62. Tunis, Ouelbani, Mèlika: University of Tunis.

———. 2003. "Seeing, Certainty and Acquaintance." In *Non-Conceptual Aspects of Experience, Proceedings of the 2000 Melbu Conference on Non-Conceptual Content*, edited by Halvard Fossheim, Larsen M. Tarjei, and John Rickard Sageng, 27–44. Oslo: Unipub Vorlag.

Mulligan, Kevin, Peter Simons, and Barry Smith. 1984. "Truth-Makers." *Philosophy and Phenomenological Research* 44: 287–321.

Nagel, Thomas. 1997. *The Last Word.* New York and Oxford: Oxford University Press.

Nakahara, Kiyoshi, and Yasushi Miyashita. 2005. "Understanding Intentions: Through the Looking Glass." *Science* 308: 644–45.

Nef, Frédéric. 1998. *L'objet quelconque. Recherches sur l'ontologie de l'objet.* Paris: Vrin.

———. 2004. *Qu'est-ce que c'est la métaphysique?* Paris: Gallimard.

Nietzsche, Friedrich. 1886–87. *Nachgelassene Fragmente Herbst 1886—Herbst 1887.* In *Werke. Kritische Gesamtausgabe.* Edited by Giorgio Colli, and Mazzino Montinari. Berlin: De Gruyter, 1967.

———. 1889. *Die Götzendämmerung oder Wie man mit dem Hammer philosophirt.* In *Werke. Kritische Gesamtausgabe.* Edited by Giorgio Colli, and Mazzino Montinari. Berlin: De Gruyter, 1967.

Nozick, Robert. 1981. *Philosophical Explanations*, Cambridge, MA: Belknap.

———. 2001. *Invariances: The Structure of the Objective World.* Cambridge, MA, and London: Belknap Press of Harvard University Press.

Nyíri, Kristóf, ed. 2002. *Allzeit zuhanden: Gemeinschaft und Erkenntnis im Mobilzeitalter.* Wien: Passagen Verlag.

———, ed. 2003a. *Mobile Learning. Essays on Philosophy, Psychology and Education.* Wien: Passagen Verlag.

———, ed. 2003b. *Mobile Communication. Essays on Cognition and Community.* Wien: Passagen Verlag.

———, ed. 2003c. *Mobile Democracy. Essays on Society, Self and Politics.* Wien: Passagen Verlag.

————, ed. 2005a. *Seeing, Understanding, Learning in the Mobile Age*, Conference organized by T-Mobile Hungary and the Institute for Philosophical Research of the Hungarian Academy of Sciences, Papers. Draft version.

————, ed. 2005b. *A Sense of Place. The Global and the Local in Mobile Communication*. Wien: Passagen Verlag.

————, ed. 2006. *Mobile Understanding: The Epistemology of Ubiquitous Communication*. Wien: Passagen Verlag.

————, ed. 2007. *Mobile Studies: Paradigms and Perspectives*. Wien: Passagen Verlag.

Ok, Hye R. 2005. "Cinema in Your Hand, Cinema on the Street: The Aesthetics of Convergence in Korean Mobile(phone) Cinema." In Nyíri 2005a, 223–30.

Okabe, Daisuke et al. 2005. "Location-based Moblogging as Method: New Views into the Use and Practice of Personal, Social, and Mobile Technologies." In Nyíri 2005a, 65–69.

Ong, Walter J. 2002. *Orality and Literacy. The Technologizing of the Word*. London: Routledge.

Orilia, Francesco. 2002. *Ulisse, il quadrato rotondo e l'attuale re di Francia*. Pisa: ETS.

Ortega y Gasset, José. 1940. *Ideas y Creencias-Sobre la razón histórica*. In José Ortega y Gasset. *Ideas y Creencias (y otros Ensayos de Filosofía)*, 23–57. Madrid: Alianza Editorial, 1986.

Peirce, Charles S. 1902. "Simplest Mathematics." In *The Collected Papers of Charles Sanders Peirce*. Vol. 4. Edited by Charles Hartshorne and Peter Weiss. Cambridge, MA: Harvard University Press.

Plato. 2009. *Selected Dialogues of Plato: The Benjamin Jowett Translation*. New York: Random House.

Poggi, Stefano. 2001. "William James e la filosofia europea. Un capitolo da approfondire." *Rivista di storia della filosofia* 2: 257–73.

Poli, Roberto, and Peter M. Simons, eds. 1996. *Formal Ontology*. Dordrecht: Kluwer.

Preston, John. 2005. "Is your Mobile Part of Your Mind?" In Nyíri 2005a, 313–24.

Putnam, Hilary. 1997. "James's Theory of Truth." In *The Cambridge Companion to William James*, edited by Ruth A. Putnam, 166–85. Cambridge: Cambridge University Press.

————. 1999. *The Threefold Cord: Mind, Body and World*. New York: Columbia University Press.

Quine, William V. O. 1941. "Whitehead and the Rise of Modern Logic." In William V. O. Quine. *Selected Logic Papers*, 3–36. New York: Random House, 1966.

————. 1948. "On What There Is." *Review of Metaphysics* 2: 21–38.

————. 1951. "Two Dogmas of Empiricism." *Philosophical Review* 60: 20–43.

————. 1953. *From a Logical Point of View*. Cambridge, MA: Harvard University Press.

———. 1958. "Speaking of Objects." In *Proceedings and Addresses of the American Philosophical Association* 31: 5–22. In William V. O. Quine. *Ontological Relativity and Other Essays*, 1–25. New York: Columbia University Press, 1969.

Reid, Thomas. 1827. *Essays on the Active Powers of the Human Mind: To which are added an essay on quantity and an analysis of Aristotele's logic.* London: Tegg.

Reinach, Adolf. 1913. "The a priori Foundations of Civil Law." Translated by John Crosby. In *Aletheia* III (1983): 1–142.

Rilke, Rainer M. 1910. *The Notebooks of Malte Laurids Brigge.* Translated by William Needham. https://ia700209.us.archive.org/11/items/TheNotebooksOfMalte LauridsBrigge/TheNotebooksOfMalteLauridsBrigge.pdf.

Rorty, Richard. 1979. *Philosophy and the Mirror of Nature.* Princeton, NJ: Princeton University Press.

———. 1982. *Consequences of Pragmatism.* Minneapolis: University of Minnesota Press.

———. 1991. "Objectivity, Relativism and Truth." *Philosophical Papers.* Vol. 1. Cambridge: Cambridge University Press.

Rousseau, Jean-Jacques. 1993. *First Discourse.* Vol. 1. New York: Knopf Doubleday Publishing Group.

Runggaldier, Edmund, and Christian Kanzian 1998. *Grundprobleme der analytischen Ontologie.* Paderborn: Schöning.

Russell, Bertrand. 1905. "On Denoting." *Mind* 14: 479–93.

———. 1908. "Transatlantic 'Truth.'" *The Albany Review* 2: 393–410

———. 1912. *The Problems of Philosophy.* London: William & Norgate.

———. 1923. "Vagueness." *Australasian Journal of Psychology and Philosophy* 1: 84–92.

———. 2012. *The Conquest of Happiness.* London: Routledge.

Ryle, Gilbert. 1949. *The Concept of Mind.* London: Hutchinson.

Sacco, Rodolfo. 1989. "Criptotipo." *Digesto IV.* Vol. 5, 39–40. Torino: Utet.

———. 1990. *Che cos'è il diritto comparato?* Milano: Giuffrè.

———. 1993. "Il diritto muto." *Rivista di diritto civile* 1: 689.

Salice, Alessandro. 2004. "Gewalt als sozialer Gegenstand." In *Erfahrung und Analyse,* edited by Johann C. Marek and Maria E. Reicher, 318–20. Beiträge des 27. Internationalen Wittgenstein Symposiums, vol. 12, Kirchberg/Wechsel, Österreichische Ludwig Wittgenstein Gesellschaft.

Sartre, Jean-Paul. 2003. *Being and Nothingness.* London: Routledge Classics.

Scheler, Max. 1916. *Der Formalismus in der Ethik und die materiale Wertethik.* In Max Scheler, *Gesammelte Werke,* vol. 2. Bern-München: Francke, 1966.

Schoggen, Phil. 1989. *Behavior Settings. A Revision and Extension of Roger G. Barker's Ecological Psychology.* Stanford, CA: Stanford University Press.

Schreber, Daniel P. 1903. *Denkwürdigkeiten eines Nervenkranken.* Leipzig: Mutze.

Schuhmann, Karl, and Barry Smith. 1987. "Adolf Reinach: An Intellectual Biography." In Mulligan 1987.

———. 1990. "Elements of Speech Act Theory in the Work of Thomas Reid." *History of Philosophy Quarterly* 7: 47–66.

Schulthess, Daniel. 1983. *Philosophie et sens commun chez Thomas Reid (1710–1796)*. Bern: Lang.

Searle, John R. 1969. *Speech Acts*. Cambridge: Cambridge University Press.

———. 1975. *A Taxonomy of Illocutionary Acts*. Cambridge: Cambridge University Press.

———. 1977. "Reiterating the Differences: A Reply to Derrida." *Glyph* I: 172–208.

———. 1980. "Minds, brains and programs." *Behavioral and Brain Sciences* 3: 417–58.

———. 1983. *Intentionality. An Essay in the Philosophy of Mind*. New York and Cambridge: Cambridge University Press.

———. 1992. *The Rediscovery of the Mind*. Montgomery, VT: Bradford Books.

———. 1993a. "Rationality and Realism, What is at Stake?" *Daedalus* 122, no. 4: 55–83.

———. 1993b. "The World Turned Upside Down." In Madison 1993, 170–88.

———. 1993c. "Reply to Mackey." In Madison 1993, 184–88.

———. 1995. *The Construction of Social Reality*. New York: Free Press.

———. 1998. "Postmodernism and Truth," *TWP BE (a journal of ideas)* 13: 85–87.

———. 1999. *Mind, Language and Society. Philosophy in the Real World*. New York: Basic Books.

———. 2001. "Neither Phenomenological Description Nor Rational Reconstruction: Reply To Dreyfus." In *Searle with his replies. Revue internationale de philosophie* 216: 277–97.

———. 2001/2002. "Neither Phenomenological Description Nor Rational Reconstruction: Reply to Dreyfus," in *Revue internationale de philosophie* no. 216: 277–97.

———. [2002] 2003. "The Construction of Social Reality: An Exchange." *American Journal of Economics and Sociology* 62, no. 2: 299–309.

Shakespeare, William. 2005. *The Complete Works*. Oxford: Oxford University Press.

Smith, Barry, ed. 1982. *Parts and Moments. Studies in Logic and Formal Ontology*. München and Wien: Philosophia Verlag.

———, ed. 1988. *Foundations of Gestalt Theory*. München and Wien: Philosophia Verlag.

———. 1993. "An Essay on Material Necessity." In *Return of the A Priori, Canadian Journal of Philosophy*, edited by Philip Hanson and Bruce Hunter. Supplement 18: 301–22. Calgary: University of Calgary Press.

———, ed. 1994. *European Philosophy and the American Academy, The Monist Library of Philosophy*. La Salle: Hegeler Institute.

———. 1995a. "The Structures of the Common-Sense World." *Acta Philosophica Fennica* 58: 290–317.

———. 1995b. "Ontology." In *A Companion to Metaphysics*, edited by Kim Jaegwon and Ernest Sosa, 373–74. New York: Routledge.

———. 1998. "Ontologie des Mesokosmos: Soziale Objekte und Umwelten." *Zeitschrift für philosophische Forschung* 52: 521–40.

———. 1999. "Social Objects." http://wings.buffalo.edu/philosophy/ontology/socobj .htm.

———. 2002. "The Ontology of Social Reality." http://ontology.buffalo.edu/smith// articles/searle.PDF.

———. 2003a. "John Searle: From Speech Acts to Social Reality." In *John Searle*, edited by Barry Smith, 1–33. Cambridge: Cambridge University Press.

———. 2003b. "Un'aporia nella costruzione della realtà sociale. Naturalismo e realismo in John R. Searle." In Di Lucia Paolo 2003, 137–52.

Spinicci, Paolo. 2000. *Sensazione, percezione, concetto*. Bologna: Il Mulino.

Stevenson, Robert Louis. 1891. "The Bottle Imp." *New York Herald*.

Stout, George F. 1910–11. "The Object of Thought and Real Being." *Proceedings of the Aristotelian Society*: 187–208.

Strawson, Peter F. 1959. *Individuals. An Essay in Descriptive Metaphysics*. London: Routledge.

Swift, J. 2004. *A Modest Proposal, the Battle of the Books and Other Short Pieces*. Digireads.com Publishing.

———. 2011. *Gulliver's Travels*. London: Plain Label Books.

Thomasson, Amie L. 1999. *Fiction and Metaphysics*. Cambridge and New York: Cambridge University Press.

Tuomela, Raimo. 1995. *The Importance of Us*. Stanford, CA: Stanford University Press.

———. 2002. *The Philosophy of Social Practices*. Cambridge: Cambridge University Press.

Treadgold, Warren. 2001. *A Concise History of Byzantium*. Houndmills, Basingstoke, Hampshire, New York: Palgrave.

Twardowski, Kazimierz. 1894. *Zur Lehre vom Inhalt und Gegenstand der Vorstellungen*. Wien: Alfred Hölder.

Tye, Michael. 1990. "Vague Objects." *Mind* 99: 535–57.

Ukritwiriya, Chaensumon. 2005. "Mobile Phone 'Mue Tue'–'An extension of the Hand'; Cool Brand Cool Self in Everyday Lives." In Nyíri 2005a, 259–65.

Van Caenegem, Raoul C. 1973. "History of European Civil Procedure." *International Encyclopedia of Comparative Law* 16. Tübingen: J. C. B. Mohr (Paul Siebeck).

Van Inwagen, Peter. 1983. "Fiction and Metaphysics." *Philosophy and Literature* 7: 67–77.

———. 1998. "How to Reason about Vague Objects." *Philosophical Topics* 16: 255–84.

Varzi, Achille C. 2001. *Parole, oggetti, eventi e altri argomenti di metafisica*. Roma: Carocci.

———. 2001b. "Vagueness, Logic, and Ontology." *The Dialogue* 1: 135–54.

———. 2002. "Ontologia e metafisica." In *Storia della filosofia analitica*, edited by Franca D'Agostini and Nicla Vassallo, 157–93. Torino: Einaudi.

———. 2003. "Entia successive." *Rivista di estetica* n.s. 22, no. 1: 138–58.

———. 2005. *Ontologia*. Roma-Bari: Laterza.

Vassallo, Nicla. 2003. *Teoria della conoscenza*. Roma-Bari: Laterza.

Vattimo, Gianni, and Pier Aldo Rovatti. 1983. *Il pensiero debole*. Milano: Feltrinelli.

Vico, Giovan Battista. 1744. *La scienza nuova*. In *La scienza nuova e altri scritti*, edited by Nicola Abbagnano, 247–748. Torino: Utet, 1952.

Villiers de l'Isle-Adam, Auguste. 2001. *Tomorrow's Eve*. Champain, IL: University of Illinois Press.

Wertheimer, Max. 1923. "Untersuchungen zur Lehre von der Gestalt." *Psychologische Forschung* 4: 301–50.

Wiggins, David. 2001. *Sameness and Substance Renewed*. Cambridge: Cambridge University Press.

Williamson, Timothy. 1994. *Vagueness*. London: Routledge.

———, ed. 1998. *Vagueness. The Monist* 81: 193–348.

Wittgenstein, Ludwig. 1953. *Philosophical Investigations*. Edited by Gertrude E. M. Anscombe and Rush Rhees. Oxford: Blackwell.

———. 1969. *On Certainty*. Edited by Gertrude E. M. Anscombe and George H. von Wright. Oxford: Blackwell.

———. 1980. *Remarks on the Philosophy of Psychology*. Edited by Gertrude E. M. Anscombe, Heikki Nyman, and George H. von Wright. Oxford: Blackwell.

Znamierowski, Czesław. 1924–30. *Podstawowe pojecia teorji prawa. I. Uklad prawny i norma prawna*. Fiszer i Majewski: Poznan.

INDEX

COMMONALITIES

Timothy C. Campbell, series editor

Roberto Esposito, *Terms of the Political: Community, Immunity, Biopolitics.* Translated by Rhiannon Noel Welch. Introduction by Vanessa Lemm.

Maurizio Ferraris, *Documentality: Why It Is Necessary to Leave Traces.* Translated by Richard Davies.

Dimitris Vardoulakis, *Sovereignty and Its Other: Toward the Dejustification of Violence.*

Anne Emmanuelle Berger, *The Queer Turn in Feminism: Identities, Sexualities, and the Theater of Gender.* Translated by Catherine Porter.

James D. Lilley, *Common Things: Romance and the Aesthetics of Belonging in Atlantic Modernity.*

Jean-Luc Nancy, *Identity: Fragments, Frankness.* Translated by François Raffoul.

Miguel Vatter, *The Republic of the Living: Biopolitics and the Critique of Civil Society.*

Miguel Vatter, *Between Form and Event: Machiavelli's Theory of Political Freedom.*

Maurizio Ferraris, *Where Are You? An Ontology of the Cell Phone.* Translated by Sarah De Sanctis.